The Toxic Classroom

The Toxic Classroom offers a wide-ranging look at education today and explores in detail the pressures children experience as a result of constant change, digital technology and political interference. Beginning with what it is like to be a child in the classroom, the book goes on to provide a detailed analysis of the curriculum, assessment and accountability, school structures, educating for global citizenship and the plethora of social issues schools are now expected to solve.

Written from the perspective of a successful headteacher with over 30 years' teaching experience, the book considers what needs to be done to put things right and outlines a more equitable and effective school system. Each chapter outlines the steps schools can implement immediately and the longer-term policy changes that are needed to de-toxify the classroom and facilitate a genuine love of learning.

Offering a challenging yet compelling argument for putting education back into the hands of teachers, this book will be of great interest both to the general reader and to those working within education such as teachers and professionals who wish to improve the ways in which children learn and develop.

Richard Steward is an educational consultant with extensive experience as a teacher and headteacher. He has taught in a variety of schools in a 30-year career and has worked as a part-time lecturer with The Open University. He has worked with the National College for Teaching and Learning and been involved in a wide range of national educational research projects. His previous book is titled, *The Gradual Art of School Improvement*, and he can be found on twitter @StewardRichard.

The Toxic Classroom

And What Can Be Done About It

Richard Steward

LONDON AND NEW YORK

First published 2021
by Routledge
2 Park Square, Milton Park, Abingdon, Oxon OX14 4RN

and by Routledge
52 Vanderbilt Avenue, New York, NY 10017

Routledge is an imprint of the Taylor & Francis Group, an informa business

© 2021 Richard Steward

The right of Richard Steward to be identified as author of this work has been asserted by him in accordance with sections 77 and 78 of the Copyright, Designs and Patents Act 1988.

All rights reserved. No part of this book may be reprinted or reproduced or utilised in any form or by any electronic, mechanical, or other means, now known or hereafter invented, including photocopying and recording, or in any information storage or retrieval system, without permission in writing from the publishers.

Trademark notice: Product or corporate names may be trademarks or registered trademarks, and are used only for identification and explanation without intent to infringe.

British Library Cataloguing-in-Publication Data
A catalogue record for this book is available from the British Library

Library of Congress Cataloging-in-Publication Data
A catalog record for this book has been requested

ISBN: 978-0-367-42468-8 (hbk)
ISBN: 978-0-367-42469-5 (pbk)
ISBN: 978-0-367-82431-0 (ebk)

Typeset in Melior
by Apex CoVantage, LLC

To Jonathan

Contents

	Introduction	1
1	What is it like to be a child in a school today?	4
	An early start	*4*
	Working with others	*6*
	Parents	*7*
	Poverty and neglect	*9*
	Fear of failure	*10*
	Social media	*12*
	Mental health	*14*
	Boredom	*17*
	Schools are the answer	*18*
	Toxic schooling	*19*
	What can schools do now to put things right?	*20*
	What should policymakers do to put things right?	*22*
2	The curriculum	24
	The background	*24*
	Where are we now? The foundation stage	*26*
	Where are we now? Primary education	*29*
	Where are we now? Secondary education	*30*
	Where are we now? Post-16 education	*33*
	Destination university	*36*
	What should children be learning in school?	*39*
	What can schools do now to put things right?	*41*
	What should policymakers do to put things right?	*41*
3	The core subjects	43
	English	*43*
	Mathematics	*48*

	Science	*53*
	Computing	*56*
	Languages	*58*
	The humanities	*61*
	Conclusion	*65*
	What can schools do now to put things right?	*66*
	What should policymakers do to put things right?	*67*
4	Beyond the core	69
	The arts	*69*
	Design technology	*72*
	Physical education	*74*
	PSHE/citizenship	*77*
	Studies and 'ologies'	*80*
	Vocational subjects	*83*
	Extra-curricular	*86*
	Conclusion	*88*
	What can schools do now to put things right?	*89*
	What should policymakers do to put things right?	*90*
5	Assessment and accountability	92
	Early years testing	*94*
	Primary testing	*96*
	Secondary assessment	*100*
	Assessment post-16	*104*
	Ofsted – a new hope?	*106*
	What can schools do now to put things right?	*107*
	What should policymakers do to put things right?	*108*
6	Structures	109
	Academies	*110*
	Free schools	*111*
	Multi-academy trusts	*113*
	Grammar schools	*115*
	Independent schools	*116*
	Faith schools	*118*
	Beyond the mainstream	*120*
	Admissions	*123*
	Departures	*124*
	A final thought on age	*126*
	What can schools do now to put things right?	*128*
	What should policymakers do to put things right?	*129*

7	A wider view	130
	What happened to the learning culture?	*130*
	Education, childcare or social service?	*134*
	Educating for global citizenship	*136*
	What can schools do now to put things right?	*139*
	What should policymakers do to put things right?	*139*
8	A vision for the future	140
	Independent, grammar and faith schools	*140*
	Structural confusion	*142*
	Age and stage	*144*
	Governance	*147*
	What can schools do now to put things right?	*149*
	What should policymakers do to put things right?	*150*
9	A 21st-century curriculum	151
	The curriculum	*151*
	A 21st-century curriculum – a modest proposal	*152*
	Summary: a curriculum model for the future	*164*
	Conclusion: de-toxifying the classroom	167
	Why are children learning and what for?	*168*
	Putting things right	*169*
	Painting in oils	*171*
	Appendix: list of common SEND acronyms	173
	Index	175

Introduction

> 'When we were little,' the Mock Turtle went on at last, more calmly, though still sobbing a little now and then, we went to school in the sea.'[1]

Alice's conversation with the Mock Turtle in *Alice's Adventures in Wonderland* may be considered an odd place to begin an analysis of the current state of the education system in Britain. However, with its combination of surrealism and twisted logic, it offers a compelling vision of the muddle and confusion which many children in today's system experience. Children in schools, who spend hours every day focussing on exercises aimed at gaining good marks in a relentless series of tests, could be forgiven for mistaking reading and writing for the Mock Turtle's 'regular course' of 'Reeling and Writhing'.

The Mock Turtle's topsy-turvy outline of the school curriculum is linguistically only a step or two away from reality, with 'Ambition, Distraction, Uglification and Derision' an obvious parody of addition, subtraction, multiplication and division'. He goes on:

> 'Well, there was Mystery,' the Mock Turtle replied, counting off the subjects on his flappers – 'Mystery, ancient and modern, with Seaography: then Drawling – the Drawling-master was an old conger-eel, that used to come once a week: *he* taught us Drawling, Stretching, and Fainting in Coils.'[2]

History becomes a 'Mystery' and we are left with an image of pupils not painting in oils but 'Fainting in Coils', a profound metaphor for a child's experience of contemporary education.

The experience of the pupil in the classroom is often described by politicians and educationalists, but what is it really like to be a child in school today? Any attempt to look through a child's eyes is inevitably a deeply subjective activity, but it is surely worth attempting. Talking to children about their experience of education is always fascinating, but teasing out what they really think about their schools and their teachers is fraught with difficulties. Young children are keen to please, and getting at what they really think can be almost impossible; asking older children about their early experiences is equally problematic since they often look back with rose-tinted spectacles.

When we look back at our own education, it is not uncommon to experience a strange dichotomy. We sometimes bask in sunlit memories of our school days, drawing heavily on games with friends, school trips, the comfort of once familiar but now lost classrooms and the fun we had when we were young. More often than not, however, we recall a bleaker vision: school bullies, terrible teachers, hours of irrelevant study, tests and exams and the ever-present threat of authority. And yet, we cling to a view of education that affirms 'it was better in my day', even though most of us know in our hearts that it wasn't.

As a society, we have been getting education wrong for years, and yet we are often intensely nostalgic about such a formative period in our lives. I wonder, however, if the current generation will be similarly nostalgic. Will today's youngsters look back on their school days with the same degree of fondness and warmth, or is the experience of education significantly worse today than it has been in the past?

People have always complained about going to school. William Blake, in 1794, was typically gloomy:

> But to go to school in a summer morn, –
>   Oh it drives all joy away!
> Under a cruel eye outworn,
>   The little ones spend the day
>   In sighing and dismay.[3]

Even Churchill, that great symbol of fundamental British values, said, 'How I hated this school, and what a life of anxiety I lived there for more than two years'.[4]

Dickens, ever an acute observer of society's terrors, paints a suffocating picture of education in *Dombey and Son* which is not too far away from the experiences of today's children:

> The young gentlemen were prematurely full of carking anxieties. They knew no rest from the pursuit of stoney-hearted verbs, savage noun-substantives, inflexible syntactic passages, and ghosts of exercises that appeared to them in their dreams.[5]

The Year 4 pupil struggling to find an example of a fronted adverbial would doubtless sympathise with Dickens' young gentlemen.

Education has always toyed with our memories as we veer between nostalgia and nightmare, and it has blighted the childhoods of many a famous figure, and yet we have survived it. Are we getting to the stage now, however, where so much damage has been done to the system, where there are so many changes in society, and where social media dominates our lives, that we are entering a new age of educational despair? I hope not.

Some children endure rather than enjoy education – it has always been so – but many would argue that children growing up today face more difficulties than ever before. Childhood has become 'toxic', schools deeply politicised and society fractured. Social media dominates children's lives in ways that were unimaginable a decade ago, and mental illness is on the rise. It is surely time, therefore, to step outside the system and think about what went wrong and how we might repair the damage we have done.

The purpose of this book is to do exactly that: my intention is to take an unflinching look at contemporary education but, more importantly, to suggest ways in which we may be able to put things right. Some may be mere ambitions; others will be more practical suggestions which could easily be implemented tomorrow. What does need to be done to ensure that education becomes de-politicised? What can we do to prepare children to cope with the complexities of modern society? And, above all, what can we do to ensure that classroom learning becomes the priority of everyone in society, from teachers and parents to politicians and business leaders?

Every chapter begins with a consideration of what has gone wrong and some of the dilemmas school leaders face today as they struggle to provide a good education for their pupils against a background of complex changes in society and the increasing politicisation of the school system. I begin by painting a picture of what it is like to be a child in school today, before moving on to explore the key areas of debate: the curriculum, assessment and accountability, systems and structures, and attitudes to learning. In an effort to dispel the gloom, at the end of each chapter, I suggest practical ways improvements can be made now, as well as some optimistic – some might say naively optimistic – suggestions that policymakers ought to, but probably won't, consider.

Ultimately, the aim of the book is to suggest ways to enable today's children to enjoy rather than endure their schooling. In other words, to help prevent them from 'fainting in coils'.

Notes

1 L. Carroll. 1865. *Alice's Adventures in Wonderland*, London, Macmillan & Co, chapter IX, p. 141.
2 Ibid. p. 144.
3 W. Blake. 1794. 'The Schoolboy', in *Songs of Innocence and Experience*, Oxford, Oxford University Press 1967, p. 154.
4 W. Churchill. 1930. *My Early Life*, London, Eland, Kindle Edition 2013, chapter 2.
5 C. Dickens. 1848. *Dombey and Son*, London, Everyman 1997, p. 140.

# What is it like to be a child in a school today?

We all have memories of our school days, but few of us can recall the events of our early lives clearly enough to construct an accurate portrait of what it was like to be a child of 5 or even 15. Even if we have excellent memories and are able to recall what we did in school in extraordinary detail, it is with adult eyes that we see things now. Childhood memories are mediated through our experiences of adulthood, and it is almost impossible to get at the true nature of our experiences in the past. We must therefore attempt to distance ourselves, putting aside our own experiences in order to think like a child in the classroom today.

Many children find novelty unsettling, and, for some, starting school can be a fairly traumatic experience. From the peace and quiet of home, where there are familiar faces and familiar surroundings, children suddenly find themselves coping with what must seem like a world of noise and confusion. All at once they have to adapt to new surroundings, new rules, new authority figures and lots of other children. On top of that, learning, which begins as play, quickly becomes increasingly formalised. Children are adaptable but, nevertheless, the first experience of school marks a huge change in their lives.

An early start

Children in England start school early in comparison with many other countries, and the age at which they first enter classrooms has fallen steadily in recent years. From entry at 5, through 'rising 5s', to the current, almost universal assumption that children start school at 4, the age of formal education has begun earlier and earlier. Many primary and infant schools now have nurseries attached, and it is not uncommon for children as young as 2 to be in school on a regular basis.

Early years education is strictly regulated and, in many institutions, even the youngest of children follow some kind of syllabus. The Early Years Foundation Stage (EYFS) profile, completed at the end of the Reception year, sets out a detailed list of accomplishments the child is expected to have achieved. Formality sets in early.

In countries like Finland, where children don't start school until they are 7, formal education begins much later, and advocates of the Finnish system suggest that the later start has little impact on their subsequent educational attainment. Research evidence is unclear on the advantages and disadvantages of starting school early. Black, Devereux and Salvanes, for example, make the point clearly:

> First, much research has shown a consistent pattern that children who start school at older ages tend to score higher on in-school tests. The second broad conclusion in the literature is that, when tested at the same age, very young children score better on in-school tests if they started school younger and hence have spent more time in school. These findings suggest that school starting age may have significant effects on the outcomes of adults. In this paper we find that this is, for the most part, not the case.[1]

Sharp's conclusion is equally uncertain:

> International comparisons are indirect evidence at best, because they involve such different cultures and educational systems. What we can say is that a later start does not appear to hold back children's progress (although it is important not to forget the important contribution made by children's experiences at home and in pre-school). Certainly, there would appear to be no compelling educational rationale for a statutory school age of five or for the practice of admitting four-year-olds to school reception classes.[2]

Most academic studies of school starting ages focus on attainment, but surely the impact of an early start on a child's well-being is a more important consideration. In both 2007 and 2011, a UNICEF study of the well-being of children in England showed that England compared poorly to other OECD countries for child well-being.[3] Children may do better in tests if they start school early, but what is the impact of an early start on their happiness and well-being?

The debate continues. The issue in England, of course, is not simply the age at which children start school but the degree of formality they experience in the early years classroom.

Although teachers and nursery leaders work hard to ensure that children learn through play wherever possible, most would surely admit to an increasingly academic approach, though they probably wouldn't use the word academic. The EYFS profile, while supposedly only an outline of what an individual child can do, inevitably acts as a set of targets so that, as soon as a child enters any kind of educational setting, he or she is under pressure to succeed. The EYFS profile summarises and describes children's attainment at the end of the EYFS. It gives the child's attainment in relation to the 17 early learning goal (ELG) descriptors, and a short narrative describing the child's three characteristics of effective learning.[4] Seventeen early learning goals is clearly a significant assessment burden, as most early years teachers would doubtless attest, and it is bound to have an impact on a child's experience of life in the classroom.

Successive governments seem to have been obsessed with national comparisons and the need for our children to keep up with those in other countries. Some would argue that this has led to an increasingly centralised approach to education. More to the point, however, it is an approach which involves increasingly bureaucratic systems for measuring and testing children's attainment. Baseline testing, for example, was strongly opposed by teachers when it was first proposed. In their paper, 'They are children . . . not robots, not machines: The Introduction of Baseline Assessment', Bradbury and Roberts-Holmes noted that 'Teachers and school leaders have serious doubts as to the accuracy of the Baseline Assessment and its use in measuring progress' and stressed that it was 'of little use in terms of the identification of additional needs'.[5] It would be easy to conclude, therefore, that it was introduced to meet the demands of politicians, not the needs of children.

Play has been replaced by purpose in our schools; children are to be educated formally as soon as possible and their progress measured at every stage. Formal education can be planned and the outcomes measured; play is simply that – play – and therefore, in political terms, of no value. Despite the fact that a huge amount of learning takes place through play, schools and nurseries face ever-more detailed instructions on what to teach and how to teach it. There is almost a Dickensian ethos underlying current early years pedagogy: children are the workers and leaders of the future; therefore, they should start work as early as possible. It could well be that many of the problems experienced by children as they move up through the system find their origins in their very first experiences of early schooling.

The confusion and excitement of a child's first experience of school, so memorably described by Laurie Lee in *Cider with Rosie*, is now amplified by increasing formality and constant testing. Starting school has now become a daunting prospect.

Working with others

For children, schools are competitive environments. This is not a comment on school sports but simply an indication of the way children inter-act with one another. It is in school where we first learn to co-operate, to listen to each other's ideas, to work together to make a task easier or simply to socialise. Many constantly feel the need to keep up, and as soon as children begin to mix with others, they start to measure themselves against them. This is perfectly natural, of course, but the moment we introduce regular testing into the picture, the nature of competition becomes more acute. Children soon become aware that they are not as good at some things as their peers, and a level of anxiety quickly creeps into both their learning and their play. In his book *Transformative Classroom Management*, John Shindler talks about longer-term dangers of competition in the classroom.[6] He writes,

> When a student sees his/her school performance as a contest, it leads increasingly to a helpless pattern . . . [this] develops through perception of

himself/herself as having a fixed quantity of ability. This incites the need to prove adequacy relative to others. While on the surface it may appear that students are motivated to perform it is rather evidence of motivation to avoid the pain of feeling inadequate and inferior.

As they move through the system, high stakes testing and the national focus on academic achievement ensure that anxiety levels continue to rise. In classrooms where play predominates, children are less anxious; where testing comes early, competition quickly follows. Kenneth Ginsberg neatly summarises the importance of play:

> Play allows children to create and explore a world they can master, conquering their fears while practicing adult roles, sometimes in conjunction with other children or adult caregivers.[7]

When play is controlled, its benefits are less obvious. In the increasingly tightly controlled world of the early years classroom, the value of play is clearly under threat.

It is worth pausing at this point to reflect on perhaps one of the most striking aspects of the school system which we rarely consider. School is probably the only time in our lives when we spend our days entirely with people of almost exactly the same age. Once we are out of the school system, this never happens again and we find ourselves mixing with people of all ages, whether in the workplace or socially. Could it be that working with our precise contemporaries adds yet another layer of potential anxiety to the experience of being in school in that our comparisons are likely to be so much sharper? If my spelling is not as good as my friend who is two years older than me, it is easy to see that in two years' time I could be of the same standard. If my friend is almost of exactly the same age, I am clearly not as good at spelling as him. Interacting with their peers in the classroom, many children must inevitably experience this sense of comparative underachievement hundreds of times a day.

Parents

Fear of failure sets in early and is often fuelled by parental expectations. In recent years we have seen the emergence of so-called helicopter parents who hover over their children and seek to fill every moment of their waking lives with educational activities. We frequently see examples in the media of parents who have created absurdly detailed weekly timetables which allow virtually no time for play or to socialise or even simply to step outside into the fresh air. Although there are, thankfully, relatively few such parents, I think it is fair to say that most of us would admit to feeling a degree of pressure to ensure that our children learn enough to keep up and get ahead.

Parental anxiety begins early. Finding a place in a good nursery is quickly followed by the need to find the right school. In 21st-century Britain, parents have more information than ever before on the nature and performance of schools in their area. What used to be a matter of local reputation has now been repackaged into a complex collection of national data sets, social media information, school websites and inspection reports. Choosing a school can be something of a nightmare, especially for parents with no direct knowledge of how the system works, other than to have been pupils in schools themselves.

A concerned parent nowadays will already have a good idea of which schools in the area are regarded as 'the best schools', but they will soon find themselves being sucked into discussions around inspection judgements: is it ok to send your child to a school that 'requires improvement'; what is really meant by an 'outstanding' school? A glance at the published data does little to clarify matters. How many parents really understand the latest progress scores published in the Department for Education (DfE)'s performance tables, especially since a score of 0.0 is actually quite good?

Parental anxiety around choosing the right school is understandable, particularly as there are so many factors to take into account. Not only is there the question of which school is considered to be the best school, but parents now need to consider what type of school it is. What exactly is an academy, or a free school, for example? Then there is the question of the admissions process, a system almost designed to generate uncertainty and anxiety as parents are forced to apply for places early in the autumn term before waiting until March of the following year to see if they have been successful. Hours can be spent poring over catchment areas and house prices, checking to see if moving to a new house is a realistic possibility. And those parents whose ambition is to get their children into grammar schools face an even more anxious time as they wait to see if their offspring have passed tests for which they have spent months preparing. There is also growing concern regarding the number of school places available. In 2019, almost a fifth of pupils in England missed out on their first-choice secondary school.[8]

As concerned parents, it is natural that we should seek to ensure that our children receive the best education on offer, but it is all too easy to see the admission process as a game we have to win at all costs. Performance data, inspection reports, the various types of school available, all add to the sense that getting into a particular school is an absolute necessity. Despite the fact that common sense tells us that, for example, a bright child will do well in virtually any school (and this is a view backed up by the data), or that a grammar school's results will obviously be better than neighbouring schools if it is allowed to select only the very brightest pupils in the area, government policy encourages us to believe that some schools are much better than others. The economics of the marketplace also lead us to believe that private education must be better than state education simply because we are paying for it, even though we are all aware that there are some terrible private schools still in operation all over the country. It is vital for parents to have a choice. This means, therefore, that parents must work incredibly hard to make the right choice, and woe betide them if they get it wrong.

It is inevitable that this level of anxiety and complexity is passed on to children. Instead of being left to become quietly excited about starting school, or moving up to the 'big school', they often become embroiled in their parents' concerns regarding the choice of the right school, or the best school. It is not surprising that, for many children, the start of school represents the culmination of an intense period of anxiety in the home, which means that they begin their education at best unsettled and sometimes genuinely distressed. Children who have failed the grammar school tests, or whose first choice of a school has been unsuccessful, face an even more troubled start.

Poverty and neglect

The other side of parental pressure is, of course, parental neglect, and this is a much larger topic and a more distressing one. There is much more focus on disadvantaged children today than there has ever been before, with school leaders acutely conscious of the need to enable pupils who have suffered neglect, or who come from deeply troubled homes, to catch up with their peers. The intensity of focus on disadvantaged pupils, and the introduction of the Pupil Premium (financial help to support schools in providing extra resources), has meant that we now have much greater awareness of the levels of poverty in our society and the extent of neglect in many homes.

Physical and emotional neglect, poverty and deprivation all lead to educational disadvantage. These children start school well behind their peers, socially, emotionally and intellectually. What has become known as 'closing the gap' between disadvantaged children and their more privileged peers is now, quite rightly, a priority in schools, but the difficulties in doing so are only now becoming clear. Children learn so much in the first few years of their lives that catching up later becomes incredibly difficult for them, as well as for the teachers trying to overcome years of neglect.

The now famous American study by Hart and Risley, which came to be known as 'the word gap', provides a good illustration of just how difficult this process of catching up really is. In their book *Meaningful Differences in the Everyday Experience of Young American Children*,[9] they recorded hundreds of hours of language used by children in different households over a two-and-a-half-year period. Families were classified by their socio-economic status. Their findings were quite shocking: they discovered that in four years, an average child in a professional family experienced almost 45 million words, an average child in a working-class family 26 million words, and an average child in a family on welfare 13 million words. Put simply, a child from a disadvantaged background enters the education system 30 million words behind children who have grown up in professional homes.

The outlook becomes even more bleak when we consider the recent rise in the numbers of children below the poverty line. According to the Resolution

Foundation, in 2018 the official poverty rate – defined as those families living on incomes of less than 60% of the median after accounting for housing costs – rose from 22.1% to 23.2%, the biggest single-year jump since 1988. The jump in the child poverty rate was much worse, however, rising from 30.3% in 2017 to 33.4% in 2018.[10] These figures are obviously a snapshot, but it is clear that child poverty is a serious issue in our society and, inevitably, an important factor in a child's experience of school.

A child from a poor background is likely to find coping with school especially difficult. He or she may well be behind others in the class in terms of vocabulary development, as well as 'social capital', the knowledge of the world that middle-class children take for granted. When we think of children from disadvantaged backgrounds, we inevitably focus on the outward facing aspects of poverty: poor diets and under-nourishment, hand-me-down clothes, non-working parents. In other words, the Dickensian pauper. What we don't consider are the huge intellectual gaps – poor vocabulary, limited experience and understanding of the world, limited social interaction and so on. If a child from a professional family, with supportive, well-heeled parents, sometimes finds school difficult with which to cope, how much worse is it likely to be for disadvantaged children?

Fear of failure

Fear of failure is the root cause of a huge amount of childhood anxiety and distress. First, there is the fear of letting one's parents down, especially when, without realising it, they have made it clear to you the extent to which their hopes and dreams are invested in their child's academic progress. Second, there is the fear of not living up to the standards set by one's teachers. Finally, and perhaps most potent of all, is the fear of not being accepted by one's peers.

We have already seen how parents' anxiety around finding the right school can be passed on to the child, but anxious parents, motivated by the best of reasons, continue to exert pressure on their children throughout their school careers. As a result, many children become anxious almost by osmosis. Parents are encouraged by schools to ensure that their children are dressed in the appropriate uniform, have the right equipment and are never taken out of school for frivolous reasons such as family holidays. They are asked to monitor their homework, check their homework diaries, and, increasingly, attend evening sessions so that they can keep up with whatever their children are learning. Regular school reports allow them to monitor their sons and daughters' academic progress, and conversations at the school gate with other concerned parents plant seeds of doubt about almost every aspect of what is happening in the classroom. Research has shown that parental anxiety is easily transmitted to children.[11] Children pick up on their parents' concerns, and if mum and dad are worried about finding a school place, or a myriad of other worries they may have about the start of school, it is almost inevitable that the child will become anxious too.

There is also a huge amount of parental anxiety around attainment. If a child is not attaining high enough standards, it is unlikely that parents will put this down to the fact that he or she may not be as bright as others in the class. Every parent is struck by how bright their children are when they are very small – young children learn at a phenomenal rate – but when the rapid pace of learning slows, the tendency today is to assume it must be due to poor teaching. Fear of failure drives parents to complain, to harass teachers and sometimes to move schools. More and more frequently, they turn to private tutors to fill the perceived gaps.

A recent article in *The Guardian* described the growth in private tuition over the last decade.[12] The proportion of pupils who have had a private tutor rose from 18% in 2005 to 25% in 2016 and stands at 42% in the capital. In 2018 alone, one in 10 of all state-educated 11- to 16-year-olds in England and Wales were tutored. These are quite striking figures and point both to the potential of education inequality, as only the relatively well-off can afford this kind of support, but also to the level of parental anxiety driving the rush towards private tutoring. For many parents, such is the need to ensure that their children achieve academically; no expense will be spared to help them get there. Whether private tuition really helps is another matter. At best it ensures that a pupil gets one-on-one support for a few hours and thus provides the individual attention that hard-pressed teachers are not able to give; at worst, it further increases stress levels, making the pupil feel that he or she has already failed if this expensive additional support is required.

Teachers are less influential than one might think, but most children don't want to let their teachers down and therefore become particularly anxious to please them when it is time for a test. Some children are frightened that they will have to endure their teacher's wrath or disdain if they do not do well and so become acutely conscious of the importance of good marks. Sometimes, it is the anxiety caused by worrying about doing well in the tests, which is the reason for their poor performance. At other times, it is because having failed before, they see no point in preparing for another test they will inevitably fail.

The tests, of course, are not the teacher's tests. Most teachers are not great advocates of frequent testing. Behind the primary school multiplication tables test, or the secondary school mock GCSE examination, sits the whole panoply of national assessment policy. Most children undertaking a simple test sitting at their desks in the classroom detect the presence of much more powerful forces underlying the tasks set by the teacher. They may not be able explicitly to identify the governmental mechanisms underlying the tests, but they feel their presence and tighten the grip on their pencils accordingly.

There is a great deal of research to suggest that the most powerful influence on children is other children.[13] Failure in the eyes of their peers is perhaps the most disturbing form of failure there is for a child. Children are acutely aware of the social gradations within a classroom. They know who the high-flyers are, they know the social trend-setters and they are very aware of the ones to avoid. They are also often cruelly dismissive of other children, the oddballs, the ones who don't fit in for whatever reason. Navigating the social hierarchy of the classroom is fraught with difficulties and can lead to huge anxieties.

Above all, children want to fit in. This means that they have to learn to adapt to the personalities around them. Sometimes this takes the form of emulation, sometimes confederacy. For an adult observer, it is easy to assume that children divide the world in simple binary terms: them and us. In reality, the world of the classroom is much more complex than this as friendships are made and broken, interests change, new people join and others leave, and arguments split the most loyal of comrades. At times, children celebrate their group identity, their class or their school; at others, they focus on their intimates, their close friends, a closeness which often excludes others. Anyone who has worked in a school can see this in action. Pupils talking to inspectors about their school are nearly always fantastically loyal. Even the most difficult children, when confronted by outsiders, sing the praises of the establishments they spend most of their lives fighting against. On the other hand, every teacher is aware of the way in which children fall out with one another on a regular basis, often over the most trivial of events, and the impact this can have both on their learning and those around them. Navigating the choppy waters of the classroom adds yet another layer of anxiety to the already-troubled child.

'It was ever thus', one might say. Perhaps so, but the world has changed, and the rise of social media has added levels of complexity to the jungle of childhood, and life is more difficult for the young than it has ever been before.

Social media

Once upon a time, a pupil bullied at school was able to go home and escape, if only for the evening or the weekend. Now, the bullying is unremitting. Whether it is via Snapchat, Instagram or a dozen other social media apps aimed squarely at young people, the messages keep coming – all through the day and all through the night. Even the most socially confident young people can easily be thrown off course by a stray remark, such is the lethal damage to their self-esteem an unkind posting can inflict.

Children, as William Golding so memorably pointed out in *Lord of the Flies*, are not always kind to one another. Learning to socialise and to empathise are key lessons of early childhood. Bullying is therefore part of growing up. However hard teachers work to prevent bullying in the classroom or on the playground, it will always be there. Bullies are powerful and subtle and, though it is a dreadfully overused word nowadays, bullying is everywhere, and children have to learn to cope with it. Unless we can find a way fundamentally to alter human nature, it is unlikely ever to be eradicated in our schools. It is yet another aspect of education with which the child must learn to deal and another source of anxiety that diverts many away from their learning.

The irony of what has been described as an epidemic of bullying is that most of the so-called bullies are unaware of what they are doing. If one person takes a swipe at an individual, others join in. For each of them, their individual comment seems fairly harmless, a light-hearted remark or a joke; for the child on the receiving end of the joke, who may have read dozens or even hundreds of such jokes, the cumulative effect turns the joke into a full-blown onslaught. In the real world, it is easy to cope with a sarcastic remark from a friend, easy to respond and easy to divert the conversation onto more comfortable territory. Online, it is much harder. Everything is public and everything is magnified. The minor squabbles and disagreements of childhood can easily take on a much darker tone and, put simply, ruin children's lives.

Adolescents have always struggled with self-image, especially if they are not the best-looking students in the class. It was even more difficult for the over-weight, the under-sized or those who were physically different in some way. I can vividly remember the misery of having to wear glasses and the first time I wore them in school. There are similar stories about children forced to wear braces on their teeth. These are all fairly straightforward things with which to deal – they may have seemed like the end of the world horrors at the time but, in the wider scheme of things, they were minor bumps on the road to adulthood. How much more difficult it must be for young people today surrounded by media images of perfection and the apparently perfect lives of online celebrities.

Young people have always looked up to others; it is part of looking forward to becoming adults. In the pre-teenage era, they longed to be grown up, dressing like adults as early as they were able to and imitating adult manners and styles. Film stars were admired for their beauty but also the freedom they possessed as grown-ups able to go about the world freely.

Once the idea of the teenager was invented, their idols grew younger. They were always out of reach, but they were, on the whole, real. The constructed fantasies of boy bands like The Monkees may have involved actors, but their audiences knew that. The Spice Girls may have appeared to live in a world of miraculous glitz and glamour but, fundamentally, they were ordinary young women living in a world of pop make-believe.

Contemporary role models are much more sophisticated and, in many ways, really quite dangerous. Computer technology offers young people images of perfection impossible to replicate in everyday life. The stunningly beautiful 'influencer' is not an ordinary person; he or she will have been electronically enhanced, and often surgically enhanced, and every image will have been filtered and shaped. The spots we might have noticed under the make-up on the face of one of the Spice Girls will have been carefully removed by the magic of Photoshop or something similar; the awkward pose, the tired look, the yawn, or the blank expression will never be seen, so carefully are the images curated.

If the images of their idols online aren't enough with which to cope, the always-on Instagram culture of their friends and acquaintances makes social interaction so much more difficult. People of all ages today construct their lives using social media. They don't present the reality of day-to-day living; they offer only the best bits. The aim is to make it look as if one is living a perfect life. The beautiful images, once the preserve of film stars and glamour models, are available to us all to construct. We may have had a terrible day, but we can still post an image of ourselves pretending to party and having the time of our lives. For the teenager sitting alone in his or her bedroom, it must sometimes seem as if everyone they know is living a perfect life apart from them. Even if they are happy and well balanced, the pressure to post perfect images in order to maintain the illusion of their online life must at times seem overwhelming. Once upon a time, a child may have worried about what their friends would say if they turned up to school wearing glasses; now they worry about how they measure up in a world of impossible online perfection.

The sinister corollary of online glamour is, of course, the increasing sexualisation of childhood. Not only do younger and younger children have access to all sorts of sexual content on the internet, but they are confronted by highly sexualised images presented to them by media influencers and mainstream advertisers. Whatever their parents think, and however tightly they regulate their children's internet use, virtually all children access online porn at an early age. What this does to their understanding of adult sexual behaviour is a topic well beyond the scope of this book, but what is clear is that children begin to see themselves as sexual beings at a much younger age. Pop culture is no longer about love; it is about sex. The sex that was once hidden in double meanings and metaphors is now explicit and a feature of a huge amount of music aimed directly at teenagers and pre-teens alike. Fashion is shot through with sexual imagery, and even the health industry closely aligns sex and fitness.

For young people concerned about how they look and how they present themselves to the world, this highly sexualised culture is a real problem. It adds yet another layer of difficulty in their attempts to grapple with increasingly complex and confusing social situations. Young girls want to look like their on-screen idols; they want to keep up with their friends, and so they join in with the heavily promoted hyper-sexual pre-teen fashion culture. Having seen sex online and seen sexual imagery everywhere they look, they are then at a loss as to how to cope with members of the opposite sex. For young women, the clash of values they later experience as the toxic culture of the media confronts feminism must seem like an intellectual and social nightmare. For boys, too, there is no escape. How do they align the pornographic imagery they have secretly been absorbing in their bedrooms with real girls in the real world? Moreover, as the 'me too' movement takes hold, how do boys feel about the way men are increasingly demonised in the press as sexual predators?

Mental health

Given the problems now faced by our young people, is it really any surprise that mental health disorders are on the rise? Barely a day goes by without some kind of reference to mental health in the media, and the word 'crisis' is used repeatedly to describe what many now see as a problem which is only going to get worse. The issues outlined earlier – social anxiety, constant testing, parental pressure, neglect, fear of failure, social media, a highly sexualised culture – seem to offer a toxic mix which will inevitably lead to mental health problems for all of us, not only the young. But is there really a mental health crisis?

According to figures published by the NHS in 2018, one in eight children under age 19 in England have a mental health disorder.[14] Boys were found to be more likely to have problems than girls until the age of 11; between 11 and 16 the balance is even, but by the time they reach 17, girls were more than twice as likely to have a mental disorder. The findings relating to teenage girls are particularly shocking, with almost one in four 17- to 19-year-olds having some kind of mental disorder, with half of those saying that they had self-harmed or attempted suicide. The impact of concerns regarding body image fuelled by social media will undoubtedly have played a part but, as we have seen, there is much more to it than that. The 2018 survey also looked, for the first time, at the mental health of pre-school children, noting that one in 18 children were affected, with boys twice as likely to have problems as girls.

However, it is not strictly accurate to talk about a sudden dramatic rise in the numbers of children suffering from mental health disorders: the 2018 survey estimated that 11.2% of children have mental health issues, but the previous survey, undertaken in 2004, was not dramatically different at 10%. Mental health disorders in the young have always been with us, but it seems that nowadays the causes are both increasingly complex and much more widely known, understood and publicised. In addition to poverty, family dysfunction, sexual assaults, examination stress and friendship issues, children have to cope with eating disorders, drugs, globalisation and, above all, social media.

Part of the problem is undoubtedly due to the fact that we now know so much more about mental health, and information about it is so much more easily available. On the face of it, this is a good thing: when mental health issues are suspected, we can easily find out information online to help lead us to the appropriate help and support. The undoubted downside, however, is that it is now all too easy for young people to access information which could well do more harm than good. The anxious teenager worried about forthcoming examinations can jump easily from web pages covering revision techniques to tips for coping with stress, to pages discussing depression and serious mental illness. In addition, instead of sharing their concerns with a few like-minded friends, they can easily be drawn into chat rooms where teenagers around the world talk obsessively about their problems. The magnifying effect of electronic media presents real dangers for young people.

The self-harm 'epidemic' is a case in point. How many of us, 20 or 30 years ago, knew anything about self-harm? If we were aware of it, more likely than not, it would be in reference to someone with a severe mental disorder, possibly someone in a psychiatric ward. Today, it is everywhere. Anyone who works in a school will know how often youngsters talk about self-harm and how common the practice has become. One has to ask the question, therefore, how do young people know about it? The answer is obvious: they learn about it on the internet. A brief search will turn up hundreds, if not thousands, of sites discussing self-harm, with many of them containing explicit images and even live streams of children deliberately cutting themselves. It is easy to see how a mildly depressed teenager could be lured into thinking that self-harm is commonplace and the obvious way to relieve anxiety. Relatively rare expressions of mental instability are thus normalised and become widespread. Minor issues that once upon a time would have been talked out amongst friends are magnified in the dark corners of the internet and turned into much more serious disorders.

Readily available information has had another side effect – another unintended consequence of the information age – and this relates to parental anxiety. Just as children turn to the net to seek solutions to their problems and discuss issues with online acquaintances, parents rush to the net to express their own anxieties regarding their children. *Mumsnet*, for example, is awash with parental concern. It also means that parents have become 'experts' in 'diagnosing' their children's supposed conditions and needs.

This has become a serious problem for schools. School leaders nowadays face a constant stream of parents demanding support for their children. In addition to concerns regarding teaching, parents are forceful in demanding mental health assessments and special needs diagnoses. More often than not they confuse the term 'description' with 'diagnosis', the latter implying a medical condition susceptible to treatment. It is easy to create a caricature of the middle-class parent whose son or daughter is not as bright as they would like them to be, demanding a 'diagnosis' of dyslexia to explain away the problem at dinner parties. 'Tristram didn't do very well in his exams but he is dyslexic, you see'. A caricature, yes, but for many school leaders, a familiar one.

Parents and teachers now have access to reams of information regarding 'conditions' of all kinds, and they are supported by a veritable industry of pseudo-psychologists. Most schools have regular contact with an educational psychologist, but the internet grants access to hundreds of online pundits who peddle misinformation with gleeful abandon. Virtually all headteachers and special educational needs coordinators will be familiar with the privately commissioned psychologist's report, or the independent dyslexia survey, and therefore have to do battle with parents demanding hundreds of hours of extra support for children who more often than not have very few problems at all. For many, their real problem is their parents.

The growth of the psychology industry has been accompanied by the growth in acronyms which almost seem to be aimed at providing parents with comfort blankets rather than being of any use in supporting children in difficulties. Special education needs and disability (SEND) is now broken down into dozens of subsections. Poor behaviour has done particularly well with wondrous conditions such as the now infamous Oppositional Defiance Disorder (ODD), commonly known to teachers as bad behaviour, now available to parents (see Appendix).

The combination of childhood anxiety, the magnifying effects of social media and the pseudo-scientific information industry has ensured that the mental health of our children is one of the most pressing problems of contemporary society. Once again, it is not easy being a child in the 21st century.

Boredom

One of the more popular solutions to stress and anxiety disorders is mindfulness, which can best be described as the latest, most fashionable version of meditation. With its roots in the Buddhist tradition of 'sati', it has been taken up by clinical psychologists who have used it to develop a number of therapeutic applications to address a variety of psychological conditions. Schools are increasingly investing time into exploring its effectiveness in a bid to lessen stress levels, particularly in the run-up to the examination season, and more and more medical professionals are promoting mindfulness as a means of coping with today's increasingly complex world. It does, of course, work because it is based on the simple premise that taking time out of a busy day to pause and to relax reduces tension and lowers levels of anxiety.

Until recently, of course, children were expert exponents of mindfulness thanks simply to long periods of time when there was nothing to do. Before the internet tightened its grip on children's lives, they had to work harder to find things to do. It is tempting, at this point, to drift into a nostalgic account of the ideal childhood fixed into the nation's consciousness thanks to Enid Blyton's *Famous Five*, with children spending hours and hours outdoors making their own fun. Considering the British weather, I doubt whether children ever really lived out their young lives like Julian, Dick, Anne and George (not forgetting Timmy the dog). However, there were obviously times when children did have to find things to do and times when they undoubtedly became overcome with boredom. I can clearly remember periods in my own childhood when I was bored and had to force myself either to endure the boredom or come up with something to do. Today, boredom lasts no longer than a few minutes as children reach for the computer and lose themselves in online worlds or catch up with social media.

Could it be, therefore, that a super-abundance of entertainment options has almost removed boredom as an option for children? This may sound like a good thing, but if we think of boredom as the analogue predecessor of mindfulness, children may no longer have natural periods of mindfulness built into their day and be losing out as a result. Instead of having natural breaks – down time – children are now able to occupy themselves much more easily. More and more children spend hours every day in front of screens. Tiny children are given iPads to occupy them. Teachers frequently encounter pupils who have spent half the night online playing games or chatting to friends. When a child's mind is stimulated, and often over-stimulated throughout the day, there is bound to be a psychological impact.

Schools are the answer

For politicians, schools offer the obvious solution to so many of the problems confronting children today. Schools are, of course, essentially part of the state, although the ties have been weakening since the advent of academies and free schools, and as such they are relatively easy to direct. Politicians can have little control over parents – parents are their constituents so they need to be placated wherever possible – and they have no way of influencing children directly. The only way forward, therefore, is to use schools to solve society's ills.

If issues were tackled thoroughly and systemically, with carefully worked out interventions based on solid research, then schools could well be effective in dealing with many of the problems which seem to baffle politicians. Unfortunately, most policies are knee-jerk reactions to high-profile events: they are imposed far too quickly, and schools are more often than not left to sort things out for themselves. In recent years, for example, schools have been tasked with tackling extremism and radicalisation, female genital mutilation (FGM), forced marriage, childhood obesity, racism, homophobia and so on.

All these things have to be built into the school's curriculum, and everyday there are calls for schools to introduce more and more topics to ensure that children are fit to enter society. As I pointed out in my previous book, *The Gradual Art of School Improvement*, schools are in danger of becoming overwhelmed by the expectations heaped upon them.[15] Headteachers are expected to ensure that they prepare children for virtually everything life has to throw at them, from sex education to drug taking, from economic literacy to environmental awareness and so on.

In the course of writing that book, I kept a daily record of the issues presented in the media which schools are expected to solve. After two months, I gave up because I was simply overwhelmed by the sheer number of the demands. The list is comprehensive, to say the least; all life is there. It covers everything from the vital topics which plague us in the modern world – racism, mental health issues, poverty and so on – to the truly bizarre: pigeon racing clubs, for example. From Darcy Bussell stressing the importance of physical education (PE) to Prince Harry warning us about the dangers of Fortnite, it seems as if everyone is entitled to a view on what schools should be doing. It is simply not possible for schools to do everything. It is a shame that the media, and politicians in particular, don't appreciate that.

Schools do their best, however, and school leaders go to great lengths to ensure that curriculum subjects such as personal, social and health education (PSHE) and citizenship[16] have thorough schemes of work which attempt to cover as many of society's concerns as possible. Most schools cover key topics in regular assemblies, and virtually all of them invite speakers into schools in order to ensure that children get the most up-to-date information. However, one of the key problems overlooked by politicians anxious to make their mark by adding yet another topic to the curriculum is the simple fact that teachers cannot be expected to be experts in everything. How many teachers were even aware that FGM existed before they were asked to talk about it in schools; how many have the kind of detailed knowledge of the 'dark net' from which children have to be protected?

Safeguarding is now a central part of school life and a key element of the school inspection framework. Its significance is a mark of the distance schools have travelled from being providers of an academic education to being expected to help shape almost every aspect of a young person's life. The teacher who entered the profession to share his or her love of literature, or languages, or chemistry now fulfils a role which is perhaps closer to that of a social worker than a teacher. *The Guardian*'s Secret Teacher described this dilemma succinctly: 'I have three roles in my classroom: teacher, parent and social worker. Sometimes the actual teaching part is the least important'.[17]

Most children say they feel safe in school, and the vast majority of inspection reports comment on the effectiveness of safeguarding in schools. However, given the complex world young people now inhabit, great care must be taken to ensure that subjects such as PSHE and citizenship don't add to their stress. It is bad enough worrying about friendships, parents, social media, body image and so on without having a whole new world of horror in the form of FGM, radicalisation and, more recently, knife crime, being opened up before you. Could it be that in seeking to protect our children, we sometimes do more harm than good?

Toxic schooling

In her influential study *Toxic Childhood*, Sue Palmer explored children's changing lifestyles, with each chapter covering a key aspect of their daily lives.[18] These are all now familiar themes: junk food; playtime and the decline of the free-range child; disrupted bed times and the lack of sleep; poor literacy in the home and the rise of the 'screen' generation; changing roles in the family; the impact of childcare; consumer culture and the rise of the entertainment media; technology for tots; and the importance of parenting. Much of her thesis focussed on education, with real concern expressed regarding the decline in children's literacy, the dominance of digital technology, the rise of assessment and the constant interference of politicians in the lives of children. Her analysis of the relationship between schools and parents was really quite prescient, and she explored the pressurised relationships between children and their parents with great insight. Throughout, however, she remained optimistic, offering a wide range of solutions aimed at 'detoxing childhood'.

Unfortunately, Palmer's optimism is yet to bear fruit, and many, if not all, of the problems identified in her book are still with us today. Indeed, many are exacerbated by what has been done to our school system in the last decade. Palmer's toxic childhood has become almost institutionalised; her damaged children are now falling victim to toxic classrooms.

What can schools do now to put things right?

- **Celebrate play**. Match the Foundation Stage profile to a rich and vibrant early years curriculum rather than matching the curriculum to the Foundation Stage profile. The revised Ofsted framework encourages school leaders to think about the rationale underpinning the curriculum, with the needs of the pupils at the heart of any discussion about what subjects to include and how to teach them. This approach offers great scope for the re-invention of the curriculum.

- **Naturalise testing**. In the best schools, testing is built into day-to-day activities so that they become ordinary activities. Children are therefore often unaware that they are doing tests, and their significance is reduced. They are significant for teachers, not children. Similarly, schools need to work hard to play down the importance of tests with parents.

- **Work with parents to decrease anxiety**. Schools need to be much more aware of the impact of the admission system on parents and work with them to allay their fears, explaining the systems as clearly as possible and stressing the positives of second- and third-choice school places. Similarly, they need to supply the detailed information parents need; the more information schools give to parents, the less likely they are to turn to the internet or to rumours and gossip.

- **Be clear about the school's strengths**. It is undoubtedly true that an RI judgement turns parents away from schools, but if school leaders are open and transparent about what went wrong and what they are doing to put things right, parents are much more likely to stay on side and support the school. Ignoring or hiding weaknesses will lead only to further weakness and to parental suspicion. An open and honest leader is likely to be much more convincing and thus more likely to be trusted with their child's future.

- **Really focus on disadvantaged pupils**. Since Pupil Premium children became a central plank of the Ofsted framework, many schools have used the framework to guide their approach to supporting disadvantaged children. This is a very positive approach, but in the best schools, leaders and teachers really think about how to help children who have fallen behind their peers to catch up and there is a real sense of passion. However, in some schools, even though a panoply of intervention strategies is in place, little thought is given to their effectiveness. It is vital to evaluate the impact of the work done with pupils of all abilities in order to ensure that they are really making progress.

- **Reading and reading**. Time must be found to read with children. It is a simple thing, but its importance cannot be underestimated. In too many schools, from primary to secondary, it is built into the timetable as just another thing to do. In reality, for many children, it is the only thing to do.

- **Private tuition**. Most schools pretend this doesn't happen. They need to be open about it, engage with private tutors, recommend the good ones, be honest about their impact and work with parents. And though it goes against the grain, teachers must not shy away from working with tutors. If they do, they retain a measure of control over what pupils are learning.

- **Social media**. How to use it safely and its impact must be taught from a very early age. Children need to learn how to live in the always-on world. Media studies has never been more important. Schools must acknowledge that teachers simply do not have the expertise to teach children about the dangers of social media without intensive training or help from expert advisors such as police officers.

- **Self-image and sexualisation**. PSHE should be taught by specialists – not class teachers – and as early as possible. Again, this is something too important to be left to amateurs. Most teachers have PSHE thrust upon them to teach in tutor time or in one lesson a week; most have very little expertise in what is becoming one of the most complex subjects in the school curriculum. Schools need to invest time in recruiting and training specialist teachers with the skills pupils need to help them understand the world today.

- **Mental health**. This must be taught without hysteria and with a degree of common sense. Pupils must be taught the skills they need to surf the web with discrimination, care and understanding. Above all, schools must work with mental health professionals and be very wary of volunteers, counsellors and others purporting to have expertise in children's mental health.

- **Mindfulness or Monopoly**. Teach children to play games. And not computer games. Board games are social activities which encourage social interaction, turn-taking, fair play and so on. Above all they are relaxing. But today children don't play these games at home, so they need time at school – and they need to be taught how to play them.

> **What should policymakers do to put things right?**
>
> - Understand that testing isn't always the answer.
>
> - Leave teaching to teachers.
>
> - Avoid the knee-jerk 'schools will fix it approach' and look for better answers to social problems.
>
> - Reform the admissions system and acknowledge the fact that there aren't enough school places for a growing population.
>
> - Recognise that teachers today are highly skilled professionals, not the old men in tweed jackets with leather patches on their sleeves they remember.

Notes

1. S.E. Black, P.J. Devereux & K.G. Salvanes. 2008. *Too Young to Leave the Nest: The Effects of School Starting Age*, Cambridge, MA, National Bureau of Economic Research.
2. C. Sharp. 2002. *School Starting Age; European Policy and Recent Research*, NFER.
3. UNICEF Office of Research. 2013. *Child Well-Being in Rich Countries: A Comparative Overview. Innocenti Report Card 11*, Florence, UNICEF Office of Research. www.unicef-irc.org/publications/pdf/rc11_eng.pdf
4. *Early Years Foundation Stage Profile*, DfE, 2018. STA/19/8311/e.
5. A. Bradbury & G. Roberts-Holmes. 2016. *They're Children, Not Robots, Not Machines: The Introduction of Baseline Assessment*, London. www.teachers.org.uk/sites/default/files2014/baseline-assessment-final-10404.pdf
6. J. Shindler. 2009. *Tranformative Classroom Management*, Jossey Bass.
7. K.R. Ginsburg. 2007. The Importance of Play in Promoting Healthy Child Development and Maintaining Strong Parent-Child Bonds, *The American Academy of Pediatrics*, Volume 119, Issue 1.
8. *The Guardian*, Thursday 13 June 2019. www.theguardian.com/education/2019/jun/13/fifth-of-pupils-in-england-miss-out-on-first-choice-of-secondary
9. B. Hart & T. Risley. 1995. *Meaningful Differences in the Everyday Experience of Young American Children*, P.H. Brookes.
10. The Resolution Foundation. 2018. *The Living Standards Audit 2018*. www.resolutionfoundation.org/publications/the-living-standards-audit-2018/
11. C. Eley, T. McAdams, F.V. Rijsdijk, P. Lichtenstein, J. Narusyte, E.L. Spotts, J.M. Ganiban & J.M. Neiderhiser. 2015. The Intergenerational Transmission of Anxiety: A Children-of-Twins Study, *The American Journal of Psychiatry*. https://doi.org/10.1176/appi.ajp.2015.14070818
12. S. Weale. 2016. *Sharp Rise in Children Receiving Private Tuition*. www.theguardian.com/education/2016/sep/08/sharp-rise-in-children-receiving-private-tuition
13. J. Hattie. 2009. *Visible Learning*, Oxon, Routledge.
14. Mental Health of Children and Young People Survey, *NHS Digital*, 22 November 2018. https://digital.nhs.uk/data-and-information/publications/statistical/mental-health-of-children-and-young-people-in-england/2017/2017

15 R. Steward. 2019. *The Gradual Art of School Improvement*, London, David Fulton.
16 I have always enjoyed the irony of the title Citizenship because, living in the UK, we are not citizens, of course, but subjects. Perhaps we should therefore change the name of the subject from Citizenship to Subjection?
17 The Secret Teacher, *The Guardian*, Saturday 10 January 2015. www.theguardian.com/teacher-network/2015/jan/10/secret-teacher-social-worker-emotional-students
18 S. Palmer. 2015. *Toxic Childhood*, Second Edition, London, Orion Books.

2 The curriculum

The background

The school curriculum presents us with something of a paradox: on the one hand, it seems to be subject to continual change; on the other, it is not that different from the basic curriculum offered in schools in the 19th century. Following the 1870 Education Act, children in establishments run by the school boards studied a set of subjects recognisable in schools today. Elementary schools catered for pupils up to the age of 14 and concentrated on the 'three Rs': reading, writing and arithmetic. Pupils in the higher years, or 'standards' as they were known then, were granted access to a broader range of subjects, including grammar, geography, history and 'plain needlework', a list which was sometimes expanded to include foreign languages and both pure and applied science.

The progression from the 'three Rs' in 19th-century elementary classes to a mixed bag of additional subjects is not too different from the current intensive focus on reading, writing and mathematics in the early years, through to the GCSE option system in secondary schools today. The 'basics' of the curriculum have remained largely unchanged; it is the details where the real battles take place.

The introduction of the National Curriculum was an attempt to fix and codify the curriculum in state schools. The 'Great Debate', initiated in a speech given by James Callaghan in 1976 at Ruskin College, led eventually to the 1988 Education Reform Act, introduced by Kenneth Baker, which saw the launch of the first statutory National Curriculum. It was, to say the least, a thorough document, with detailed programmes of study covering both 'core' and 'foundation' subjects. Teachers in schools had never seen such detail coming directly from central government and, as a consequence, discussions around what the curriculum should and should not include intensified. The idea of fixing the curriculum once and for all served only to stimulate debate and led to an era of continual change, the consequences of which are still evident in our schools today.

Over the next few years, successive education ministers took delight in responding to the national debate by introducing a series of reforms, the aims of which were both political and practical. The 1994 review of the National Curriculum sought to slim down what was, by then, regarded as a wildly over-prescriptive document. The review was led by Ron Dearing, a respected educationalist who, it is fair to say, had considerable support amongst teachers and education professionals. His report led to a slimmed-down curriculum, with lots of the detail trimmed to sensible levels and a new focus on assessment. Many of his key ideas were, of course, rejected by politicians, but he deserves credit for the revised National Curriculum introduced in 1995, which undoubtedly made the lives of teachers, and by extension the pupils they taught, much more manageable.

The 1999 revision continued to rationalise what was still seen by many as a burdensome, over-stuffed curriculum, particularly at the primary level. David Blunket, the education secretary at the time, decided to reduce the content of foundation subjects in primary schools to allow more time to be spent on the core subjects of English, mathematics and science. Ed Balls continued the rationalisation process, slimming down the curriculum still further in 2008 and commissioning yet another review, this time focussing largely on the primary curriculum and led by Jim Rose. The results of this review were overtaken by events – a change of government in 2010 – and the advent of Michael Gove, whose own review, led by Tim Oates of Cambridge Assessment, resulted in a revised National Curriculum introduced in 2013. Gove's insistence that GCSEs and Advanced Levels, more commonly referred to as A-levels, were no longer fit for purpose and introduced an intense period of change in schools, as teachers struggled to come to terms with new syllabuses (now to be termed 'specifications') and complex new assessment systems.

Gove's vision of a properly academic curriculum was, of course, intensely traditional. He advocated the reintroduction of the 'canon' of English literature, insisting that pupils should be reading Austen, Dickens, Hardy, Keats and Byron, among others. He commissioned Simon Schama to develop a history curriculum which told the story of 'our island', a patriotic vision of the past which marginalised the more global concerns of historians in order to concentrate on the achievements of empire. He also made the study of foreign languages compulsory up to the age of 16 and insisted upon a basic grounding in the fundamentals of science for all pupils. With Gove's reforms, we came full circle back to the traditions of the 19th century and much closer to the English public school curriculum so much admired by conservative politicians. In the current academic year, teachers continue to wrestle with Gove's reforms as the new examination specifications take hold and new assessment rules begin to bite.

Each successive secretary of state is under an obligation to make his or her mark, and the office of the Secretary of State for Education is perhaps the most accessible for ambitious politicians desperate to attract attention and further their careers.

They all know about education because they have all been to school; changes are therefore easy to make. The developments outlined earlier make this clear. Every new education secretary seems desperate to make changes, but very few consider educational professionals worth listening to. Gove's description of the teaching profession as 'the blob' was widely criticised, but one cannot help thinking that he was merely saying out loud what many politicians have thought for years.[1]

A school curriculum is more than a list of subjects. There are a number of key elements. First, there is the statutory National Curriculum which the majority of schools still follow, despite the freedoms given to academies and free schools. Second, there are those subjects which are prescribed by law but which, for many, sit outside the academic curriculum: religious education, sex education, careers advice and guidance, and work-related learning. Finally, there is all the other stuff: extra or co-curricular activities which, though rarely included in school prospectuses as part of the curriculum, are often vital to the life and culture of the school.

The definition can then be broadened still further if we consider the philosophy underpinning the curriculum. Sean Harford, Ofsted's Director of Education, used the following working definition in a recent speech:

> The curriculum is a framework for setting out the aims of a programme of education, including the knowledge and understanding to be gained at each stage (intent); for translating that framework over time into a structure and a narrative, within an institutional context (implementation) and for evaluating what knowledge and understanding pupils have gained against expectations (impact/achievement).[2]

In other words, the curriculum is a framework involving both skills and knowledge which schools deliver as a coherent narrative to their pupils. As this is a definition prepared for Ofsted, it perhaps inevitably moves on to include impact and achievement. This strikes me as more about evaluating the curriculum rather than the curriculum itself. However, the only way to check that a curriculum is doing what one wants it to do is to evaluate it, though not necessarily in terms simply of achievement in examinations but the wider achievements of pupils who have been through the system. Is it all about success in exams, paths to employment, or more about developing a love of learning to sustain them in later life?

The curriculum in schools today is a result of almost constant change and is therefore a contributory factor to the toxic atmosphere in the classroom. It is worthwhile, therefore, taking a few moments to outline exactly where we are before exploring the complexities of the curriculum discussion in more detail.

Where are we now? The foundation stage

The basic curriculum currently taught in state schools in England is broken into several stages: The foundation stage, key stages 1 to 4, and the 16–19 programmes of study. Children begin their journey through the system by entering what an objective observer might regard as perhaps the most complex area of the curriculum. The Early Years Foundation Stage Statutory Framework (EYFS) covers seven areas of learning:

- communication and language
- physical development
- personal, social and emotional development
- literacy
- mathematics
- understanding the world
- expressive arts and design

To make things simpler, at the end of their Reception year, the Foundation Stage Profile measures children's attainment in 17 areas of learning known as Early Learning Goals (ELGs). These are:

Communication and language

- Listening and attention
- Understanding (e.g. following instructions, responding to questions)
- Speaking

Physical development

- Moving and handling (showing good control and coordination in large movements, like climbing, and small, like using scissors)
- Health and self-care

Personal, social and emotional development

- Self-confidence and self-awareness
- Managing feelings and behaviour
- Making relationships

Literacy

- Reading
- Writing

Mathematics

- Numbers
- Shape, space and measures

Understanding the world

- People and communities
- The world
- Technology

Expressive arts and design

- Exploring and using media and materials (including music and dance)
- Being imaginative

In each of these areas, the ELGs set out what the average child is expected to be able to do at the age of 5. For example, the number goal says that pupils should be able to count reliably from one to 20, place these numbers in order, and say which number is one less or one more than a given number. They should be able to add and subtract two single-digit numbers and count on or back to find the answer. They should also be able to solve simple problems like doubling, halving and sharing.

In addition to the 17 ELGs, the EYFS profile includes information about how a child is developing in three 'characteristics of effective learning'. These are:

- playing and exploring
- active learning
- creating and thinking critically

These three characteristics are regarded as playing an important part in children's ability to learn. They also enable their Year 1 teacher to understand their level of development and their learning needs as they move into key stage 1.

The slimmed-down National Curriculum introduced by Ron Dearing in 1995 has given way to a complex and demanding early years curriculum which teachers struggle with on a day-to-day basis, the complexities of which few parents really understand. What children make of all this is harder to determine, but this will be explored in the next chapter.

Where are we now? Primary education

Once pupils enter the primary phase, the National Curriculum becomes the guiding light. Its grip on the curriculum is tempered, however, by the influence of the various tests pupils encounter as they move up through the system, with each according more or less importance to the various aspects of the programmes of study. The impact and influence of these tests will be explored later. For now, let's concentrate on the basics.

The subjects to be studied at key stages 1 and 2 are the same, with the only difference being the addition of languages at key stage 2. They are divided into core subjects: English, mathematics and science, and the foundation subjects: art and design, computing, design and technology, geography, history, music and physical education. All schools are also required to teach religious education at all key stages.

The balance between these subjects is difficult to determine and, to an extent, up to each individual school. However, over the past few years there has been an increasing focus on the basics, English and mathematics, with much less attention paid to the foundation subjects, especially at key stage 1. Since it is vital for pupils to learn basic communication and numeracy skills before progressing further in their learning, this emphasis is hardly surprising. Some would argue, however, that the pendulum has swung too far. A not uncommon pattern in primary schools is the morning spent on English and mathematics, and the afternoon used to fit in everything else. Obviously, where this happens, it leads to a very distorted curriculum, with some subjects neglected almost entirely. This often occurs in schools where the teachers do not feel appropriately equipped to deliver specialist subjects such as science or technology. It is not unusual, therefore, to find that pupils in one school have an excellent grounding in, say, geography but very little understanding of science. This is a common lament among secondary subject teachers.

Most primary leaders would argue that the foundation subjects are taught alongside English and mathematics, with many using either topic books or simply one common exercise book with all subjects taught through the prism of the core subjects. This approach has a lot to recommend it, but it is likely, nevertheless, to lead to, at best, a fragmented approach to the foundation subjects or, in the worst cases, a haphazard scamper through various bits and pieces of random, disconnected knowledge.

There is a particular issue with languages in primary schools because there are simply not enough teachers with the skills necessary to teach languages, or, indeed, a common approach. Most schools do their best to provide a good grounding in languages, but the variety of approaches, or often simply the neglect of this vital area of learning, means that most secondary linguists feel obliged to start again from scratch. A secondary school with, say, five feeder primaries, may well take in Year 7 pupils whose experience of languages ranges from those who have had an hour a week of specialist teaching to those who had a day in Year 5 singing songs in French or Spanish. Although language teaching in many primary schools is both exciting and inspiring, inculcating a love of languages from an early age, in many it is barely paid lip service and thus regarded by pupils as largely irrelevant. In comparison with language learning in European schools, pupils in the UK are severely disadvantaged, with the systematic study of a language delayed in practice until the age of 11.

Languages are undoubtedly a special case, but advocates of the other foundation subjects are able to make compelling cases for increased attention being paid to their areas of interest. Scientists, for example, often point out that serious science teaching starts far too late in a society where scientific expertise is increasingly demanded by the industrial sector. The same is said of computing, with frequent calls for coding to become the language children should be learning from an early age. Others, with equal conviction, argue that the current focus on the basics undermines the development of creativity and artistry. While art is still a key feature of the majority of primary classrooms, music, where specialist skills are again required, receives less and less attention.

As we shall see, the balance between English and mathematics and the foundation subjects is shifting, especially following the appointment of Amanda Spielman as Chief Inspector. There is now a much sharper focus on curriculum design and implementation, and much more awareness on the part of school leaders of the need to offer a genuinely broad and balanced curriculum. The tension between the contents of the National Curriculum and the demands of the tests at key stage 2 is still at the heart of the primary curriculum debate, nevertheless. Headteachers now face a real dilemma: focus on the curriculum in order to offer pupils rich, logical and stimulating learning experiences, or prepare for the tests in order to safeguard the school's reputation in the community. In the majority of schools, skilled leaders do both, but it is by no means an easy task.

Where are we now? Secondary education

Secondary schools follow the same basic curriculum as their primary counterparts with, at key stage 3, the addition of citizenship and compulsory sex education. At key stage 4 things open up, but the following subjects are still compulsory and must be studied by all: English, mathematics, science, computing, citizenship and physical education. Religious education remains a legal requirement. In addition, schools offer a range of optional subjects with the number on offer dependent on the size of the school, the specialisms of the staff, and a range of other factors including the type of school, the demands of the local community and the priorities of senior staff and governors.

The secondary National Curriculum builds upon and extends the primary curriculum, but there is nevertheless a considerable disconnect between the two sectors. Before the advent of multi-academy trusts and all-through schools, there was something of a gulf between primary and secondary education, with teachers rarely crossing the great divide between the two. Things are changing now, but it is still true to say that links between the primary and secondary school curriculum are far from secure. In most secondary schools, teachers tend to start again from scratch. They assume a basic level of knowledge in English and numeracy and build from there.

This disconnect between primary and secondary education must be one of the great lost opportunities of the education system in the UK. Secondary teachers feel that they cannot rely on the knowledge and skills taught in primary schools, not because the quality of teaching is considered to be inadequate, far from it, but because the primary curriculum is regarded as fractured and too varied to form a reliable base on which to build. A secondary geography school teacher will be aware of the topics suggested in the primary National Curriculum but may quickly find that a pupil's knowledge of the various topics depends largely on what primary school he or she attended. Pupils from one school will have a detailed knowledge of one area of the curriculum and know little about other areas; pupils from a neighbouring school may have a very different bank of knowledge. The safest route forward is to start again.

The overall effect of this disconnect is that anything beyond the basic English and mathematics curriculum is simply abandoned or, at best, left dormant. The annual debate in the press about the length of the summer vacation and its deleterious effect on pupils' learning seems little more than a red herring when the real primary/secondary gap is understood.

The removal of the key stage 3 tests has had a significant impact on curriculum planning, with more and more schools choosing to begin teaching GCSE specifications in Year 9. Given the pressure schools are under to perform in the league tables, this is hardly surprising. Many school leaders, anxious about results and concerned about the amount of content in the new GCSE specifications, have looked at the curriculum and come to the conclusion that the best way forward is to extend key stage 4. This allows more time to be spent on GCSE preparations and should, therefore, result in improved GCSE grades. Of course, the impact on key stage 3 has often been profound: pupils have less and less time to experience aspects of the curriculum which do not relate directly to examination specifications.

While a two-year key stage 3 does not necessarily mean that pupils will experience an impoverished curriculum, the intensification of the focus on examination specifications points to a much more fundamental question: what is the curriculum for? The extension of GCSE courses into the lower school suggests that the main function of the curriculum is to prepare pupils for examinations, as if the *raison d'être* of schools is to enable pupils to pass exams. In schools where this idea has been pursued to its logical extreme – and there are a few – GCSE courses are seen as the sole destination as soon as children cross the school threshold. In effect, key stage 4 has become a five-year GCSE course. Discontented parents who feel that their children are not being fairly treated by the school frequently accuse school leaders of operating examination factories: 'All you care about is the school's league table position'. If schools focus solely and relentlessly on GCSE preparation, they may have a point.

The lower secondary school National Curriculum is undoubtedly fairly prescriptive, but a three-year key stage 3 does allow pupils to experience a broad range of subjects and to experience them in some depth. With the abolition of the key stage 3 tests, it also means that teachers have had more time to explore learning opportunities not directly tied to examination specifications. This is surely one of the school system's great areas of opportunity: the chance to spend three years focussing on learning for the sake of learning, a chance to stimulate and inspire, a time to inculcate a genuine love of learning to last a life time. With the increasing use of tests in primary schools – the foundation stage profile and the ELGs; the phonics test in Year 1 (and Year 2 if it is failed); the new times tables tests; key stage 1 tests taken in Year 2; and preparations for the key stage 2 tests taken early in Year 6 – there are very few school years where pupils are left alone to enjoy their learning without some kind of examination in view. The early years of secondary school should therefore be regarded as a golden opportunity to engage and excite, a chance to make learning both enjoyable and stimulating. The obvious antidote to the toxicity of the examination treadmill is surely a period of unencumbered learning, a time when teachers can really explore their subjects, adapt lessons to the interests of pupils and lay the foundations for further study. The extended key stage 4 is clearly a threat to the brief moment of freedom the first three years of secondary schools are able to offer.

Children who are engaged by and interested in their learning at key stage 3 are much more likely to approach their GCSEs positively; children in schools where examination success shapes the curriculum are much more likely to regard learning as a daily grind and a means to an end. This is a distinction, however, which very few politicians recognise. The political imperative is always shaped according to outcomes; learning as something to be celebrated per se is rarely considered. Schools which are outcomes focussed are therefore the darlings of the state. It is hardly surprising, therefore, that school children pick up on this idea and have begun to regard schools as places to prepare for examinations. For them, the notion of learning for enjoyment or personal enrichment is nonsense. They attend school to pass examinations.

Most secondary schools operate an 'options' system at key stage 4, allowing pupils a choice of subjects to be studied to GCSE level. In recent years, however, the degree of choice has lessened significantly, with most schools insisting upon a compulsory suite of core subjects with only two or three options. Though sharpened by the introduction of the English Baccalaureate (Ebacc), the core offer has, in reality, held sway in school for years. All pupils, in virtually every school in the country, are expected to follow a course of study embracing English, mathematics and sciences, a language and a humanities subject. In addition, they are legally obliged to study religious studies, citizenship and physical education. The introduction of the Ebacc meant that most schools firmed up their key stage offer, insisting on a language and either history or geography.

A further constraint was added thanks to the Progress 8 (P8) measure introduced in 2016. This meant that schools wishing to gain a good P8 score had to ensure that virtually all of their pupils pursued the correct combination of subjects: English, English literature, mathematics, two or three sciences, and geography or history. The combination of the Ebacc and the Progress 8 measure meant that, in practice, most pupils got to choose two, possibly three optional subjects. The chance to pursue personal interests therefore took a further step back as the majority of pupils were locked into a truly national curriculum.

The unforeseen consequence of the Ebacc/Progress 8 lock was a dramatic decline in the take-up of arts subjects, with schools finding themselves unable to offer art, music and drama, as numbers opting for these subjects made them financially unviable. Similarly, with very few vocational qualifications attracting Progress 8 points, schools were quick to replace their vocational courses with more academic choices attracting points. Pupils with genuine artistic talent find that schools no longer offer a range of arts subjects – and with fewer pupils taking arts subjects, the various option blocks operated by schools become more and more restrictive – so that they are often able to choose only one arts option. Similarly, those who would genuinely benefit from vocationally oriented courses are presented with a very limited selection chosen by the school according to the points available rather than the needs of the individual. The notion of choice, therefore, is an illusion. Children in English schools today follow a highly standardised, tightly controlled curriculum where opportunities for individual development are severely restricted.

Where are we now? Post-16 education

All young people are now expected to take part in education or some form of recognised training until they are 18. While education is compulsory until age 18, this doesn't necessarily mean schooling. Post-16 education can take a number of forms and may be academic or vocational. Students can stay on at school into the sixth form to take A-level qualifications or a number of alternative Level 3 qualifications such as courses offered by the Business and Technology Education Council (BTEC), the International Baccalaureate (IB) or the Cambridge Pre-U. They can move to other sixth forms, or sixth form colleges, or they can transfer to the local Further Education (FE) college to pursue more practical vocational courses. Alternatively, they can opt for work-based apprenticeships or traineeships.

This sounds like a great offer but, for many, the choices are really quite limited. A-levels are still regarded as the 'gold standard', and they remain the first choice for the majority of students and their parents. In schools with sixth forms, the decision is often fairly straightforward for young people: they stay on if they do well enough in their GCSEs to qualify for A-level study or move on to FE college if they don't meet their school's sixth form entry requirements. Some schools offer alternative courses for students not considered capable of A-levels: these include BTECs at Level 3 and the occasional Level 2 course. Advocates of BTECs argue strongly that they are equivalent to A-levels but, to be frank, they simply do not have the same status.

A-levels have been around since 1951. Consequently, they are hard-wired into the system. Any attempt to replace them is met with horror, and changes over the years have been gradual rather than radical. Critics argue that the most significant change has more to do with standards than the nature of the examinations themselves. Far more candidates today gain the highest grades, and there are constant accusations of grade inflation. The figures would seem to bear this out, with over 25% of students now attaining A or A* grades compared to around 8% in the 1960s achieving A grades. On the face of it, this seems fairly conclusive. However, on closer examination, it becomes clear that comparisons over time are not as easy as just comparing percentages. A-levels have changed, both in terms of content and structure; they now test different skills; students have changed and sixth form study is taken much more seriously than in the past; competition for university places has also had an impact, encouraging students not simply to pass but to do as well as they can; students are not only more committed but possibly brighter than their 1960s counterparts; and, whisper who dares, the quality of teaching in schools has improved dramatically. Detailed studies of grade inflation always turn out to be inconclusive. However, the general feeling that it's easier to get an A than it used to be still holds sway across large sections of society.

Sixth form courses remained much the same until the year 2000, when it was proposed that students were to take between five and six subjects, as opposed to the traditional three or four. Advanced Supplementary (AS) courses had been introduced in 1989 to encourage A-level students to take an additional subject, but this proved to be something of a damp squib. Students were initially encouraged to begin three and a half A-levels, but many quickly realised that the AS level was unnecessary and quickly abandoned it to concentrate on the A-level courses essential for university entrance. This resulted in the creation of Curriculum 2000, which changed the shape of A-levels, at least for a while (see Chapter 4).

Sir Ron Dearing's wide-ranging review of the curriculum suggested a number of far-reaching changes, including an attempt to introduce greater parity between academic and vocational qualifications with the introduction of Advanced Vocational Qualifications (AVCs). A-levels were broken into two parts, with three modules taken in the first year of study, leading to an Advanced Subsidiary (AS) qualification, followed by A2 examinations at the end of the second year. Students would therefore be offered a much broader range of qualifications in Year 12 before specialising in Year 13. They would also be encouraged to mix traditional A-level study with AVCs which adopted the same two-part structure.

This sounds like a great idea, and the changes were broadly welcomed by schools and politicians alike. However, as ever, the conservatism of the system prevailed, and Dearing's radical changes quickly failed to take root. Grammar and independent schools led the way in rejecting AVCs, continuing to focus strictly on A-levels. School curriculums were adapted to take account of the new AS levels, but most moved to a four/three pattern: four AS levels leading to three A-levels in Year 13. Consequently, three A-levels remained the goal, and AS levels were often seen as merely a somewhat clumsy step on the way. It came as no surprise, therefore, that when A-levels were revised again in 2015, AS levels were effectively abandoned, although they do still exist as stand-alone qualifications. The majority of sixth form students now study for three A-levels once again. Throughout all this, universities have looked on, with most sticking firmly to traditional three A-level offers, effectively ignoring AS levels and AVCs.

A-levels may have retained their status and appeal, but what happens to the thousands of students for whom A-level study is too demanding? Schools have always felt obliged to offer something for these students, and the financial pressures on sixth forms mean that the more students enrolled, the better the finances. In general terms, a school sixth form needs to be fairly large, with around 200 or 250 students, to be considered financially viable, and with most schools desperate to hang on to their sixth forms, the search for courses which would enable weaker students to continue post-16 became a priority. Unfortunately, this quest resulted in a somewhat half-hearted approach, with most schools offering a few BTECs, or their equivalents, in addition to the now-compulsory English and mathematics GCSE re-take courses for those not achieving good enough passes at the end of Year 11.

Many of the BTEC courses undoubtedly have a great deal to recommend them, but far too many students choose them for the wrong reasons. Many just want to stay on at school and therefore opt for subjects in which they have very little interest, and they underachieve or drop out as a result. Others are attracted to courses which look fabulously entertaining – the BTEC sports diplomas are a good example – but which ultimately offer little in the way of genuine career progression. Students who stay in school following Level 2 courses have even fewer choices: they are often doomed to endless re-sits of English and mathematics, plus a mixture of pseudo vocational courses which leave them bored and dissatisfied.

There are much more positive choices to be made at FE colleges, including industry standard training and apprenticeships, but the attraction of the school sixth form is strong. Far too many students therefore opt either for A-level courses with which they can't cope, or BTECs taken as a last resort. And, it has to be said, parents are often complicit in these poor choices as they always see A-levels and sixth form study as the best way forward for their sons and daughters, despite evidence to the contrary. For many, of course, the school sixth form is the safe choice and not surprisingly so: many 16-year-olds are not mature enough to venture out into the world, and they crave the care and support offered by their schools.

With a third of Year 11 pupils failing to gain five good GCSEs, and a significant proportion of post-16 students poorly catered for outside of the traditional A-level system, it is clear that there is a lot wrong with the curriculum as it stands. Thousands of young people are let down by the system every year and will continue to be failed unless radical solutions are found. The failure of Curriculum 2000 is a potent symbol of the paralysis of the education system in this country. Despite the fact that educational alternatives for those who don't follow the traditional A-level route lack both the status and acceptance necessary to ensure that the needs of all students are met, it is hard to see how a truly radical and effective system can ever be introduced. With grammar schools, independent schools and middle-class comprehensives, all supported by universities insistent on traditional A-levels, very little is likely to change. One can only hope that the efforts that have gone into supporting disadvantaged pupils, and the developing understanding of the importance of cultural capital, will eventually work its way through the system to enable the establishment of an approach more sympathetic to the needs of all students, and not just those who take A-levels.

Despite these concerns, however, it is important to acknowledge both the value and the success of A-levels. The fact that they have fundamentally changed very little since 1951 must say something about their appeal and their effectiveness. After five years of secondary schooling following a timetable crammed with subjects the student doesn't necessarily enjoy and with very little choice over what they study, the chance to choose three A-levels is a real pleasure, and generations of people are able to look back fondly at their sixth form careers with a genuine sense of warmth and intellectual growth. The charge often levelled at the English system is that it is too narrow, and that students specialise too early, but the opportunity to study a handful of subjects in real depth is surely something of tremendous value. Education post-16 is undoubtedly in need of reform, but it could be that the depth of study offered by A-levels is key to a more equitable system. As I write, the government is preparing to introduce yet another group of vocational qualifications, T Levels, and these do seem to offer the depth and detail of traditional A-levels, as well as strong links with industry. Whether they will achieve the status necessary to be considered as a genuine alternative to A-levels remains to be seen. One can only hope they do.

Destination university

Whenever politicians announce changes to the educational system, the rhetoric is usually focussed on preparing children for the world of work and meeting the needs of industry. More often than not the curriculum in schools is seen as an assembly line which moves relentlessly towards the production of perfect citizens, educationally and ideologically equipped to be productive and, above all, gainfully employed. This accounts for the frequency of speeches about skills, and the political obsession with what has become known as 'a world class education'. The function of schools, therefore, is to supply the country with workers and managers appropriately equipped to compete with their counterparts internationally, thus securing the UK's position on the world stage. In simple terms, this is a function not-too-far removed from the 19th-century colonial system designed to prepare young gentlemen (and, of course, it was only gentlemen then) for managerial roles across the empire. Education is about preparation for work.

Ironically, despite the rhetoric, the curriculum in schools moves unerringly towards universities rather than employment. In practice, the majority of students are prepared not for employment but academia.

As we have seen, a great deal of energy has gone into addressing the skills gap identified by industrialists, and successive governments have attempted to put things right by focussing on a huge range of vocational initiatives. From TVEI to T Levels and STEM, politicians seem determined to focus the attention of schools on industry. In reality, however, the system continues, as it always has done, to focus on preparing students for university. University courses may well be vocational in content, but the prevailing ethos in academic institutions is less about preparation for work and all about learning. Universities are still regarded as centres of learning, whereas schools seem to be regarded very differently. While politicians argue about how to shape the curriculum in schools to meet the needs of industry, schools still head steadily towards these centres of learning. Could it be that, despite the political debate, society still values the notion of education as an end in itself?

GCSEs prepare pupils to take A-levels; A-levels prepare students for university. Although around a third of 16-year-olds do not meet the 'good standard' of education required at key stage 4, the school curriculum is nevertheless shaped by a university progression model. Primary school pupils are equipped with the literacy and numeracy skills they need to tackle the secondary curriculum; and the Ebacc ensures that schools across the country follow a curriculum that is fundamentally academic. And, as we shall see in the next chapter, assessment systems are designed to foster and support an academic approach to education. Consequently, the needs of pupils who are unlikely to meet the 'good standard' are marginalised, despite the efforts of teachers and school leaders to help them succeed. The curriculum is simply not designed for them.

We should acknowledge, of course, that the raft of vocational initiatives introduced into schools in the past 25 years clearly indicates a political awareness of the failure of the current system to meet the needs of the forgotten third of pupils. The dominance of the idea of a university education as the ultimate goal, however, tends always to undermine this aim. Indeed, many of the changes to education post-18 support this charge.

It is now easier than ever to gain a university place. In a speech to the Labour party conference in 1999, Tony Blair pledged that 50% of all young people should take part in higher education, a target that has now been reached. A great deal was done to enable this to happen: the university system was expanded; more and more university places became available; foundation courses were introduced to help students with poor A-level grades access degree-level study; offers were lowered; bursaries and grants were introduced to support young people from disadvantaged backgrounds; and unconditional offers began to proliferate to attract as many students as possible. Even the introduction of eye-watering student fees has not halted the rise in university numbers, and there is now a general assumption that the majority of young people are destined for university.

While we should applaud the efforts taken by universities to reach Blair's somewhat arbitrary target, it is clear that the rise in student numbers serves to reinforce the notion that the paramount aim of the curriculum in schools is to prepare pupils for university. This, of course, is a worthy aim, but it raises all sorts of awkward questions which society has yet to address. Do so many young people really need a university education? How many of them now compete for jobs which really don't require degree-level study? How many students head off to university to undertake courses with which they don't really have the academic skills to cope? One of the unintended consequences of the rise in university numbers has been the disappearance of jobs for those who want to leave school at 18. Employers who used to recruit sixth formers now target university leavers, and why wouldn't they? Why employ a sixth former if, for not much more money, an employer can recruit a 21-year-old with a degree?

Young people now work their way through schools with one destination in mind – a university education. With demanding assessments at every stage, and the fear of failure ever present, they face constant pressure to succeed. More able students compete to gain places at Russell Group universities, with an Oxbridge place still regarded as the ultimate achievement, while the less able worry about achieving good enough grades at A-level simply to gain a place anywhere. Is it any wonder, therefore, that there has been a dramatic decline in the mental health of young people?

The nature of university courses is beyond the scope of this book, but it is impossible to ignore the impact of the university system on the school curriculum and the lives of pupils in the classroom. Genuine curriculum change cannot be achieved by isolated adjustments to primary or secondary education. If politicians really want to improve education, they need to consider the whole system, from nurseries to universities and beyond.

What should children be learning in school?

There is a certain irony in the fact that, despite constant change, the curriculum today is not wildly different from that offered to children in the 19th century. The conclusion of Raymond Williams' *The Long Revolution*, though written over 50 years ago, makes the point: 'The fact about our present curriculum is that it was essentially created by the 19th century, following some 18th century models and retaining elements of the medieval curriculum near its centre'.[3]

The English curriculum has become something of a national monument to be repaired, repurposed and restored but never replaced. The notion of tearing up the curriculum and starting again from scratch is as unthinkable as knocking down the palace of Westminster and building something much more fit for purpose. However radical the thinking of the politicians who delight in meddling with schools, the changes they make rarely address the fundamental question: what should children be learning in schools? Society has changed dramatically in the last hundred years: the pre-war order of the Edwardians, elegantly captured in Kenneth Grahame's *Wind in the Willows*, is a world away from the globalised digital age. The riverbank where Ratty, Mole, Toad and Badger contemplated the beauty of nature and communed with Pan is now polluted, threatened by global warming and fenced in by digital advertising displays. And yet, the education we offer our children is broadly the same.

John White's study of the aims of the National Curriculum, *Rethinking the School Curriculum*, reinforces the view that, despite revisions to the 1988 blueprint, schools are growing increasingly out of touch with the world beyond the classroom.[4] He describes schools as being 'in the grip of custom' and ends by suggesting a number of 'general lessons for the curriculum as a whole'. In particular, he mentions the need to 'reverse introspection' and encourage individual subjects to look beyond themselves; he advocates 'interconnectedness', suggesting that subjects need to be aware of connections across the curriculum; the 'primacy of the practical' is also important in the sense that students need to be active and independent learners; and the notion of greater student choice, beginning at key stage 3, is felt to be vital in order to make education more interesting and more enjoyable for all students.

Custom and practice is still the most powerful feature of contemporary curriculum design. As a headteacher, I once conducted an interesting experiment: I asked the school council to design a brand new curriculum for the modern era. They were asked to think about the needs of contemporary society and to forget about the subjects they were currently studying. Inevitably, after hours of discussion, they came up with a curriculum that was virtually the same as the one followed by the majority of secondary schools in the country. The challenge was simply too demanding and consensus almost impossible. If young, flexible minds cannot break out of the cage of convention, what chance do our politicians stand?

Is it really possible, is it even thinkable, therefore, to put aside current curriculum thinking and start again? It could well be that every question to be asked on the journey to a new curriculum leads to such complex debates that the only solution is to fall back on the tried and trusted model we have all been following for years.

There are undoubtedly aspects of modern society for which the contemporary education system does not prepare children. The digital age has changed forever the way we communicate, and young people today are simply not properly prepared to cope with the social media world they now inhabit. Mental health is more of a concern than ever, and there is no doubt that the sudden – and in historical terms it is sudden – switch to a digital rather than analogue culture has contributed to the increasing awareness of such issues. It is also possible that easy access to information is in itself part of the problem.

Employment patterns have changed, and young people face very different working lives from previous generations. Not for them the age-old route of university or training followed by half a lifetime in a secure, well-paid job; they are likely to have careers switching from job to job, with re-training a constant feature of their working lives. And all this is underpinned by the spectre of climate change. Although there is a growing understanding in western society of the threat of climate change, politicians are still reluctant to take it seriously. Action to halt climate change involves long-term planning and global cooperation, whereas politicians focus intensely, and sometimes almost exclusively, on short-term electoral goals and national or local issues. For young people, however, climate change is real and a source of huge concern.

None of this really features in the school curriculum. Certainly, aspects of climate change may be touched upon in geography or science, various social issues are explored in English lessons, and social media is sometimes considered as part of computing or information technology teaching, but the issues which really concern the younger generation, and the ideas they need to understand in order to cope with the modern world, are marginalised and, more often than not, neglected almost completely. The introduction of personal, social and health education (PSHE), and more recently citizenship, has gone some way towards introducing these vital topics into schools, but they have become catch-all subjects attempting to cover huge issues in too little time. Moreover, as they are non-examined, they are accorded very little value by teachers and pupils alike in schools where examinations are everything.

The dominance of an examination culture built upon the firm foundations of a curriculum that has changed very little in the past hundred or so years means that young people today are doubly disadvantaged. They not only face the stress and anxiety of constant testing, but they are forced to study subjects which for many of them seem to have very little relevance in the modern world. The things in which they are interested, and really need to know about, are neglected in favour of subjects dictated more by the conservatism of politicians than their needs or, indeed, the needs of society. Conservatism and neglect are therefore key features of the toxic classroom.

What can schools do now to put things right?

- **Broaden the curriculum.** School leaders should think about the curriculum not only in terms of timetabled subjects but in a wider sense to include all aspects of school life, including extra-curricular or co-curricular activities and community links.

- **Extend the curriculum.** Primary schools should ensure that their curriculum is firmly linked with that of the local secondary school; secondary schools should work hard to ensure that Years 5 and 6 blend seamlessly into Years 8 and 9. A good idea would be for schools to include the additional years as shaded boxes in their curriculum diagrams.

- **Raise the status of non-core subjects.** The importance of subjects other than English and maths in primary schools needs to be re-asserted. This means detailed curriculum plans, greater time allocation, less attention to the tests and stronger links with secondary schools.

- **Simplify testing and assessment.** One of the key duties of school leaders is to make compulsory national testing as straightforward as possible. This means a light touch approach to foundation stage profiles in the early years; much less emphasis on key stage 2 tests; and delaying preparation for GCSEs until Year 10.

- **Be careful with Progress 8 and the Ebacc.** Too many schools adapt their plans to achieve success in the league tables; success in the league tables should be seen as a good outcome of a curriculum that meets the needs of pupils, not as an end in itself.

- **Fly a flag for the arts.** School leaders should do everything possible to reverse the national decline in the take-up of arts subjects. Similarly, they should offer strong support for languages and vocational subjects.

- **Listen to students.** If students are to be fully engaged in their learning, then their concerns must be taken into account. This means seeking opportunities to introduce their key concerns – climate change and globalisation, for example – not only in assemblies and tutor periods but into the curriculum itself.

What should policymakers do to put things right?

- Allow schools much more flexibility in curriculum design so that they can adapt it more successfully to the needs of their pupils.

- Recognise the importance of extra-curricular activities and fund them appropriately, without relying solely on the good will of teachers.

- Abolish key stage 2 tests and allow teachers to assess pupils' abilities.

- Recognise that the primary curriculum has come to be dominated by English and maths due to the testing regime, and encourage schools to raise the status of subjects such as science, history, geography and art.

- Be honest about the lack of language teachers in the UK and make the recruitment and retention of skilled linguists a high priority.

- Understand that schools are not just about examinations and recognise that schools are being driven to adapt their curriculums to meet the needs of league tables and not the needs of pupils.

Notes

1 Gove's view of the teaching profession as 'the blob' is far from an individual, isolated view. Toby Jones, in a paper, the title of which really says it all, explains the origin of the term and why he regards it as so appropriate:

> What is The Blob and what has a 1950s sci-fi movie got to do with education policy? Michael Gove, the Secretary of State for Education, uses it as a catch-all term to describe the opponents of education reform, but he's thinking in particular of the leaders of the teaching unions, local authority officials, academic experts and university education departments. In this, he's following the lead of William J. Bennett, the former US Education Secretary, who originally coined the term to describe the army of educationalists, lobbyists and government officials who obstructed his attempts to reform America's public education system in the 1980s. He used it specifically to refer to the 'bloated educational bureaucracy'.
>
> It's a good term, and not just because it conveys the sheer scale of the opposition reformers like Gove and Bennett face. (In the film the amoeba-like alien threatens to consume an entire town.)

T. Young. 2014. *Prisoners of the Blob: Why Education Experts Are Wrong about Nearly Everything*, London, Civitas.

2 From a presentation given by Sean Harford at the Ofsted/NASUWT BME Consultation Conference, 27 January 2018 ICC Birmingham.
3 R. Williams. 1965. *The Long Revolution*, London, Penguin, p. 188.
4 J. White et al. 2004. *Rethinking the School Curriculum*, Oxford, Routledge, Falmer, p. 180.

3 The core subjects

So far, we have considered the curriculum in general terms, but arguments over the content of the curriculum are not restricted to which subjects are included, however. Indeed, some of the fiercest debates have raged over the content of individual subjects. One might expect teachers and educationalists to engage enthusiastically with subject-specific details but, even here, in the minutiae of subject content, politicians feel that they have every right to intervene. Michael Gove may have been the most overt meddler in curriculum detail in recent years, but politicians have never been afraid to interfere directly in the classroom. Virtually every subject has been a matter of public debate at one time or another. The brief summary which follows will serve to emphasise the degree to which children are prey to the ideological whims of politicians, journalists and educationalists. The classroom has always been a political battleground. I wonder how often politicians reflect upon the effect of these constant hostilities on the children sitting behind the desks.

English

Many teachers would argue that the English curriculum has seen the most dramatic changes in the past few years, albeit characterised by something of a lurch towards the past. There is now a strong focus on the explicit teaching of grammar, and there are new GCSE specifications shaped around an intensely traditional view of the canon of English literature. There is perhaps no better example of curriculum change where custom and practice predominate.

The curriculum for English has gone through several incarnations since the inception of the National Curriculum for English in 1990. The increasing emphasis on the teaching of phonics culminated in the Primary National Strategy, which placed systematic phonics at the heart of the teaching of reading (DfES 2006).[1] This, in turn, led to the explicit teaching of grammar which, it is fair to say, caused widespread anxiety amongst teachers who found that the levels of subject knowledge required to teach children about language were considerably greater than most had acquired during their own secondary schooling. Teachers suddenly found that they were expected to teach parts of speech and their functions; they had to focus much more explicitly on punctuation; and, above all, they found themselves confronted by a raft of linguistic terminology which even the most grammar literate individuals found confusing.

The impact in the classroom of this intense focus on grammar and linguistics has generated a huge amount of debate. Traditionalists insist that children must have a good grounding in grammar, they should be able to name the parts of speech, and they should have strong punctuation skills. More progressive thinkers, however, are concerned that by focussing on the mechanics of language, the joy of reading for pleasure and writing for fun will be driven out. Children will be able to point to verbs and adverbs, but they may not be able to write with any flair or creativity. There is nothing new about these arguments, of course; educationalists and politicians engaged in exactly the same debate in the 19th century.

The revised GCSE English specifications have been particularly contentious. Employers were perhaps hoping for a qualification which gives every pupil a chance to demonstrate that they are able to speak and write English to a degree of competency; instead they now have an examination which tests much more traditional skills. The reforms introduced in 2015, and the conditions set out by The Office of Qualifications and Examinations (Ofqual) require examination boards to assess students on unseen texts from the 19th, 20th and 21st centuries. These must include a literary fiction text and a literary non-fiction text. The reading assessment accounts for half of the new examination and is based on unseen texts from the past three centuries, both fiction and non-fiction. Pupils are expected to evaluate the writer's choice of vocabulary, form and structural features.

The writing assessment makes up the other half, with pupils expected to write clear and coherent texts. A hefty 20% of the marks for this examination are awarded for the range of vocabulary and sentence structures, spelling and punctuation (an extension of the previous SPaG marks – spelling, punctuation and grammar). It is unsurprising, therefore, that many now question whether the English GCSE is fit for purpose.

The English Literature GCSE specification is consequently even more traditional with its focus on 'classic literature' and 'substantial whole texts in detail' taken from the following categories:

- Shakespeare

- The 19th-century novel

- A selection of poetry since 1789, including Romantic poetry

- Fiction or drama from the British Isles from 1914 onwards

Advocates of the new specifications argue that a renewed focus on whole texts, and those written by our greatest writers, leads not only to higher standards but to a much greater enjoyment of reading. Critics respond by pointing out that the prescribed texts are too demanding and completely inaccessible to many of the pupils reading them. The fear is that the struggle to work their way through a 19th-century masterpiece may well put them off reading for good. There is also the awkward focus on English texts, rather than those written in English. Not only does this exclude American literature but texts from around the world. For many, this is seen as highly inappropriate in multi-cultural Britain.

Most of the changes to the English curriculum could be described as mere tinkering with ideas that have been in place for hundreds of years. How often do politicians consider what they hope children get from their learning in English? What, at the end of at least 12 years of English lessons, should children be able to do?

There is likely to be universal agreement that everyone should be able to read and write with sufficient fluency to be able to participate in society. Thereafter, almost every aspect of the curriculum becomes a matter of contention. Do children really need a detailed understanding of punctuation, grammar and the parts of speech to be considered fluent in English? And what kind of English should they be learning – 'standard' English, contemporary English or even American English? This, in turn, leads to complex discussions regarding spoken English and, in particular, pronunciation and dialect. Should all pupils in England be taught to speak received pronunciation (RP) or be encouraged to celebrate their local dialects? The study of English is not, of course, restricted to reading and writing; the ability to speak clearly and accurately should surely be a key part of any child's education. The inclusion of oral examinations in English GCSE syllabuses led to howls of outrage from traditionalists who regarded them as pointless extras, and yet, these were likely to be the same people who were, at the same time, decrying the decline of RP and the insidious influence of regional and international dialects. Although the term 'oracy' has been around since the 1960s, it is still yet to be universally accepted by anyone other than English teachers as a fundamental feature of language learning in English.[2]

The question of what children should be reading is another minefield. From the debate over whether children in the early years should be reading texts specifically designed to teach them phonics, rather than classic picture books and books for young readers, to the contents of A-level specifications, there is always scope for debate. There are arguments around both style and content. Issues of style often concern the technical accuracy of books written for children: should they, for example, be allowed to read slang or American English? How appropriate is text-speak, or other forms of language which have evolved as a result of digital technology? Is it fair to make young readers battle their way through the often complex and sophisticated diction of 19th-century novels? Should teachers focus mainly on technical writing or creative writing?

Debates over the content of children's reading are seemingly endless. First, there is the assumption that children must read 'the classics', but even here there is very little agreement. The 'canon' of English literature is constantly questioned.

The traditional view, undoubtedly favoured by Michael Gove and his followers, is that there is a standard set of texts which every child should study. Anyone who has studied English to A-level will have a clear understanding of what this means: Chaucer, Shakespeare, Dickens, Austen, the Brontës, Lawrence, Orwell and so on There is also an understanding that some more modern texts are considered to have attained classic status and are therefore part of the canon. From Michelle Magorian's *Goodnight Mister Tom* in primary schools to Sebastian Faulks' *Birdsong* at A-level, there are books regarded as of sufficient literary quality to be given to children. The choice of texts used in the sixth form is likely to be more open to updating, whereas lower school choices are more conservative and resistant to change. For example, J.B. Priestley's *An Inspector Calls* is one of the most popular 'modern' texts taught at key stage 4 despite having been written 75 years ago.

The new GCSE specifications focus on English books as opposed to books written in English. This means that novels such as F. Scott Fitzgerald's *The Great Gatsby*, J.D. Salinger's *The Catcher in the Rye* and Harper Lee's *To Kill a Mockingbird*, which have fired the imagination of thousands of children over the years, are no longer specified as set texts. A Department for Education 'myth buster' attempted to defend this decision, but the attempt to do so was not entirely convincing:

> We consulted on the minimum requirements for the new GCSE criteria last year: the final categories (a work by Shakespeare; a selection of poetry; a 19th century novel; and a British work since 1914) are the product of that consultation. We were always clear that exam boards could add further works if they wanted – and the criteria explicitly say they can.
>
> We would also not expect any school to think that pupils should only be reading their GCSE set books. Our new national curriculum sets out that all pupils should read a wide range of fiction and non-fiction, including 'seminal world literature', and we have made questions on unseen texts compulsory at GCSE in order to reward those who read widely.[3]

The plain fact is that schools are following the GCSE specifications and, as a result, American texts will become less and less common in English classrooms. In a multi-cultural society where children are learning to become global citizens, is it therefore appropriate to focus solely on texts written in the British Isles? Most writers and educationalists agree that children should be introduced to literature written in English from all round the world – from the USA, from Africa, from India, from the Caribbean. This is particularly important for English children whose heritage derives from other parts of the world. Is it right that the reading habits of our children are to be defined – and perhaps limited – according to the whims of the secretary of state for education?

Discussions regarding spoken English and the canon of English literature continue to be a matter of heated debate, but they are nothing compared to the frequent and furious eruptions of rage concerning the content of children's reading which we see in the press almost on a monthly basis. More often than not, these outbursts concern matters of sexuality and/or religion. These range from the mildly absurd – the Harry Potter novels banned from Catholic school libraries because of their promotion of witchcraft and wizardry – to debates which have led to public outrage, widespread demonstrations and even violence. The recent debacle over the so-called promotion of homosexuality in primary schools is a shocking example of the way in which debates over curriculum content seem to ignore the impact of political and religious arguments on pupils in the classroom.

In 2019, the headteacher at Anderton Park Primary School in Birmingham had to endure eight weeks of protests outside her school gates over her decision to teach LGBT-inclusive content to her young pupils, the vast majority of whom were Muslim. As well as shouting and threatening behaviour, one protest resulted in LGBT campaigners and their children being pelted with eggs. The row centred on whether the local authority-run school was teaching children about LGBT relationships, gender and sexual orientation in an 'age-appropriate' manner. Of course, this raises the question, what is age-appropriate LGBT content in primary schools? And who should decide this?

Of course, many of the protesters will not have read the offending books or have understood the schemes of work followed by the teachers in the classroom. This did not stop them, however, from taking issue with what they perceived to be inappropriate curriculum content. In trying to follow the government's guidelines, the unfortunate Anderton Park headteacher found herself at the sharp end of an intensely political argument. Like the infamous section 28 debacle,[4] which banned the promotion of homosexuality by teachers, issues such as this have the power to turn schools across the country into places of protest and classrooms into battlefields. Was it really worth eight weeks of poisonous protest outside the school, during which children were in serious danger of becoming traumatised by the anger and outrage of their parents, in order to make sure that they did not have to experience the occasional lesson presenting LGBT relationships in a positive light? Never has the classroom been more toxic.

The Anderton Park experience is an extreme example, but every day school leaders find themselves having to respond to parental complaints regarding the books read in the classroom. Over the years, as an English teacher and as a headteacher, I have dealt with complaints regarding the sexual content of set texts, the political leanings of the writers, religious issues, the way in which mental health issues are dealt, and, like Anderton Park, the promotion, or the lack of promotion, of LGBT issues. In addition, there are always concerns from parents of ethnic minority children regarding the lack of positive role models drawn from non-white backgrounds. English teachers work hard to find books that boys will enjoy, and yet, in doing so, they often lay themselves open to the criticism that these books don't project positive images of girls.

Whether it is Michael Gove insisting on the traditional canon of English literature and a thorough grounding in grammar, or a parent with genuine concerns about the way girls are represented in teen fiction, everyone feels they are entitled to have a say in the English curriculum taught in schools. Sadly, however, the children who read the books are rarely consulted. It is, of course, important for school reading lists to reflect the society in which pupils are growing up, and it is right for politicians and parents to have their say, but surely it should be up to teachers to decide what's best for children. Their decisions are more likely to be based on the value of a text as a stimulus for learning rather than its social, political or religious status. If parents and politicians trusted teachers a little more, the classroom would be a much less toxic place.

Mathematics

The new mathematics curriculum has been equally controversial, if not attracting the same degree of attention in the media afforded to the revised English GCSEs. The main concern here is the question of difficulty. The new GCSE was developed in response to requests from employers for more students to be able to apply their knowledge in a real-life context and a desire to introduce more rigour. One of the main results is that questions are more contextual, meaning students must solve problems rather than simply doing mathematics with no obvious real-world application. This increased problem-solving element is something with which many students struggle, and how relevant to the real world the questions actually are is open to question. There is also a requirement for learners to memorise important mathematical formulae by heart, with few formulae allowed to be provided to students in examinations. Formulae to be memorised include the quadratic formula, Pythagoras' theorem and trigonometry ratios.

Examinations have also become more demanding in terms of content, with topics previously part of the old AS level specifications moved down to the higher tier of the new GCSE. For example, students now need to be able to expand the products of more than two binomials or deduce expressions to calculate the nth term of quadratic sequences. There is therefore a degree of difficulty inherent in the new mathematics GCSE which prompts some serious questions about the purpose of mathematics in schools.

In an article titled 'What's Wrong with Maths GCSE?', Charlie Stripp, the chief executive of Mathematics, Education, Innovation (MEI) and director of the National Centre for Excellence in the Teaching of Mathematics (NCETM), considered the intended purposes of the GCSE specifications. He made three points:

1 To identify those who have not reached the minimum national expectation of maths competence at age 16. On the new maths GCSE this is considered to be a grade 4.

2 To prepare as many students as possible to study maths to a higher level.

3 To identify which students are ready to study maths to a higher level, and which maths qualification pathway will best support their aspirations.[5]

The first point concerns basic competence; the other two focus on preparedness for higher study. Does this apparent imbalance tell us something about traditional notions regarding the purpose of the study of mathematics in schools? Ensuring pupils have a basic competence is important, but the real driver of the mathematics curriculum is preparation for A-level and university courses.

Most people would agree that ensuring pupils have reached 'the minimal national expectation of maths competence' is a worthy aim, but what does it really mean? What mathematical skills should a 16-year-old have? Here we get to the heart of the debate and, again, it is about curriculum content. Politicians have been reluctant to engage with the details of mathematics study with the same level of enthusiasm they reserve for the English curriculum, but there is a general consensus that mathematics is a good thing and that difficulty is to be welcomed. The question asked by almost every key stage 4 pupil, 'What is the point of all this?', is rarely asked by politicians. Do 16-year-olds really need to understand calculus, for example, and should the ability to handle complex algebra be necessary to be considered mathematically competent?

It is something of a cliché to consider how much of the mathematics taught in schools is used by the majority of the population in their everyday lives, but it is nevertheless a valid question. Despite having spent my working life in education and, as a headteacher, having had to deal with the complexities of balancing a £5 million budget, I must confess to using a very limited set of mathematical skills. I have never felt the need to delve into calculus or algebra; my requirements have always been restricted to basic numeracy. In most professions, and in people's everyday lives, a basic skill set is sufficient: addition, subtraction, multiplication; the ability to understand percentages and, occasionally, probability; and a basic grasp of trigonometry. Why, therefore, do we expect pupils to learn an incredibly sophisticated set of skills, the vast majority of which they are never likely to use again? Of course, the same question could be asked of the curriculum content in most subjects taught in schools, but since mathematics occupies such a central position in education, it is fundamental to a consideration of the relevance of the current school curriculum.

The intense focus on mathematics starts at a very early age. For some time, politicians have been concerned that young children are not properly prepared to compete with their international counterparts. According to the Education Policy Institute, 21 countries have less of a gap between the best and worst primary maths results, exposing a long tail of underperformance in which pupils are left behind before they reach secondary school.[6] The think-tank compared key stage 2 maths results for primary school pupils with equivalent tests in 56 countries, using data from the 2015 Trends in Mathematics and Science Study (TIMSS), to establish how English pupils fare against their peers overseas.

In order to address the problem of the attainment gap, the Department for Education introduced a £41 million 'maths mastery' curriculum in primary schools, an approach which involves whole class teaching and taking all pupils through calculations in minute detail before moving on. It was initially deployed in a thousand schools, subsequently to be rolled out to 8,000 in 2020.

However, while we should undoubtedly be concerned about the gap between the best and worst performers, we should not overlook the more positive aspects of the report. It concluded, for example, 'this new analysis finds that England performs relatively well on international rankings for primary aged pupils'.[7]

Primary mathematics is far from basic. By the end of the Reception year, 4-year-olds in primary schools are expected to be able to:

- count reliably to 20,
- order numbers from 1–20,
- say 1 more or 1 less to 20,
- add and subtract two single-digit numbers, and
- count on or back to find an answer.

By the end of Year 6, they should be able to:

- use negative numbers in context and calculate intervals across zero,
- compare and order numbers up to 10,000,000,
- identify common factors, common multiples and prime numbers,
- round any whole number to a required degree or accuracy,
- identify the value of each digit to three decimal places,
- use knowledge of order of operations to carry out calculations involving four operations,
- multiply: 4-digit by 2-digit,
- divide: 4-digit by 2-digit,
- add and subtract fractions with different denominators and mixed numbers,
- multiply simple pairs of proper fractions, writing the answer in the simplest form,
- divide proper fractions by whole numbers, and
- calculate % of whole number.

Difficulty sets in early. It is hard to argue that our primary school children are not set high enough expectations in mathematics. Nor is it surprising that so much curriculum time is now devoted to mathematics in primary schools, often, as we have seen, to the detriment of other subjects.

Mathematicians argue that the real benefit to pupils of learning complex mathematics at an early age – aside from the obvious advantages in terms of access to higher education – is the development of problem-solving skills. Most mathematicians concede that most of the higher skills taught at GCSE and A-level, where the content is even more demanding, are rarely used by pupils in their subsequent careers. They all argue strongly, however, that the ability to solve problems is fundamental to virtually all walks of life. It is hard to gainsay this view, but couldn't the same argument be made for language learning? Advocates of the study of Latin in schools are always keen to point out the benefits for pupils engaging with complex grammar, demanding vocabulary and sophisticated texts in developing intellectual capacity.

We also need to question the emphasis on preparedness for higher education. The political obsession with mathematics in schools is largely driven by the view that Great Britain lags behind the rest of the world in terms of science, technology, engineering and mathematics (STEM). This contention is largely driven by our performance in the Programme for International Student Assessment (PISA) implemented by the Organisation for Economic Co-operation and Development (OECD) in 2000. Measuring the mathematics, science and reading skills of 15-year-old students every three years, PISA relies on broad international participation. In the 2015 test published in 2016, 72 countries took part, including some from outside the OECD, and the UK's performance was far from scintillating, coming 27th in mathematics, 15th in science and 22nd in English. Singapore was ranked number one in all three categories. It is clearly the political view that the UK should be up there with Singapore and other high-performing countries such as Hong Kong, China and Taiwan. The fact that the comparability of the tests across the 72 countries is highly dubious is rarely taken into account. The assumption is that students in the UK are not very good at mathematics and must do better. This is hardly fair, however. Mathematics is flourishing in British universities, and students are trained to a very high level at both A-level and degree level. Where we have lagged behind is in the numbers completing higher-level courses.

It is probably true to say that in the past, universities have not been training enough engineers to allow the nation to face an increasingly technological future. This is not because the universities were not offering courses of sufficient quality but because of the reluctance of students to undertake STEM courses in the first place. Mathematics, science and engineering courses have always been perceived as 'difficult'; they have also been regarded as courses not really suitable for women. A huge amount of effort has gone into promoting STEM subjects in schools and a great deal of work has been done to try to address the gender imbalance, but there is still some way to go. Whether the revised A-level is going to help is another matter. By increasing the difficulty of the higher-level examinations, students are just as likely to be put off continuing on to university as encouraged to do so. And, of course, if the A-level specifications have been revised to ensure that students are well prepared for degree-level study, this doesn't necessarily mean that GCSEs have to do the same. In making sure that the mathematics GCSE is more demanding, more closely aligned to A-levels and thus more academic, it could be argued that it has been made even less relevant to key stage 4 pupils.

We also need to consider whether engineers need the kind of mathematics taught at GCSE and A-level, or is it really the preserve of elite pure mathematicians? Although they are always keen to meddle in curriculum minutiae, politicians rarely explore the relationship between the content of mathematics examinations and the demands of industry. The assumption is that more mathematics, and more difficult mathematics, is the solution. Clearly, this may not be the case. Companies that employ students with A-levels or degrees are employing them on the basis that they are ready to be trained to do very specific roles. In a sense, therefore, the onus is on industry to ensure that their employees have the mathematical skills they need; it is not necessarily the responsibility of schools to do so. This brings us back to the question of basic skills and Charlie Stripp's notion of 'the minimum national expectation of maths competence'. Instead of insisting on increasing difficulty, it might be more appropriate for us to consider what we actually mean by mathematical competence and what skills are needed to achieve it.

The political obsession with mathematics and STEM subjects in schools is also based on a distorted view of the employment landscape in the UK. For example, the largest employer in the UK – and the fifth largest in the world – is the National Health Service, with somewhere between 1.4 and 1.7 million employees. Nor should we ignore the fact that the creative industries in the UK are flourishing and admired around the world. I wonder how many of the politicians who see STEM subjects as the future appreciate the irony of the fact that, while we have been sending our teachers to China to learn from their expertise in mathematics pedagogy, Chinese teachers have been travelling in the opposite direction to learn how to make their students more creative.

It is undoubtedly true that mathematicians are in demand, but we need to be careful that we do not give students the impression that the study of STEM subjects is the only reliable route towards full-time employment. Yes, the cultural assumption characterised by the fact that far too many people, including highly educated professionals, are happy to say 'I am no good at maths', has to be addressed, but we should not overlook the fact that there are many routes into full-time employment, most of which require very little expertise in mathematics.

Once again, as with the English curriculum, we are left to consider the impact of all this on pupils in the classroom. From the 7- and 8-year-olds struggling with fractions and Roman numerals, to 16-year-olds feeling compelled to study mathematics in the sixth form when they would have preferred, and been much better suited, to following courses in the arts or humanities, we should never forget that debates around the contents and demands of the mathematics curriculum have a direct impact on the lives of children in schools.

Science

Debates relating to the science curriculum in schools reflect some of the issues affecting both English and mathematics. The new science GCSEs are undoubtedly more demanding than those they have replaced, especially with regard to the level of mathematics required, but it is over content where most of the concerns have been raised. Teachers have been alarmed by the sheer quantity of information they have to impart, whereas parents, politicians and religious groups tend to focus on the nature of the topics to be taught. At the primary level, there are concerns that teachers are not properly equipped to teach science to the necessary standards and that the subject is afforded too little time due to the dominance of English and mathematics.

Anyone who has looked at a selection of pupils' secondary science exercise books cannot fail to be struck both by the number of facts recorded and the number of experiments described. The repetitive nature of the books is also quite striking. It is not an exaggeration to say that once pupils have learned the scientific method in their first year, and been trained to record experiments according to a set formula, their written work in science consists largely of records of the experiments they have conducted, all recorded in exactly the same way. Finding evidence of the development of skills in science books is notoriously difficult. Of course, most science teachers are aware of this problem but justify the tedious repetitiveness of the contents of their pupils' exercise books by referring to the vast amount of content they have to get through both at key stage 3 and as part of the new GCSEs.

One of the key methods employed by Ofsted to assess progress and the effectiveness of the curriculum is the scrutiny of pupils' books, but I am sure that many inspectors would agree that science books present the most difficulties in this regard. They can look to see if the content is appropriate to the age and ability of the pupil in view but, since most of the writing consists of formulaic recording of information, it is often impossible to determine whether progress has been made. They can also look to see if the learning is sequential and properly planned but, with so much information to get through, the sequence is often little more than a succession of loosely related topics to be covered at speed.

Evidence of content overload is also apparent in the classroom. Although science teachers today adopt a panoply of techniques to capture pupils' interest and engage them in their learning, they often find themselves rushing through activities and experiments simply because they have so much stuff to get through. Rarely do they have opportunities to explore ideas beyond the examination specifications, and class discussions, where the real learning often takes place, are cut short because of the need to move on to the next topic.

The Ofsted science subject survey published in 2013 noted the challenges faced by teachers of science when attempting to ensure that syllabus content was covered. This was particularly true with regard to practical activities:

> Most science teachers wanted to use practical activities to engage and interest students, but many of them, as well as subject managers, described the

challenges they faced. Time in the laboratory was the most pressing concern. Those attempting to squeeze triple science GCSEs into less than 20% of a week's timetable, starting in Year 10, faced this problem most acutely. In these situations, any practical work that students did was the necessary minimum for controlled assessments. As a result, opportunities for illustrative and investigative scientific enquiry were limited, and so was the achievement of students. They achieved their GCSE grades but not the science practical skills they needed at the next stage. Sixth-form teachers told inspectors that this lack of practical skill is revealed starkly for many students at A level, as they try to catch up with the demands of accurate, individual practical and experimental work.[8]

This was a survey carried out some time ago and well before the introduction of the new, more demanding GCSEs. How much worse, then, is the situation now? And, of course, if teachers are under pressure to make sure they cover all the topics they need to, what is it like for pupils? With lessons cut short and practical work curtailed, how effectively are they learning?

But is so much content really necessary? How much of it do pupils take in and remember until forced to do so when they begin to revise for their examinations? Are they learning skills, are they developing the curiosity identified by Ofsted as one of the key features of the best science lessons, or are they simply learning facts to regurgitate in examinations?

The obvious answer to the problem of curriculum overload in schools is often the demand from heads of science for more time. However, most schools already devote around 20% of the timetable to science. This therefore prompts us to ask the question, do we really need to devote so much time to science in secondary schools? As with mathematics, how much of the science learned at school do the majority of us use in our everyday lives, and how much do we need to pursue careers outside of the science industry?

The National Curriculum for 2014 sets out why we teach science in schools:

A high-quality science education provides the foundations for understanding the world through the specific disciplines of biology, chemistry and physics. Science has changed our lives and is vital to the world's future prosperity, and all pupils should be taught essential aspects of the knowledge, methods, processes and uses of science. Through building up a body of key foundational knowledge and concepts, pupils should be encouraged to recognise the power of rational explanation and develop a sense of excitement and curiosity about natural phenomena. They should be encouraged to understand how science can be used to explain what is occurring, predict how things will behave, and analyse causes.[9]

These are very worthy aims but, with such an overloaded curriculum, are teachers really able to 'develop a sense of excitement and curiosity about natural phenomena'? Surely, with less content, more time could be devoted to topics and discussions which really fire children's imaginations. This, in turn, is likely to stimulate more interest in the subject and lead ultimately to more pupils choosing to study science at A-level and beyond. With young people's passionate concern about climate change, typified by the teenage campaigning superstar Greta Thunberg, there are flames ready to be fanned. If teachers could take more time exploring the ideas that really mean something to young people today, science teaching could be transformed in schools.

The issue in primary schools is not really a question of content; it is about the time spent on science in a curriculum seemingly dominated by English and mathematics. The Ofsted survey referred to previously found that most primary schools allocated one afternoon a week to science:

> Science lessons took place once a week in the majority of the primary schools visited, usually in the afternoon. The length of time for a lesson varied, with the better practice allowing the lesson to extend into the next day, if this was necessary to complete the investigation. A strong feature of the Early Years Foundation Stage was that teachers allowed children to complete the activity they had chosen; the older the pupils were, the less likely it was that they had the freedom to take time to explore ideas, find solutions and get to the bottom of their enquiry.[10]

One afternoon a week in a primary school means about an hour, and an hour after lunch when children are tired after a long morning. Moreover, the survey was written before the focus on English and mathematics had grown in intensity. It is hardly surprising therefore that secondary science teachers lament the lack of science in primary schools and consider pupils woefully ill prepared to tackle the secondary curriculum. As we have seen, the result of this is that virtually all secondary schools start science education from scratch in Year 7.

More positively, the Ofsted survey indicated that concerns regarding primary teachers' lack of scientific knowledge were largely unfounded:

> Despite concerns raised by various government agencies and professional associations about the lack of science subject specialists in primary schools, the evidence from this survey indicates that this was not a serious barrier to pupils' achievement in terms of teachers' knowledge and understanding.[11]

There is not enough time in secondary schools to deliver the content required by the National Curriculum programmes of study and the GCSE specifications, and yet far too little time seems to be devoted to science in primary schools. Nor is this due to a lack of teacher expertise; it is down to deliberate curriculum decisions. There is clearly a contradiction in the Department for Education's thinking here: if science is so important that an allocation of 20% of curriculum time in secondary schools is not enough to deliver the specified content, why is so little time devoted to its study in primary schools? What are children to make of a subject to which the odd afternoon in their primary schools was devoted which then becomes one which dominates their secondary school timetables?

Putting the debate about the sheer quantity of curriculum content aside, we come to the second key area of contention: the choice of topics to be covered. It is here that politicians and the press are more likely to get involved, especially since most of the arguments revolve around either religion or sex, and sometimes both. Although the teaching of evolution is compulsory in publicly funded schools, there are nevertheless frequent stories in the press concerning religious groups attempting to make creationism, or its more modern counterpart 'intelligent design', part of the mainstream curriculum. For example, there was a huge outcry when, in 2003, the Emmanuel Schools Foundation sponsored a number of faith-based academies where evolution and creationist ideas were to be taught side-by-side in science classes. Ofsted reviewed the situation and decided that the matter did not need to be pursued, but it nevertheless led to a sustained public debate involving both Richard Dawkins and Rod Liddle, an unlikely pairing if ever there was one.

Creationism as a matter of contention comes and goes in the press, but it would be wrong to assume that the rationalists have won the battle. As recently as September 2019, the proposed new Welsh curriculum revived the controversy with distinguished figures such as David Attenborough, Steve Jones and Alice Roberts expressing their concerns that the proposed changes could increase the possibility of creationism being taught as a science in Welsh schools.

The other key area for debate is the inclusion of Sex and Relationships Education (SRE) in science lessons, particularly in primary schools. According to the National Curriculum, the basics of sex education fall within the science curriculum. The statutory content requires maintained schools to teach children about human development, including puberty, and reproduction. In the spring of 2019, in response to a consultation period, the Department for Education announced an overhaul of SRE in both primary and secondary schools. The result was that health and relationship education became compulsory in schools, with sex education optional in the primary phase. As we saw with the Anderton Park debacle described earlier, it is not necessarily the scientific aspects of sex education where the problem lies but with the more contentious issues of LGBT education. Sex education as part of the science curriculum nevertheless remains a sensitive subject and one which is almost certain to continue to stimulate considerable parental debate.

As with English and mathematics, the science curriculum is subject to constant change and frequent debate and, as always, children in the classroom are caught in the middle of it all.

Computing

The role and importance of computing in schools offers us an interesting example of the difficulties schools and those involved in education have in ensuring that the curriculum remains relevant and up to date. Even though it is one of the most recent additions to the curriculum, the subject has already undergone a dramatic change from information communications technology (ICT) to computing, and there are now calls for it to focus more explicitly on computer coding. We could therefore see computing as a subject give way to computer coding before perhaps disappearing altogether.

The inclusion of coding in the school curriculum has become something of a cause célèbre for both politicians and the technology industry. Computing replaced ICT in the 2014 revision of the National Curriculum with the aim of ensuring that children were better prepared to compete in an increasingly digital age. There has been much discussion of the 'Fourth Industrial Revolution', a term coined by Klaus Schwab, and the need to ensure that schools prepare pupils for a world in which artificial intelligence, robotics, nanotechnology and biotechnology are becoming increasingly significant.[12] However, the world is changing so quickly that critics are already suggesting that the revised curriculum is out of date and the focus on coding is something of a red herring.

Once again, the degree of difficulty injected into the curriculum is not to be underestimated. Key stage 1 pupils have to learn what algorithms are as well as learning to create and debug simple programs of their own. At key stage 2 pupils move on to more complicated concepts, getting to grips with variables, sequencing, selection and repetition. Once children begin secondary school, they learn to use two or more programming languages to create their own programs. Schools are free to choose the specific languages and coding tools. Pupils learn simple Boolean logic, working with binary numbers, and they study how computer hardware and software work together. On the face of it, this would seem to offer pupils a good grounding in the basics of computer programming and a good basis on which to build for further study. Some argue, however, that this approach is already out of date.

In February 2019, the OECD's Director of Education and Skills, Andreas Schleicher, warned against coding education. Speaking at the World Innovation Summit for Education (WISE) in Paris, Schleicher said, 'In a way coding is just one technique of our times and I think it would be a bad mistake to have that tool become ingrained'. He added, 'You teach it to three-year-olds and by the time they graduate they will ask you remind me what was coding. That tool will be outdated very soon'. In a recent article on the WISE conference, James Higgins summarised the background to Schleicher's speech, making two key points:

- The UK government's 2017 autumn budget announced an investment of £84m to increase the number of computer science teachers. Computer science is officially the hardest-to-recruit-for subject with only two-thirds of places filled last year.

- By 2020, there is a predicated skills shortage of 800,000 skilled IT jobs across the EU, the EU has predicted. The UK is one of only 15 members that has embedded coding in its curriculum.[13]

There is clearly a need to make sure there are enough teachers of computing available to ensure that pupils have the skills they need to cope with the digital age, and there is no doubt that the government is committed to making computing a significant feature of contemporary schooling. Schleicher's argument, however, suggests that no matter what versions of coding pupils are encouraged to learn today, these will be out of date before they join the computing workforce. One could argue that this doesn't matter because they will be learning the skills needed to allow them to adapt and survive in workplaces of the future. However, more imaginative future thinkers point out that as technology develops, and machine learning accelerates, there will be little need for any of us to learn how to code. Coding as a skill may quickly become obsolete.

Could it be that in the rush to ensure that pupils are equipped to compete in the global, digital economy, a new subject has been accidentally introduced into the curriculum which will be out of date before it has time to become properly embedded? Once again, children are the victims of political thinking, not to mention the teachers who are being trained to teach a subject which may not exist within a few years of them starting their careers in schools.

Pupils need to learn about computers, about how they work and how to work them, but for the majority, the subject is really about communications and not technology. The now obsolete subject title, Information and Communications Technology, was not perhaps far off the mark after all. Pupils need to learn to use computers as tools to interact with the world. More importantly, they need to understand how the digital world works. The basic skills they need to operate computers diminish in importance every day: why learn to type, for example, when voice recognition technology gets better and better? What they really need to learn how to do is to communicate clearly and accurately in order to make sure they can instruct the technology effectively and efficiently. They also need to develop the skills to cope with the unreliable and potentially dangerous influence of social media. Not only do they need to understand how to communicate clearly, they need to become skilled at understanding the ways in which information is represented in digital media; in other words, to be able to understand concepts such as representation, persuasion, bias and manipulation. Ironically, these are all skills taught in the old-fashioned English curriculum and refined in that most reviled of all subjects, media studies.

Computing therefore offers us a splendid example of the complexities of curriculum planning and the consequences of both political and educational panic in the classroom.

Languages

Some have argued for computer coding to replace traditional language learning in schools but, as the technology develops, it is obvious that this is an idea that has had its day. Coding is unlikely to replace French or German; and linguists therefore can breathe a sigh of relief. However, the status of language learning in our schools is a key question in itself and yet another battleground for political debate. Here, however, the issues are not so much around content, as they are in English, maths and science, but about which languages should be taught and, more fundamentally, whether languages should be taught at all.

There is no doubt that language learning has been in decline in schools for some time, despite the government's efforts to boost take-up by designating languages as Ebacc subjects. A survey conducted for the BBC in 2019 revealed drops of between 30% and 50% in the numbers taking GCSE languages in the worst affected areas in England. A separate survey of secondary schools suggested a third had dropped at least one language from their GCSE options. GCSE examination entry figures paint a dismal picture of language learning in UK schools: data compiled by the Joint Council for Qualifications (JCQ) shows an overall 45% decline in GCSE language entries, with those for French declining by 63% and German by 67%. Spanish has bucked the trend, rising since 2002 by 75%, but this has done little to prevent the overall decline.[14]

So why have language entries declined so rapidly? First, there is the perceived difficulty of learning a language. There is no doubt that some children find language learning difficult, but the same could be said for maths and physics, both of which are becoming increasingly popular. The examination boards have not helped: most teachers and senior leaders are well aware of the fact that attaining a top grade in a language has become progressively more difficult in recent years. For students aiming for a good set of grades, this can be off-putting to say the least. Why take on the challenge of a language, where the chances of getting an A or an A* are slim, when other options offer a more straightforward route to success? With fewer and fewer pupils taking a language, and fewer gaining a good grade, the perception that languages are difficult is thus strengthened still further.

There are also budgetary issues affecting participation in languages in schools. Because of the decline in the numbers of students studying a language at A-level, class sizes have fallen, meaning that in many schools they have become financially unviable. With sixth form funding so low, it is difficult for schools to run classes for three or four students; they simply can't afford it. There is also the additional problem of staffing: not only are fewer and fewer students going on to study languages at university, even fewer decide to train as teachers. In many parts of the country, headteachers are finding it almost impossible to appoint language teachers. In some places, students simply cannot find places to study languages at A-level.

Entries for some languages are rising, however, but immigration has played its part here with, for example, entries for Portuguese up by around 50% and Polish by 45% since 2013. Unfortunately, this is not an indication of a renewed interest in languages: most secondary schools offer their pupils the chance to take examinations in their native language both to boost their self-esteem and, of course, to add to their GCSE points tally. In many cases, there is no learning involved: pupils are simply tested in a language they already know.

A great deal of effort has gone into promoting so-called global languages. Mandarin, for example, has been heavily promoted, and the Mandarin Excellence Programme[15] has been enthusiastically embraced by a number of schools across the country. The government in England is also investing in supporting Mandarin teaching, with a target of 5,000 pupils being 'on track to fluency' by 2020. Examination entries have risen accordingly but, for most schools, the same issues occur. If recruiting a teacher of French is difficult, how much more difficult is it to find a teacher of Mandarin? And with characters and tone changes to learn, the problem of perceived difficulty is even more of an issue for potential students.

Of course, the elephant in the room is undoubtedly the ubiquity of English. English has become a universal language and, as a result, many students simply don't see the point of learning a language when most foreigners they meet speak fluent English. If you are a child growing up in, say, France or Italy, there are powerful incentives for you to learn English. English is everywhere: in pop songs, in Hollywood movies and online. For a child growing up in Devon or Somerset, where is the incentive? Where is the cultural attraction? How many of them can name a French pop star or an Italian movie? Add to this the difficulty of learning a language, and the question of which language to learn in the first place and then choosing a language option at GCSE or A-level makes very little sense to them.

There are powerful arguments for learning languages. France and Germany, for example, are two of the UK's closest trading partners, and it is obvious that a business that employs people able to speak to potential customers in their own language is likely to do better than one where every conversation has to be translated or conducted in English. Spanish and Mandarin are both spoken by millions of people across the world, millions who don't necessarily speak English, and if we wish to make meaningful connections with people, a knowledge of their languages is surely essential. There is also the immense cultural value of learning a language: it is only through immersion in a language that people really get to appreciate the cultures of other countries.

Learning a language also requires a wide spectrum of valuable skills. Students of French, for example, will develop good memories and powerful analytical skills; they will become confident speakers and develop insights into other cultures which those who speak only English can never hope to attain. They are therefore incredibly valuable to industry and, of course, to society in general. And, above all, there is the sheer pleasure of learning a language: language learning offers a level of cultural and intellectual enrichment that few other subjects can match. How many of us wish we had paid more attention to language learning when we were at school?

There have been numerous attempts to revive languages in schools. Foreign languages were introduced formally within the primary school curriculum in England in 2014 for the first time. Children at key stage 2 now study one foreign language for up to one hour per week. It can be any modern or ancient foreign language, and the focus should be on enabling pupils to make substantial progress in one language. However, in reality, there is a very mixed picture. While most primary schools insist that they offer language learning, the nature of the provision varies wildly – from formal teaching by specialist teachers in some schools to the occasional hour of singing songs in French. In essence, most primary schools pay lip service to learning a language; it is done because they have to do it. To be fair, not much can be done in an hour a week, and even less if the school doesn't have a linguist on the staff.

The introduction of the Ebacc in 2015 seemed to suggest that schools where language provision has declined would be encouraged, or even impelled, to put languages back into the heart of the curriculum. Unfortunately, as the figures quoted earlier confirm, this hasn't really happened. The government's ambition to see 75% of pupils studying the EBacc subject combination at GCSE by 2022, and 90% by 2025, is currently looking increasingly unlikely. Although the 2019 Ofsted framework refers to this target, inspectors are not directed to accord it particular emphasis.

Ultimately, the debate over languages in schools is symptomatic of the UK's ambivalence to foreigners in general. The tensions highlighted in the Brexit debates between the pro-Europeans and the British 'patriots' will undoubtedly have had an impact on language learning in schools. The promotion of England as a great nation ready to stand alone in the world clearly implies a sense of superiority. English is therefore the most important language and the only one worth learning. Those with a more European sensibility are much more likely to appreciate the importance of learning a language. As always, political arguments are played out in the classroom and impact directly on children's learning.

The humanities

Like languages, the humanities are part of the Ebacc and thus promoted accordingly. However, only history and geography are recognised as humanities Ebacc subjects, and this in itself has led to considerable debate, particularly with regard to the status of religious studies.

Geography has proved itself to be fairly adaptable and, for that reason, largely immune to political debate. The National Curriculum descriptors are broad enough to allow teachers and examination boards to encompass a wide range of topics and thus adapt to changing times and changing ideas. Climate change, for example, can easily be incorporated into the human and physical geography descriptors both at key stage 2 and key stage 3, and this has allowed teachers to offer subject content in sympathy with the interests of young people. With the rise in political activism amongst young people in response to the climate crisis, geography as a subject is proving to be remarkably popular. It is not surprising, therefore, that the subject is often one of the most popular choices both at GCSE and at A-level.

There are criticisms, of course. Those who deny, or play down, the effects of climate change argue that children are being unduly influenced by their teachers, and some feel that pessimism linked to concerns about global issues is a major contributor to the mental health crisis in schools and colleges. Much of the criticism is more basic, however, deriving from pupils' lack of knowledge of the world around them. Despite the fact that at key stage 1 children study both 'locational knowledge' and 'place', many, including secondary school geography teachers themselves, decry the fact that children's knowledge of the basics is sparse, to say the least. Teachers find that when they start secondary school, very few pupils can draw a map of Britain or locate major cities. Even fewer can identify countries around the world.

The narrowing of the primary curriculum is surely the major culprit here. With the dominance of English and mathematics in some schools, very little time is afforded to geographical knowledge. There isn't time to develop a systematic approach to the subject, with the National Curriculum often covered by topics rather than the explicit teaching of geography as a separate discipline. This, as we have seen, is true of many subjects at the primary level.

History is similarly affected by curriculum narrowing in primary schools, and few would agree that schools are able to meet the key aim of the National Curriculum to ensure that pupils 'know and understand the history of these islands as a coherent, chronological narrative, from the earliest times to the present day'.[16] Children often start secondary school with a jumbled knowledge of the Romans, 1066 and all that, and a few of the more glamorous monarchs, including Henry VIII and Elizabeth I. Whether they have any sense of 'a coherent, chronological narrative', or even a workable sense of time, is another matter. To be fair, children's understanding of time develops as they grow up but, even so, many would agree that the current approach to history in primary schools addresses historical episodes rather than history as a journey through time.

In secondary schools, much has been made of the introduction of integrated humanities courses which combine geography and history (and sometimes RE). Schools with a two-year key stage 3, introduced to allow more time to be devoted to GCSE courses, lay themselves open to the criticism that history and geography have been marginalised and thus devalued. The continuing popularity of both subjects at GCSE undermines this argument to some extent, though it is hard to deny that the loss of a more general course in Year 9, not tied to an examination syllabus, may well have narrowed the curriculum for many young people, especially for those who decided not to study either subject at GCSE.

The real debates regarding history in schools, however, relate firmly to curriculum content, and it is here where politicians like to get involved. When the Ebacc was being developed, Michael Gove, the bête noir of the school curriculum, led the charge, strongly supported by the historian, Simon Schama. In an article in *The Guardian* in 2010, Schama lamented the lack of coherence in the curriculum:

> My own anecdotal evidence suggests that right across the secondary school system our children are being short-changed of the patrimony of their story,

which is to say the lineaments of the whole story, for there can be no true history that refuses to span the arc, no coherence without chronology.[17]

The concern regarding coherence is in line with the concerns of many, including history teachers, but it is with the notion of 'patrimony' where the debate really takes off. Schama went as far as outlining his own list of key topics which every child should learn: murder in the cathedral; the black death and the peasants' revolt in the reign of Richard II; the execution of King Charles I; the Indian moment; the Irish wars; and the opium wars and China. This is a very traditional list and was criticised by many as being a celebration of Britain as it once was, not how it is now. Schama's vision reflected a very traditional view of what history should be about. It is in line with the National Curriculum's aim of focussing on the history 'of these isles' but entirely out of sorts with the views of those who argue for a curriculum that recognises the diversity of contemporary British society.

The history curriculum prior to the advent of Gove was heavily criticised for its focus on skills and topics rather than chronology. Robert Skidelsky, writing in the *Independent* in August 1989, explained his opposition to the history GCSE:

> Some pupils are doing exotic syllabuses such as the history of medicine, taught by teachers who know nothing about medicine. . . . Learning by doing has become entrenched in the form of projects and coursework assignments, while chronology and factual recall have become marginalised.[18]

The Gove-Schama axis set out to reverse this position and attempted to correct both the lack of a chronological approach and the move away from traditional British history. This would address what they saw as a decline in history as a key subject in schools. The ensuing debate, however, not only explored skills in opposition to chronology but pitched nationalism, patriotism and jingoism against Britain's increasingly multi-cultural society and the need for pupils to regard themselves as global citizens.

The 2018 Windrush scandal is a recent example of how easily political headlines find their way directly into the curriculum in schools, and, of course, into the classroom. Following extensive press coverage, the Runnymede Trust, a race equality think-tank, said that Windrush had exposed a 'shocking lack of understanding' at the government level about the winding up of the empire. The trust demanded a new approach to teaching in schools to ensure all pupils learn about migration and empire. The DfE countered by pointing out that the topic of migration and the British empire are compulsory in several parts of the history and English curriculum for both primary and secondary schools.[19]

As society changes, the teaching of history will inevitably change. The debate will therefore continue, and what children learn in history lessons will always be buffeted by political and intellectual arguments. There is a positive side to the influence of politicians on the history curriculum, however: the continuing high-level debates, such as the one driven by the Windrush scandal, show children that history is a living subject and directly relevant to their daily lives.

History teaching is always destined to court controversy, but the prize for generating the most contention must surely go to the teaching of religion in schools. This is a complex issue encompassing religious observance, curriculum content, multi-culturalism and the relevance of the subject in modern Britain. A pupil sitting in a religious studies lesson today can have little understanding of the depth and divisiveness of the debate underpinning the lesson.

Current arrangements go back to the 1944 Education Act when Britain was predominantly a Christian country. A daily act of collective worship 'of a broadly Christian nature' is still a legal requirement, despite the fact that most schools interpret the phrase very broadly. Indeed, in many schools a collective act of worship is not actually possible due to the numbers of pupils involved and limitations on the spaces available. It is also quite likely that most of the potential audience are not actually Christians at all; they are much more likely to come from atheist or agnostic homes or follow a wide range of other religions. It is clear, therefore, that these assemblies have become something of an anachronism.

Religious studies as a subject is different and does attempt to offer a wider view of religion. There is always a comparative element, and pupils are encouraged to learn about the major world religions. More active Christians criticise the decline in the teaching of scripture, and the lack of attention to the Bible, but the subject in schools focuses on teaching pupils about the nature and purpose of religious faith. The National Curriculum shies away from outlining a syllabus for religious studies, even though it does so for every other subject, merely including the phrase: 'All schools are also required to teach religious education at all key stages'. Maintained schools generally follow a locally agreed syllabus which covers world religions (Christianity, Islam, Hinduism, Buddhism and so on) as well as key topics such as:

- What is religion?
- What is belief?
- Prejudice and discrimination
- Religion in the media
- A comparative study of two or more religions
- Philosophy and religion
- Religion, belief and creativity

Common sense would seem to suggest that this approach to religious education is essential to enable pupils to understand the world. However, it regularly faces challenges from all sides. Conservative and orthodox religious figures dislike the holistic approach, preferring to focus on instruction in their own particular faiths;

atheists argue that far too much attention is given to religion and insist that it has no place in schools in our increasingly secular society.

There are regular calls for a nationally determined syllabus, called something like 'Religion, Belief and Values', to replace religious education, and many insist that it should be obligatory in all state-funded schools. The aim is to equip children with the knowledge they need to understand how religion works in society and to explore the nature of religious faith without advocating any particular belief system. Others call for the abolition of faith schools which, with some justification, they see as perpetuating division and prejudice in society. Although the majority of faith schools are run by the Church of England, the rise in Islamic schools has proved to be the real trigger for debate. Church of England schools have been around for a long time, and most wear their religion lightly; Islamic schools are new and therefore threatening. Catholic and Jewish schools have been tolerated because there aren't that many of them, and they have never posed a real threat to the dominant culture; Islamic schools for many symbolise the rise of Islam in Britain, a prospect they find very worrying indeed, especially when their fears are exacerbated by a sensationalist press.

Underlying any discussion of the role of religious education in schools is the right of parents to bring up their children in their own faith and the freedom of all members of society to follow whatever faith they choose to believe. It would be a brave politician who attempted to limit this particular freedom. This certainly accounts for the DfE's reluctance to include programmes of study for religious education in the National Curriculum and its reluctance to include the subject in the Ebacc. Whether a nationally agreed approach to religious education in schools will emerge is hard to determine; if it does, it won't stop the arguments. What children learn about religion will continue to excite fierce debate.

Conclusion

One of the most fascinating exercises any school leader can undertake is the oddly named 'pupil pursuit'. This involves spending the day following a pupil from class to class simply observing what he or she is learning. At the end of the day most adults are exhausted and confused, whereas the children seem to cope remarkably well. Whenever I have undertaken a pupil pursuit, I have ended the day wondering how pupils learn anything. They move from class to class, subject to subject, teacher to teacher with apparent ease, but the constant changes of subject and context are, frankly, bewildering. After an hour of complex mathematical work, led perhaps by a teacher who is fairly distant and strict, they move on to detailed language learning in a classroom with different pupils and a teacher with a much more relaxed approach. They seem to adjust instantly to the demands of the new subject, as well as adapting to the new classroom context and the new boundaries set by the teacher. And this continues all day long, every day. Ultimately, it demonstrates just how adaptable young people really are.

However, there are limits. Children in schools already face the demands of five hours of increasingly intensive learning, switching from subject to subject, and should not, therefore, have to cope with the constant change or uncertainty deriving from constant political interference. The brief subject review outlined previously clearly demonstrates the extent to which schools are under siege. Teachers and leaders do their best to protect pupils from the more dramatic changes in political thinking, but it is becoming increasingly difficult for them to do so. Once again, it is hard not see classrooms as places of disorder rather than stability. Schools should be places of calm and ordered learning, not the battlegrounds of political ideology.

What can schools do now to put things right?

- **Choose books with care**. The revised examination specifications promote a very particular version of English literature; teachers need to work hard to ensure that pupils are introduced to high-quality writing from around the world.

- **Read more**. Far too many teachers stick to the books they read in school and university. It is incumbent on all teachers, and English teachers in particular, to read the books their pupils read and ensure that the best contemporary fiction is read in the classroom.

- **Recognise trends**. Children and young people want to play the latest games, watch the latest films, listen to the latest music. They also want to read the latest novels. Schools must ensure that funding is available to update the books read in class on a regular basis. It's surely time to replace *Goodnight Mister Tom*.

- **Join the real world**. One of the main criticisms of the mathematics curriculum relates to its abstract nature. Schools should work to ensure that, wherever possible, the teaching of maths is related directly to examples drawn from everyday life.

- **Handle the STEM agenda with care**. STEM subjects are rightly promoted in schools, but care must be taken to ensure that other areas of the curriculum are not neglected as a result. The promotion of careers in non-STEM subjects should be seen as a priority.

- **Identify what is important**. In order to tackle the problem of an overloaded science curriculum, school leaders need to encourage science teachers to distinguish between essential and desirable content. A more sensible balance can then be created to encourage depth of learning rather than simple recall.

- **Be careful with coding.** Coding may well equip students for successful careers, but schools need to consider whether they can really keep up with the requirements of an industry which changes so quickly. The real focus should be on enabling students to understand and deal effectively with the digital world.

- **Promote languages.** Students need to understand the importance of language study in terms of dealing with other cultures. Languages should not be seen simply as a requirement of the Ebacc. Work needs to be done to make language learning fun, accessible and relevant.

- **Reconsider the role of RE.** Helping pupils understand the role of religion in a multi-cultural society is a vital part of their education. RE in schools needs to move away from a traditional diet of key facts about world religions to explore the history, context and impact of religion in contemporary society.

What should policymakers do to put things right?

- Trust teachers with regard to the books they choose to teach.

- Abandon the nostalgic view of English literature as a celebration of empire and recognise the importance of English as a global language. Encourage schools to teach literature from around the world to help prepare pupils for a global society.

- Take a more balanced view of the STEM agenda in secondary schools. STEM subjects need promoting but not at the expense of the arts.

- Raise the status of science in primary schools to prepare pupils more effectively for the study of science at the secondary level.

- Acknowledge the impact of digital technology on society and enable schools to adapt their curriculums in order to ensure that children are properly equipped to survive in the digital world.

- Having recognised the importance of language learning by including it in the Ebacc, ensure that enough teachers are trained and recruited to make effective language teaching possible.

- If the Ebacc is to be retained, RE should be included as an Ebacc subject. The role of religious education should be seen as distinctly different from faith education, and all schools, faith schools and secular schools, should be required to teach the impact of religion on contemporary society.

Notes

1. Primary Framework for Literacy and Mathematics, *DfES 2006. 02011-2006BOK-EN.* www.standards.dfes.gov.uk/primaryframeworks
2. The term 'oracy' was coined by Andrew Wilkinson in the 1960s. This word is formed by analogy from literacy and numeracy. Oracy in educational theory is the fluent, confident and correct use of the standard spoken form of one's native language.
3. *English Literature GCSE: A Myth Buster*, Department for Education, Crown copyright 2014.
4. The Section 28 clause was introduced by Margaret Thatcher as part of the Local Government Act 1988 and effectively banned the 'promotion' of homosexuality by local authorities and in Britain's schools. The clause endured until it was repealed in Scotland on 21 June 2001 and in the rest of the UK on 18 November 2003.
5. C. Stripp. 2017. What's Wrong with Maths GCSE? Addressing Fundamental Problems at the Heart of the New Exams, *Teachwire*. www.teachwire.net/news/whats-wrong-with-maths-gcse-addressing-fundamental-problems-at-the-heart-of-the-new-exams
6. J. Jerrim, P. Perera & P. Sellen. 2017. *English Education: World Class in Primary?*, Education Policy Institute.
7. Ibid. p. 6.
8. *Maintaining Curiosity: A Survey into Science Education in Schools.* Ofsted 2013. Crown Copyright 2013, p. 33.
9. National Curriculum in England: Science Programmes of Study, *Department for Education*, 2013. www.gov.uk/government/publications/national-curriculum-in-england-science-programmes-of-study
10. *Maintaining Curiosity.* p. 19.
11. Ibid. p. 12.
12. K. Schwab. 2017. *The Fourth Industrial Revolution*, London, Crown Publishing, Random House.
13. J. Higgins. 2019. The Report: Is Coding 'a Waste of Time?', *Education Technology*. https://edtechnology.co.uk/Article/what-is-the-code-for-success/
14. B. Jeffreys. 2019. Language Learning, German and French Drop by Half in UK Schools, *BBC News*, 27 February. www.bbc.co.uk/news/education-47334374
15. The Mandarin Excellence Programme is an intensive language programme for schools in England, which aims to get at least 5,000 pupils on track to fluency in Mandarin Chinese by 2020. The programme is funded by the Department for Education and delivered by the UCL Institute of Education in partnership with the British Council.
16. National Curriculum 2016. p. 245.
17. S. Schama. 2010. My Vision for History in Schools, *The Guardian*, 9 November.
18. R. Skidelsky. 1989. Battle of Britain's Past Times: The Prime Minister Has Decreed a Revival of National History Teaching, *The Independent*, 22 August.
19. S. Weale. 2019. Migration and Empire 'Should Be Taught in English Schools', *The Guardian*, 3 July. www.theguardian.com/education/2019/jul/03/migration-and-empire-should-be-taught-in-english-schools

4 Beyond the core

The subjects discussed in the previous chapter are generally considered to be part of the core curriculum. Michael Gove put the cat among the pigeons by excluding religious studies, design technology and the arts from the Ebacc, but these subjects can be found in virtually every school curriculum in the country and they play a key part in the curriculum debate. Politicians, educationalists and the press regularly discuss the content of these subjects in considerable detail and, as a result, they become victims of almost constant change.

Unfortunately, however, the debate doesn't end there: as we move beyond the core, the arguments continue. Subjects which are often regarded as peripheral sometimes come under the spotlight, provoking regular speculation and, occasionally, furious debate. Everyone has been to school; everyone therefore has an opinion. It is at the ragged edges of the curriculum, however, where the discussions become particularly interesting.

The arts

The arts are in decline in schools. There can be no doubt about that. Since 2014, the number of A-level entries in arts subjects, which include drama, music and art, in England has fallen by 13,000, almost 17%. Conversely, entries in science, technology, engineering and mathematics (the STEM subjects) have increased by 15,500, a rise of 6%. The picture is the same for GCSEs where, between 2014 and 2019, the number of entries for arts GCSEs decreased by 30,000. Moreover, the proportion of pupils taking at least one arts subject fell from 57% in 2014 to 53% in 2016, a trend which is continuing today.

The promotion of the Ebacc and the introduction of the Progress 8 measure has proved to be a toxic mix for the arts, and, of course, for children in the classroom. The Ebacc is designed to ensure that there is a strong focus on a traditional set of 'core subjects': English, English literature, mathematics, science, geography or history, and a language. There is no mention of the arts. Progress 8 is similar in that it measures pupils' achievement in eight subjects, although in practice this equates to 10 subjects because English and mathematics are double counted. The measure covers progress in English, mathematics, three other Ebacc subjects and three other non-Ebacc subjects.

On the face of it, the Ebacc does seem to offer an opening for the arts in the non-Ebacc category. However, in reality, these slots are often taken up by other subjects. Virtually all secondary schools operate an options process at key stage 4 whereby pupils have to choose which subjects to study to GCSE level. In the past, they have had a reasonable degree of choice; today that choice is severely limited. In order to satisfy the demands of the Ebacc – and remember that it is the government's ambition that 75% of all pupils should begin studying the full set of EBacc subjects by 2022 – pupils now have an extended set of compulsory subjects. Most pupils in most secondary schools now have to study English, English literature, mathematics, a language, geography or history, and two or three sciences. This equates to seven or eight GCSEs. In addition, religious studies is still compulsory at key stage 4, as is physical education. There will also be some form of personal, social and health education which often includes careers education.

In order not to overburden pupils with too many GCSEs – although many would argue that eight is too many in the first place – schools now offer a very limited choice of option subjects – sometimes three but, more often than not, two. This means that pupils struggle to choose between a long list of competing subjects. These include GCSEs in physical education, business studies (both of which are very popular), design technology, geography or history (they will have chosen only one of these as part of their Ebacc options), an additional language, a third science, and a long list of what can best be described as 'newer' subjects popular in schools such as sociology, psychology, media studies, environmental studies and so on.

This leaves very little space for the arts. In schools where the arts were promoted strongly, pupils used to be offered a suite of arts GCSE including art, art graphics, music, drama, dance and, sometimes, photography. Now that these subjects face fierce competition from all the other subjects vying for attention in the two empty option blocks, schools have been forced to reduce their arts offer. Schools which ran two or three sets in art now offer one; music GCSE has disappeared from the timetable in hundreds of schools; drama is becoming less and less popular and dance is now a real rarity, seen only in the very largest comprehensive schools.

The introduction of the Ebacc and the Progress 8 measure have both played a huge part in the decline of the arts, but there are other factors to take into account. The obsession with STEM subjects, both politically and in schools, has led children to believe that the only way to prepare for life beyond school is to focus on English, mathematics and science. Nor did the intervention of the universities in the debate help improve matters: the Russell Group's now infamous list of 'facilitating A-levels' drove students even further away from considering arts subjects as suitable vehicles for academic success. The list was exclusive, to say the least: biology, chemistry, English, geography, history, maths, modern and classical languages, and physics. To be fair, these subjects were only ever recommended, and A-level students were advised to take two of them, leaving the third A-level as an open choice, but this is not how the list was interpreted. Students turned away from the arts in fear of losing the chance to gain access to the top universities. This led to absurd situations where incredibly creative and talented young men or women, who were likely to achieve the highest grades in subjects like art or drama, felt obliged to study science or maths knowing full well that they were going to underachieve. And as A-level arts subjects were seen as 'unsuitable' for universities, this filtered down into key stage 4, leaving schools struggling to offer arts subjects at any level.

The Russell Group has now thankfully abandoned the notion of preferred subjects. The facilitating subjects list has been replaced with a new website called Informed Choices, which suggests A-level options for pupils based on what they want to study at university, and more general guidance for those who haven't yet made up their mind. The damage has been done, however, and the perception of the arts as somehow inferior lingers in the minds of children in our schools today.

The arts are undoubtedly uniquely important in schools, but their value is often overlooked. E.W. Eisner, in an influential study titled *The Creation of the Mind*, outlined succinctly the reasons why the arts should be taught to all young people:

1 The arts enable children to make good judgments about qualitative relationships

2 Problems can have more than one solution and questions can have more than one answer

3 The arts celebrate multiple perspectives (there are many ways to see and interpret the world)

4 In complex forms of problem-solving, purposes are seldom fixed, but change with circumstance and opportunity

5 The arts make vivid the fact that neither words in their literal form nor numbers exhaust what we can know

6 Small differences can have large effects

7 The arts allow us to think through and within material

8 The arts allow us to say what cannot be said (a work of art can allow a release of poetic capacities to find the words that will do the job)

9 The arts give us experiences we can have from no other source and, through such experiences, allow us to discover the range and variety of what we are capable of feeling

10 The arts' position in the school curriculum symbolises to the young what adults believe is important.[1]

In September 2019 in an opinion piece in *The Guardian*, Michael Rosen, one of the most trenchant critics of the government's approach to education, summed up, with characteristic flair, the attitude of politicians to the arts in schools. After describing a joyful school poetry workshop, during which a poem evolved into a performance, he bemoaned the dismal position in England where school leavers were to be seen as little more than 'units of labour'. According to the prevailing ideology, these units, he lamented,

> should be seen as being more or less able to compete in what ministers call the global labour market; there is an agreed amount of knowledge that needs to be transferred from teachers to pupils so that they can become these competitive units.[2]

Such a vision leaves very little room for poetry.

Design technology

Whatever happened to design technology (DT)? Like the arts, design as a subject has suffered as a result of the Ebacc/Progress 8 debacle, but it is true to say that it was in a state of decline well before the influence of either of these 'innovations' took hold in schools. Put simply, design technology is a mess.

Design technology in schools is an umbrella subject, with most design departments responsible for a suite of courses yoked uncomfortably together. These include supposedly technical subjects such as resistant materials, product design and electronics, but most design leaders are also responsible for textiles and food technology. The AQA examination board, for example, offers A-level design and technology specifications in

- Fashion and textiles
- Food technology
- Product design
- Product design (textiles)
- Systems and control technology

The AQA GCSE course is designed to allow teachers to choose elements of the A-level courses by focussing on processes and materials. Its aims are expressed in typically mangled and opaque language:

> The new GCSE places greater emphasis on understanding and applying iterative design processes. Students will use their creativity and imagination to design and make prototypes that solve real and relevant problems, considering their own and others' needs, want and values.[3]

This is in line with the Design and Technology Association's somewhat optimistic view of DT as a subject:

> Design and technology gives young people the skills and abilities to engage positively with the designed and made world and to harness the benefits of technology. They learn how products and systems are designed and manufactured, how to be innovative and to make creative use of a variety of resources including digital technologies, to improve the world around them.[4]

They have strong support from their patron, the inventor James Dyson, who declares:

> Design and technology is a phenomenally important subject. Logical, creative and practical, it's the only opportunity students have to apply what they learn in maths and science – directly preparing them for a career in engineering. Policymakers must recognise design and technology's significance for the UK economy and strive not just to preserve it – but to ensure it appeals to the brightest of young minds.[5]

This all sounds impressive but, unfortunately it doesn't filter down into the classroom. Design technology in the vast majority of schools is muddled and confused. It is also true to say that design is often one of the weakest subjects, with poor outcomes and poor teaching.

There are several issues here. First, there is the notion of design itself. I am sure everyone would agree that design skills are important to society, but the image of design propagated by DT as a subject is unclear. Students aiming to follow careers in engineering design will find themselves in much greater demand if they have A-levels in maths and physics; those preparing for work in the creative industries should be advised to take art, graphics or photography. Unfortunately, design technology offers a smorgasbord of loosely related skills which fails to give students a real insight into industrial or creative design despite the grand aims of its advocates.

Despite its promotion as a STEM subject, design technology did not make it into the Ebacc and has therefore been pushed into the option blocks described earlier. With a choice of only two or three additional subjects to choose from, pupils are becoming more and more reluctant to opt for design subjects which are not perceived as suitably academic. This leads us to the second issue with the subject: who is it for?

It is undoubtedly true to say that design is more likely to appeal to less able students than the very brightest, though we are not supposed to say so. Of course, lots of very able students take design GCSEs, but the majority are those who want to do something practical as a way of escape from the relentless academic diet dictated by Progress 8 and the Ebacc. The history of the subject is relevant here because design technology has its origins in woodwork, metalwork, cooking and sewing, and there are thousands of pupils in schools who would really enjoy and benefit from learning these supposedly old-fashioned skills without the pseudo-academic theory papers which are so much a feature of current examination specifications. Indeed, many teachers of design lament the loss of practical learning in schools and find the focus on written work pointless and suffocating.

There is, of course, a natural divide in design technology departments in schools, with product design and resistant materials on one side and textiles and food technology on the other. And, despite the enormous efforts of schools to make design subjects gender neutral, it is still true to say that boys are more likely to be drawn to the former and girls the latter. It is also true to say that textiles attracts highly motivated, more able girls who see textiles as an arts subject and nothing to do with design. Indeed, in some schools, textiles is part of the art department, not the design department.

As we shall see, there is a huge and developing skills gap in secondary schools. With fewer and fewer pupils taking design subjects, and few schools able to offer vocational courses, those who would be better suited to practical rather than academic learning now have very little choice. As a consequence, young people who could well become talented carpenters, metal workers, dressmakers and tailors are now unable to learn the basic skills they need to prepare themselves for practical careers. Instead, they are forced to slog their way through academic subjects where they will undoubtedly underachieve. This, in turn, leads to disaffection and, more often than not, poor behaviour.

Instead of extolling the virtues of design technology, politicians and industrialists should perhaps be advised to lobby for a return to the practical skills of the past to ensure that schools are genuinely able to meet the needs of all pupils.

Physical education

Physical education (PE) is undoubtedly a core subject, but it is generally considered to be something other. It is a non-academic subject and regarded by many as little more than a break from classroom learning. Despite strenuous efforts to increase its academic credibility – with the introduction of GCSE and A-level courses – physical education, for most people, is 'just PE' and therefore disconnected from the core curriculum. However, contemporary concerns regarding healthy lifestyles mean that discussions regarding the nature and content of PE in schools are becoming more and more important.

In 2011, the World Health Organization claimed that childhood obesity is one of the most serious public health challenges of the 21st century. In 2016, the government published *Childhood obesity: a plan for action*[6] and, in 2018, in response to the plan, Ofsted reviewed obesity, healthy eating and physical activity in schools:

> Childhood obesity is one of the pressing issues of our generation. By the start of primary school, almost a quarter of children in England are overweight or

obese. This rises to over a third by the time children leave Year 6. Obesity in children starting Reception has risen for the second year in a row. Naturally, this issue is a high priority for the government, and the recently published obesity strategy sets out the responsibility we all have to support young people in meeting the challenge.[7]

Ofsted's advice highlights the importance of physical education in schools:

In the shared effort to tackle obesity, schools should focus on improving those things they are best placed to do:

- planning a challenging and well-sequenced curriculum, including learning about the body in PE and science about healthy eating and cooking

- providing ample opportunity for children to take physical exercise during the school day – with lots of opportunities to 'get out of breath'

- teaching particular skills like how to cook or how to dance

- updating parents on their children's physical development such as agility, balance and coordination.

The strength of this advice undoubtedly raises the status of PE in schools, but there is a problem here: PE as it is delivered in schools today is not really about fitness and healthy lifestyles; it is about games. This may seem to be a somewhat harsh judgement, and PE teachers across the country will argue that they focus intensively on fitness, but the plain fact is that PE in schools is still based on a model which ultimately derives from the one developed in 19th-century public schools. A child time-travelling from the playing fields of Eton, Rugby or Harrow in, say, 1860 to a comprehensive school in Milton Keynes in 2020 would barely notice the change of setting.

PE in schools is organised largely around traditional team games: football, rugby and netball in the winter; cricket and athletics in the summer. There are good reasons for this, of course. Although more and more schools have sophisticated fitness suites, the easiest way to conduct a PE lesson with a class of 30 pupils and one teacher is still through team games. Many schools now organise complex carousels of activities which enable pupils to spend some time working on personal fitness, and most schools have lunchtime or after-school fitness sessions, but the majority of pupils' time is spent participating in teams.

Children undoubtedly understand the importance of personal fitness, and they cannot escape the ubiquitous promotion of healthy lifestyles via social media, but many of them simply do not enjoy team games. PE for them, therefore, becomes a subject to avoid and not embrace. There is also an added problem: as children grow into teenagers, they become increasingly body conscious and so shy away from games and crowded changing rooms. This is particularly true for teenage girls, especially in mixed sex contexts where they become acutely conscious of their looks and the opinions of others.

Attempts to modernise PE in order to focus directly on fitness and health are often unwittingly undermined by those who deliver the subject. PE teachers become teachers because they love PE. They take delight in team games; they participated fully in PE when they were at school and most have been part of local, regional or national teams of some kind or other. Many are therefore baffled by the suggestion that PE as it is delivered in schools today isn't really about health and fitness and are genuinely mystified by the fact that so many young people hate PE with a passion.

A few years ago, as a headteacher, I instigated a major re-structuring of my school's curriculum: I attempted to introduce a new approach to physical education with the aim of promoting fitness and health much more successfully. I moved food technology out of the design department and linked it directly with PE, thus creating a new subject called health and fitness. The hope was that by working together, the teachers involved would create a radically new curriculum in which pupils were taught about healthy eating and healthy lifestyles in the classroom before putting them in practice via a variety of physical activities including, of course, team games if that's what pupils wanted to do, but via a wide variety of other sports and exercise routines including, for example, dance, Pilates and yoga. Although the experiment enjoyed some success, it was ultimately a failure because the PE teachers really couldn't wrap their heads around such a radical approach. For them, more time for PE simply meant more games.

This led me to conclude that PE teachers were perhaps not the people to be leading the drive for increased fitness in schools. This, of course, is far from the case, but there is a problem to be addressed here. If the government is serious about promoting healthy lifestyles, then the traditional PE culture needs to change. There are promising signs in some schools where dance is given high status and fitness suites are designed to appeal to young people in the same way that commercial gyms and leisure centres appeal to fashion-conscious millennials, but, in too many, there is still an unrelenting diet of games and a macho culture of competitive sports and team bonding.

The issue of culture is one that reaches well beyond the school gates, however. Britain has a powerful sporting culture which underpins the traditional approach to PE in schools. An alien visitor would undoubtedly find our society's obsession with football, rugby and cricket something of a surprise, especially when it dominates the media and is part of most people's everyday social chatter. Nevertheless, its dominance is rarely questioned. Any attempt to dilute the sports-based school curriculum is likely to run aground on the populist view of sports as the glue that holds society together.

Funding also has its part to play. Delivering PE lessons which are not based on team games is expensive and time consuming, and most schools do not have the indoor facilities required to offer a wide variety of individual activities. Very few schools can afford the money a truly transformative curriculum would cost. Therefore, with increasingly sedentary lifestyles and limited options for fitness beyond PE, obesity rates will continue to rise.

PSHE/citizenship

Healthy lifestyles also feature prominently in personal, social, health and economic education (PSHE). This is a relatively new subject introduced in the late 1970s in order to bring together the various threads of the health and social issues schools are tasked by politicians to deliver. The prominence of the subject has grown in recent years, particularly with the increasing focus on the *Every Child Matters* outcomes and the duty on schools to promote their pupils' well-being, but it remained non-statutory until very recently. However, despite not being mandatory until September 2020, schools in England were encouraged to enact the new PSHE curriculum in September 2019. In addition, new mandatory sex and relationships guidance was introduced for first teaching in 2020.

PSHE education is defined by Ofsted as a planned programme to help children and young people develop fully as individuals and as members of families and social and economic communities. Its goal is to equip young people with the knowledge, understanding, attitudes and practical skills to live healthily, safely, productively and responsibly.[8]

PSHE is often combined with, or subsumed in, citizenship, another National Curriculum subject area, the aim of which is

> to provide pupils with knowledge, skills and understanding to prepare them to play a full and active part in society. In particular, citizenship education should foster pupils' keen awareness and understanding of democracy, government and how laws are made and upheld.[9]

I suspect very few people would disagree with the aims of both citizenship and PSHE. They are key subjects and vital to enable young people to thrive in and understand life in modern Britain. Problems arise, however, when we get to debate not only about content but also curriculum overload. As we have seen, schools now offer a complex and academic curriculum, with key stage 4 pupils taking GCSEs in eight, nine or ten subjects. When RE and PE are added to the mix, it is not hard to see why PSHE and citizenship often become compressed and afforded very little curriculum time. Schools tend to shoehorn both subjects into the timetable wherever they can, and they are usually combined. In some, they are given a lesson a week; in others, a lesson a fortnight. More and more schools now deliver PSHE and citizenship in tutor time, with occasional whole days devoted to key aspects such as careers or health.

In many ways, PSHE and citizenship have become repositories for all the topics governments decide pupils need to learn about in order to address society's ills. The proposed content is really quite staggering when considered objectively. To satisfy the new SRE guidelines alone, for example, secondary schools need to cover:

- different types of committed, stable relationships
- what marriage is, including its legal status

- the characteristics and legal status of other types of long-term relationships
- the characteristics of successful parenting
- how to determine whether other children, adults or sources of information are trustworthy
- the characteristics of positive and healthy friendships
- how stereotypes, in particular stereotypes based on sex, gender, race, religion, sexual orientation or disability, can cause damage
- different types of bullying (including cyberbullying)
- what constitutes sexual harassment and sexual violence and why these are always unacceptable
- the legal rights and responsibilities regarding equality (with reference to the protected characteristics as defined in the Equality Act 2010)
- rights, responsibilities and opportunities online
- online risks
- how sexually explicit material (e.g. pornography) presents a distorted picture of sexual behaviours and can damage the way people see themselves in relation to others
- that sharing and viewing indecent images of children (including those created by children) is a criminal offence
- the concepts of, and laws relating to, sexual consent, sexual exploitation, abuse, grooming, coercion, harassment, rape, domestic abuse, forced marriage, honour-based violence and FGM, and how these can affect current and future relationships
- the facts about the full range of contraceptive choices, efficacy and options available
- the facts around pregnancy, including miscarriage
- choices in relation to pregnancy (with medically and legally accurate, impartial information on all options, including keeping the baby, adoption, abortion and where to get further help)
- how different sexually transmitted infections (STIs), including HIV/AIDS, are transmitted, how risk can be reduced through safer sex (including through condom use) and the importance of and facts about testing
- the prevalence of some STIs, the impact they can have on those who contract them and key facts about treatment

- ways in which the use of alcohol and drugs can lead to risky sexual behaviour
- facts about reproductive health, including fertility

This is a huge amount of information to convey in an hour a week, especially considering that SRE is only one aspect of the PSHE/citizenship curriculum. The National Curriculum programmes of study for citizenship at key stage 3 expect schools to teach children about:

- the development of the political system of democratic government in the United Kingdom, including the roles of citizens, Parliament and the monarch
- the operation of Parliament, including voting and elections, and the role of political parties
- the precious liberties enjoyed by the citizens of the United Kingdom
- the nature of rules and laws and the justice system, including the role of the police and the operation of courts and tribunals
- the roles played by public institutions and voluntary groups in society, and the ways in which citizens work together to improve their communities, including opportunities to participate in school-based activities
- the functions and uses of money, the importance and practice of budgeting, and managing risk[10]

And this is before we even get to PSHE and careers education. Is it any wonder, therefore, that schools struggle to deliver such a comprehensive programme?

One aspect many school leaders find particularly difficult to rationalise is the promotion of fundamental British values (FBV). All maintained schools must meet the requirements set out in the Education Act 2002 and promote the spiritual, moral, social and cultural (SMSC) development of their pupils. Through ensuring pupils' SMSC development, schools should also demonstrate they are actively promoting fundamental British values. Schools have to promote the fundamental British values of democracy, the rule of law, individual liberty, and mutual respect and tolerance of those with different faiths and beliefs. To many, the emphasis on specifically British values sounds overtly political, particularly against a background of global education. Consequently, FBV is accorded very little attention in many schools.

Whether it is the overt politicisation of the curriculum, sensitive issues relating to sex education, or concerns regarding the relationship between the programmes of study and religious observance, the scope for controversy is profound. Teachers of PSHE have to tread carefully in the classroom, not only to ensure that their teaching is in line with government guidelines but to avoid upsetting and alienating pupils and their parents. Ironically, given the sensitivities of the topics to be covered, most PSHE teachers are not trained to teach the subject. They are usually teachers of other subjects with gaps in their timetables. In many schools, all teachers are expected to teach PSHE and citizenship as part of their role as tutors. Unsurprisingly, for many, this is regarded as one of the least enjoyable parts of the job. A teacher with a passion for literature who joined the profession to pass on his or her enthusiasm and subject knowledge is unlikely to warm to teaching thirty 15-year-olds about the dangers of sexually transmitted diseases.

The PSHE/citizenship curriculum is clearly overloaded. It covers sex education, careers education, democracy, values and beliefs, morality, finance, Britishness, health and well-being. And yet, there is no doubt that the teachers tasked with delivering all this can assume there will be more to come. As each new government seeks to make its mark, more and more is added to the school curriculum. It surely cannot be long before both teachers and pupils simply become overwhelmed. With so much to cover, the subject is becoming unmanageable and therefore of less and less value to children in the classroom. It is clearly time for a rethink. Instead of expecting schools to help solve the next tranche of social problems, politicians would be better advised to allow schools to focus on what really matters and to provide the funding to train the specialists needed to deliver such complex and sensitive subjects effectively.

Studies and 'ologies'

PSHE and citizenship are curriculum subjects abused by politicians who see them as solutions to awkward problems in society, and yet they rarely feature in the press. The real media venom is reserved for 'soft' subjects such as media studies, business studies, psychology and sociology. The veteran broadcaster John Humphrys, for example, is well known for his sneering attacks on media studies. And yet, looked at objectively, these subjects are the ones most likely to equip children with the information and skills they need to navigate contemporary society.

Sociology has, in fact been around for some time. The first European department of sociology was established at the University of Bordeaux in 1895 and shortly afterwards, in 1904, the London School of Economics followed suit. The subject gradually made its way into schools, both at the GCSE and A-level, and is now well established across the country, especially post-16. Sociologists investigate the structure of groups, organisations and societies, and how people interact within these contexts. Since all human behaviour is social, the subject matter of sociology ranges from the intimate family to the hostile mob; from organised crime to religious cults; from the divisions of race, gender and social class to the shared beliefs of a common culture; and from the sociology of work to the sociology of sports.

Few subjects, therefore, could be more relevant to the lives of young people in schools today, and yet sociology is still regarded with disdain by the middle-class intelligentsia and, indeed, the media. Why is this the case? There has always been a distinction between the so-called hard sciences, like physics and chemistry, and the 'soft' social sciences. Hard sciences are consequently seen as more difficult, more demanding and therefore an indication of superior intellect. Bright students are still steered quietly away from social sciences if they have the capacity to study physics, maths, chemistry and biology. These subjects lead to desirable professional careers in medicine, engineering and industry; sociology has a less obvious career path.

Psychology too suffers from the same prejudices, despite being equally valid and, again, directly relevant to young people's lives. In simple terms, psychology is the scientific study of the mind and behaviour. A-level courses tend to cover key areas such as social psychology which focuses on the social interactions people have with each other; cognitive psychology which looks at how we perceive and interpret the world around us; developmental psychology which considers how people develop and change throughout their lives; psychopathology, the study of the causes of mental disorders, such as OCD, phobias and schizophrenia; and biological psychology which looks at the role of evolutionary forces and genetics in behaviour. All this is underpinned by a study of the research methods used by professional psychologists. For a young person struggling to find his or her place in an increasingly complex world, this kind of study is directly relevant and utterly fascinating. This accounts for its growing popularity: in 2018, A-level psychology was the third most popular subject after maths and biology.

Though not as popular as psychology, business studies attracts the attention of more and more students. In 2018, 32,867 pupils in the UK took business studies at A-level, an increase of 9.5% on 2017, and the subject is now more popular than geography. Concerns about future employment opportunities are doubtless behind this trend and, although it is commendable that young people are thinking about their career prospects in this way, the growing popularity of the subject is a potent symbol of the way in which the purpose of education is seen by many as simply to prepare students for the world of work. The value of business studies as an entrée into the business world is questionable, of course, and it is undoubtedly true to say that employers looking to recruit are likely to be more attracted to the analytical skills of an English student or an historian. Sociology and psychology are directly relevant to the lives of young people; the appeal of business studies relates more to their fears about the future and contemporary society's obsession with the utility of education.

Media studies has become something of a middle-class bête noir. Ironically, it is often vilified in the press by the very people who should be its strongest supporters, and, like sociology and psychology, it is often regarded as a subject taken by students who are not up to genuine academic study. Many argue, however, that is should be at the heart of every school curriculum. Children today have grown up in a world fundamentally different from the one with which their parents and teachers are familiar. To use the now somewhat clichéd term, they are digital natives. Most of them have been using mobile devices since they were toddlers, they entertain themselves with computer games and YouTube, their reading is conducted almost entirely online, their knowledge derives from Google and Wikipedia, and their social lives are conducted via Snapchat, Instagram and whatever social media app is in favour at the time. Their reach is global and their access to information unlimited.

Consequently, they inhabit an amazing yet dangerous world. They have fabulous opportunities, glorious entertainment and instant access to everywhere on the planet, and yet they are prey to psychological manipulation, fake news, online grooming, exploitation, isolation and loneliness.

Media studies looks at all of this head on and teaches children how to understand this new world, and yet it is still regarded as a soft subject for those not bright enough to take qualifications in history or English literature. Undoubtedly, both of those subjects teach vital analytical skills, the power of language and the importance of an understanding of perspective and bias, but they don't teach the basics of how the media works.

A glance at the GCSE media studies specifications demonstrates just how relevant the subject is to the lives of young people. Students generally study four key topics: media language, representation, industries and audiences. Each of these areas encourages them to think about the nature of the media, how it works, and, above all, how it influences their lives. The language element covers the forms, codes and conventions of the new media and teaches students how meaning is communicated. It then links the language of the media directly to social, cultural and political contexts by exploring a range of media texts and products. This means they explore ideas such as codes, anchorage, signs, symbols and icons and thus begin to understand how media texts are able to influence and manipulate their readers and viewers. From the study of language, the subject expands to explore the concept of representation, explaining how people, ideas and things are re-presented in different ways for different effects. In other words, students learn how, as soon as something is used by the media, its meaning changes and, more often than not, its meaning is carefully controlled. This allows them to consider how the media portray events, issues, individuals and social groups, thus learning to take nothing at face value.

Most specifications explore media industries: they look at how the processes of production, distribution and circulation affect media forms and platforms, and in doing so they encourage students to understand the power and influence of the media organisations they use on a daily basis. This then allows them to study audiences in order to consider the way media form targets, reach and address audiences, and how audiences respond to them.

Surely, young people who spend their lives engaged with digital media need to understand all this both to enable them to get the best out of the new world they inhabit but, above all, to keep themselves safe. Navigating the internet has become a skilled task; our children need to learn how to do it. They need to learn how to analyse representations, how to detect bias, how to avoid undue influence and how to keep themselves safe from predators. In other words, they must learn to approach the digital world with discrimination and care. When virtually every image can be Photoshopped and manipulated; when 'fake news' is rife; and when the personalisation of media streams means that people are encouraged to live in ever smaller online communities, it is vital that young people develop a sophisticated understanding of how this all works.

Safeguarding, internet safety and online bullying are given high priority in schools, but such dangers are usually separated out into the PSHE curriculum; it must now be time to recognise the fact that they are part of a much wider field of understanding. Media studies undoubtedly suffers from a terrible reputation, but it needs rehabilitating and placing at the heart of the curriculum.

However, before we move on from the various studies and 'ologies', it is fair to point out that sometimes these increasingly important subjects don't help themselves to gain the academic credibility they need to establish themselves in the mainstream curriculum. Media studies, for example, is often watered down with pointless projects which involve pupils making posters and adverts, supposedly to allow them to explore media concepts but which, more often than not, degenerate into primary school art projects. And then there is the vexed question of language and terminology; these newer subjects seem to delight in dressing up basic concepts in ludicrously high-flown language which, instead of affording academic credibility, become barriers to learning. PE leads the way here with A-level students expected to grapple with, for example, the difference between 'temporal' and 'spatial' anticipation or explain the 'psychological refractory period', perhaps via the 'single channel hypothesis'. Let's hope that, in order to cope with all this, they learn 'self-efficacy' and avoid 'evaluation apprehension'.[11]

Vocational subjects

Design technology is often seen as the closest thing to a vocational subject in schools but, as we have seen, as both an academic and technical discipline, it is mired in confusion. The debate over its content, or the skills it should be teaching, could be regarded as a microcosm of the discussions surrounding vocational education. If design technology is a mess, vocational education is a disaster. This is nothing new, however. Failed attempts to introduce credible and effective vocational courses stretch right back into the 19th century. In 1867 the Schools Inquiry Commission published a *Report Relative to Technical Education*, which discussed the lack of technical training offered in the UK.[12] The report observed that the provision of technical education throughout other parts of Europe was putting Britain at a disadvantage in relation to manufacturing standards. Countries such as France and Germany had in place systems of education that provided for technical education on a variety of levels from craft to large-scale engineering. The report could have been written yesterday.

Since then, there have been numerous attempts to reinvigorate vocational educational in schools and colleges, the most recent of which is the introduction of T Levels. There have been some successes – the establishment of City and Guilds in 1875 and the introduction of polytechnics a few years later – but, on the whole, vocational initiatives have begun with excited bursts of enthusiasm shortly before collapsing into chaos. Those of us who have worked in schools long enough to remember the Technical and Vocational Education Initiative (TVEI) introduced by the government in 1982, will be acutely aware of how poorly such things are thought through. TVEI saw huge amounts of money flooding into schools to virtually no effect. New kitchens were built, new workshops constructed and the virtues of technology trumpeted widely across the profession. Unfortunately, however, nothing really changed. Schools took the money, dabbled with design technology courses for a while and then returned to the curriculum they had in place before all the fuss.

The introduction of General National Vocational Qualifications in 1993 was supposed to offer students a suite of qualifications equivalent to GCSEs and A-levels, but, as always, these were badly thought out, unappealing to students and dismissed by teachers and school leaders as lacking any real credibility. It is difficult, therefore, not to be cynical about the introduction of T Levels. These are described on the Department for Education's website as 'new courses coming in September 2020, which will follow GCSEs and will be equivalent to 3 A-levels. These two-year courses have been developed in collaboration with employers and businesses so that the content meets the needs of industry and prepares students for work'.[13] This sounds depressingly familiar, and, as soon as they were announced, critics were lining up to dismiss T Levels as far from credible alternatives to A-levels.

Creating an effective system of vocational education is not, of course, simply a matter of introducing new courses; it is much more complicated than that. First, there is the dominance of the academic culture. Overturning the powerful cultural assumption that the only credible form of education is the traditional GCSE/A-level route is a huge undertaking. The route to the top via success at A-level before a traditional university degree is deeply embedded in our culture. The professions – medicine, law, finance and so on – represent aspiration and achievement; other forms of employment are still regarded as 'trade'. In a country devoted to the monarchy and re-runs of *Downton Abbey*, it is hard to see how the barriers between vocational and academic education will ever be broken down. It is, of course, possible, but politicians will need to think seriously about cultural change before rushing to introduce yet another set of qualifications which they think will solve the problem. And, as the 1867 report pointed out, vocational education works in other countries.

A few years ago, I was lucky enough to spend a week in Finland looking at the Finnish education system which, at the time, was regarded as the most successful in the world. Ultimately, I discovered that the success of Finnish schools was not down to better teaching or a more effective curriculum but thanks to two key factors: teaching in Finland is regarded as a high-status profession, equivalent to medicine or the law, and Finnish society at the time was largely middle class and affluent. What did impress me, however, was the technical college I visited. Yes, the academic route is considered to be the way forward for the very brightest students, but vocational education enjoys high status in Finland. The local Further Education college was a hive of activity and a key part of local industry. Students built houses from scratch, learning the skills needed to create well-built properties which were then sold on the open market and for which there were waiting lists. In addition, the college featured restaurants open to the public, hair salons and car repair workshops. Students were actively engaged in learning skills in real-world situations. Their academic education was not neglected, however, and all students were expected to continue their studies of Finnish, mathematics and a foreign language. Virtually all the students I spoke to in the workshops spoke English well.

To be fair, by attempting to introduce vocational qualifications alongside academic qualifications, politicians have tried to bridge the gap between vocational and academic education in English schools and thus weaken the grip of academia on the nation's psyche. Pupils were, for example, encouraged to take the General National Vocational Qualification (GNVQ) alongside traditional GCSEs, and T levels are being promoted as A-levels in another guise. The idea has always been to convince pupils and their parents of the value and credibility of vocational education in order to encourage them to move on to technical courses post-16. Due to the power of the academic culture, however, this has never really worked. Pupils and parents understand that traditional academic qualifications are still the only ones with real credibility in our society.

There have even been attempts to introduce technical schools alongside traditional comprehensives, presumably with the idea of 'catching them early'. The success of these has been variable. City Technology Colleges (CTCs), introduced in the 1980s, were set up as state-funded all-ability comprehensive schools which were linked closely to industry sponsors. They were supposed to be inner-city flagships for technical education, and yet the programme floundered. Sites for new schools couldn't be found, parents were reluctant to commit to vocational education early on in their children's careers and local authorities were reluctant to engage with schools which seemed to threaten the viability of the other schools in the area. CTCs have re-emerged in various forms over the years – City Academies, for example, or, more recently, studio schools – but none have really captured the imagination of the public.

Other problems faced by schools wishing to introduce genuine vocational qualifications relate to staffing and equipment. Most vocational subjects in secondary schools are taught by non-specialists; the skilled craftsmen and technical specialists needed to teach to a high level are simply not available in schools. A school hoping to offer a course in, say, electrical engineering, would begin by offering it for only a few hours a week. Finding an electrician, with both the technical and pedagogical skills, to deliver a course in a few hours spread across the week is almost impossible. In addition, schools simply don't have the facilities to offer genuine vocational training. Massive investment in equipment would be needed to enable students to develop real workplace skills. Difficulties over staffing and the lack of facilities in schools mean that technical education is almost inevitably left to colleges of further education. Vocational courses that do exist in schools are those which demand very little additional equipment and which can be taught by members of staff willing to get to grips with courses which are essentially information rather than skills based. Health and social care is a good example. This is a popular course which is easy to teach in schools. Many would argue, however, that it isn't really a vocational course at all and, as always, it tends to attract lower ability pupils, reinforcing still further the notion that vocational education is the poor relation of academic study.

Sir Ron Dearing's Curriculum 2000 perhaps came closest to offering a credible vocational programme in schools by encouraging students to follow four subjects in Year 12 and three in Year 13. This allowed them to combine academic study with vocational courses: Advanced Certificates of Education (AVCs) were introduced alongside Advanced Subsidiary (AS) levels. In addition, students were encouraged to take a separate key skills qualification. Although a good idea in theory, in practice the experiment quickly fell apart. Few schools were able to offer a compelling range of AVCs; the more traditional grammar and comprehensives stuck to academic AS levels; issues arose over comparability of standards; and industry, despite voicing strong support, proved reluctant to get seriously involved. As a result, AVCs were abandoned and AS levels were reintegrated back into traditional A-levels. A good try but, as always, the culture proved too strong to change.

Many Further Education colleges do a great job, however, in preparing young people for the world of work, but they are desperately underfunded and inevitably seen as inferior to sixth forms and sixth form colleges which offer A-levels. Promoting improvements in the further education sector is surely the way forward. With appropriate funding and the recruitment of well-trained specialist staff, FE colleges could become technical and vocational centres of excellence. Perhaps it is time to recognise that schools will never be capable of offering high-quality vocational education, and it will therefore be much better to leave it to institutions where such things are possible. Schools should offer a good, general education, retaining the ability to offer practical skills like woodwork and cookery to, let's be honest, less able pupils, without the constant pretence of expertise in vocational education. With investment and expertise, Further Education colleges could become centres of excellence with the pulling power and employment opportunities they need to compete with academic sixth forms. Only then will the academic culture loosen its hold on the nation.

Extra-curricular

Secondary school children spend at least 25 hours a week in class and yet, when adults are asked what they remember about school, they rarely mention their lessons. They might talk about a favourite, usually eccentric teacher, but, more often than not, they will recall events which took place outside the classroom, or the things their friends got up to. Lots of seemingly mundane things stick in the memory: the playgrounds, summer afternoons watching cricket, clouds of smoke emerging from the staff room, the bus journey home. Most of our memories involve our friends and a surprising number relate to misbehaviour and rule breaking. My most cherished memories of school, I am almost ashamed to admit, relate to an accidental fire in a newspaper store room where, unbeknown to staff, we were re-enacting battles in the First World War trenches, or a marvellous occasion when a sixth former tapped into the public address system freshly installed in the assembly hall so that, instead of hearing the headteacher's stirring words, the whole school was treated to a very loud and very long extract from *Derek and Clive Live*. In order to remember what went on in lessons, I really have to think, and, even then, much of it is a blur.

The mundane stuff is therefore important. It is at the heart of the school experience. Similarly, the extra-curricular activities in which young people take part play a huge part in their lives. It is all too easy to regard extra-curricular activities as something other, as beyond the curriculum and therefore having only a minimal impact on pupil learning. In reality, they play a vital part: instead of extra-curricular, a better name might be co-curricular, as they sit alongside the academic curriculum, supporting and enhancing it. Any genuine discussion of the school curriculum must attempt to address the co-curricular aspects of what goes on in school as they often have a significant but sometimes hidden impact on academic progress.

Despite financial pressures on schools, and spiralling teacher workloads, most schools still manage to offer a remarkable range of extra-curricular opportunities: daily sports, fitness rooms, music lessons and ensembles, drama clubs, large-scale musical productions, science clubs, art clubs, library sessions, debating societies, eco-clubs, coding and IT lessons, and so on. In addition, the past few years have seen a rise in homework clubs, revision sessions and catch-up opportunities for pupils who have fallen behind. In the majority of schools, there is also a strong culture of trips and visits, whether directly related to the curriculum or just for fun. Virtually every subject department offers some kind of day out, whether it's to see a set-text play in English, to visit a local castle in history, or to visit the science and natural history museums. Residential trips to help children get to know each other are now common in the first year of secondary schools, and most primaries arrange an extended trip to London or France.

Some secondary schools offer a range of trips which would embarrass the local travel agencies: my own school regularly ran two skiing trips a year, art department visits to New York, language department visits to France and Spain, a summer water-sports holiday in the Ardèche, a big band tour to Lake Garda, Duke of Edinburgh expeditions to Snowdonia, sixth form visits to Auschwitz, history department visits to Pompeii, and a host of other one-off trips all aimed at inspiring and encouraging pupils' participation. The angry *Daily Mail* readers who regard teachers as feckless layabouts who spend most of their working lives enjoying their long summer vacations would do well to take a look at exactly what teachers do for children in our schools today. Nor is a trip abroad ever a holiday for the teachers: anyone who has supervised a school trip knows just what hard work it really is.

In the past, schools which offered exotic foreign trips have laid themselves open to the criticism that they are elitist, catering only for middle-class children whose parents can afford such opportunities; nowadays, however, thanks largely to Pupil Premium funding, every effort is made to ensure that they are made available to all pupils. As is only right, the experience of schooling should be the same for everyone.

As we have seen, however, disadvantaged pupils often find themselves falling behind their peers as they move up through the system. Extra-curricular activities are doubly important for them, therefore. Not only is there a need to bridge the 'word gap' – remember that a child from a disadvantaged background enters the education system 30 million words behind children who have grown up in professional homes – but there should also be an intensive effort to offer some of the experiences these children have missed due to the poverty of their lives at home. One of the saddest moments in my school career occurred when I was listening to a Year 7 boy read an extract from a book about theme parks: at the end of each paragraph he excitedly told me about the parks his friends had been to until I eventually realised that he had never been to one himself. It later emerged that not only had he never been to a theme park, but he had never been on a day out with his family. How he must have felt sitting in class next to children who were used to two or three foreign holidays a year is hard to imagine.

The significance of this 'other' aspect of the school curriculum is now recognised by schools, and the importance of what has become known as cultural capital is now firmly established in educational thinking. The latest Ofsted handbook makes it clear that good schools should be thinking about pupil progress and well-being in ways that go way beyond the academic curriculum:

> As part of making the judgement about the quality of education, inspectors will consider the extent to which schools are equipping pupils with the knowledge and cultural capital they need to succeed in life. Our understanding of 'knowledge and cultural capital' is derived from the following wording in the National Curriculum:
>
> It is the essential knowledge that pupils need to be educated citizens, introducing them to the best that has been thought and said and helping to engender an appreciation of human creativity and achievement.[14]

Conclusion

In this chapter, I have tried to demonstrate the importance and relevance of academic subjects which find themselves excluded from the Ebacc and the core curriculum, as well as to stress the importance of the extra-curricular and co-curricular elements of children's experiences of schools. From the perspective of the toxic classroom, it is hard to miss the irony here. Lessons in the classroom are subject to intense political and educational debate, and vulnerable to constant change; life beyond the classroom, which politicians leave to teachers to plan and implement, is where children in schools really begin to flourish. It could be that it is there that the real learning takes place.

What can schools do now to put things right?

- **Promote the arts.** Despite the pressures of the performance tables, primary schools should ensure that arts subjects are allocated sufficient curriculum time, and secondary schools should ensure they offer a good range of arts subjects as part of the key stage 3 curriculum, as well as at key stage 4. Art, music and drama GCSEs should be the basic offer in every school in the country.

- **Redesign design.** DT is in a mess and should be replaced by genuinely practical subjects. These could be non-GCSE subjects or, better, courses delivered in conjunction with the local FE college. For pupils with artistic design skills, graphics is surely a more appropriate option choice.

- **Reconsider PE.** If funding is available, the balance between games and physical fitness needs to be adjusted to make the subject much more inclusive. Link PE directly to the healthy living agenda and make food technology a part of the package. By shifting the focus from team games to personal health and fitness, schools might begin to be able to address the obesity crisis.

- **Specialists.** Where possible, ensure that PSHE is taught by specialists and not reluctant teachers of other subjects.

- **Media studies.** Most school leaders recognise the importance of media studies in our rapidly changing digital world; the case must be made strongly to pupils, parents and politicians to dispel the snobbery that has dogged the subject for years.

- **Disadvantaged pupils.** Any consideration of support for disadvantaged pupils, and any adaptations to the curriculum, should include provision for involvement in extra-curricular activities. It is here that the weaknesses in social capital can be addressed most effectively.

What should policymakers do to put things right?

- Politicians need to understand the contribution the arts make to UK industry and promote arts education accordingly.

- There needs to be greater focus on the technology and engineering elements of the STEM agenda to help schools offer genuinely practical courses for potential engineers and designers.

- Provide funding for a root and branch re-structuring of PE in schools.

- Think carefully before proposing yet more social issues to be addressed in school classrooms.

- Recognise that the so-called ologies, subjects derided by traditionalists, are becoming vital areas of study in schools.

- Increase the funding provided for disadvantaged pupils at all levels in all schools.

Notes

1 E.W. Eisner. 2002. *The Arts and the Creation of Mind*, Yale, Yale University Press.
2 M. Rosen. 2019. Let the Music in: Why Schools Need a New Deal for the Arts, *The Guardian*, 2 September. www.theguardian.com/commentisfree/2019/sep/01/term-starting-english-schools-arts-emergency-subjects
3 AQA. 2019. *GCSE Design Technology*. www.aqa.org.uk/subjects/design-and-technology/gcse/design-and-technology-8552
4 The Design and Technology Association. www.data.org.uk/campaigns/what-is-design-and-technology/
5 Ibid.
6 Cabinet Office. 2016. *Childhood Obesity: A Plan for Action*. Updated January 2017. https://www.gov.uk/government/publications/childhood-obesity-a-plan-for-action/childhood-obesity-a-plan-for-action
7 HMCI's Commentary. Ofsted. 2018. *Obesity, Healthy Eating and Physical Activity in Primary Schools*, July, 180017, p. 3. https://assets.publishing.service.gov.uk/government/uploads/system/uploads/attachment_data/file/726114/Obesity_healthy_eating_and_physical_activity_in_primary_schools_170718.pdf
8 Ofsted. 2010. *Personal, Social, Health and Economic Education in Schools*. 090222. Archived 4 March 2016 at the Wayback Machine. https://web.archive.org/web/20160304070557/http://www.surreyhealthyschools.co.uk/downloads/Personal__social__health_and_economic_education_in_schools.pdf
9 National Curriculum Programmes of Study Statutory Guidance. *DfE*, September 2013. www.gov.uk/government/publications/national-curriculum-in-england-citizenship-programmes-of-study/national-curriculum-in-england-citizenship-programmes-of-study-for-key-stages-3-and-4
10 Ibid.

11 Cf. AQA Subject Specific Vocabulary, October 2019. www.aqa.org.uk/resources/physical-education-and-sport/as-and-a-level/physical-education/teach/subject-specific-vocabulary
12 The Schools Inquiry Commission. 1867. *Report Relevant to Technical Education*, London, Her Majesty's Stationery Office. https://babel.hathitrust.org/cgi/pt?id=mdp.39015074762728&view=1up&seq=7
13 Department for Education, *Introduction of T Levels*, October 2019. www.gov.uk/government/publications/introduction-of-t-levels/introduction-of-t-levels
14 Ofsted. 2019. *School Inspection Handbook*, September, p. 43. 190017. The Ofsted quotation refers to the *National Curriculum in England: Framework for Key Stages 1 to 4*, Department for Education, December 2014. www.gov.uk/government/publications/national-curriculum-in-england-framework-for-key-stages-1-to-4/the-national-curriculum-in-england-framework-for-key-stages-1-to-4

5 Assessment and accountability

A child's first day of school can be a fairly traumatic experience, not necessarily for the child but certainly for his or her parents. It marks the first real step away from home and the first step towards independence. Parents worry endlessly about how the very small person they have kept so close for so long will fare in the noisy classroom, cut off from mum and dad. They worry about other children, whether their children will be able to cope, whether the teacher will understand them, whether they will be bullied and whether they will shine academically as they move up through the school. A few parents will think about the exciting learning journey their child is about to undertake, but how many contemplate the assessment journey they face?

It is not too much of an exaggeration to say that a child starting school in England today is staring down the barrel of a gun – an assessment gun. He or she will be formally assessed in virtually every school year and continually assessed as lessons unfold across the year, the term or even the week. Assessment will determine, for example, where they sit in the classroom – will they sit with the bright-eyed squirrels or the slow-witted pheasants? It will determine the classes to which they are assigned; the sets they are put in; the subjects they study; the support they receive; the opportunities they are offered; the secondary schools they attend; the GCSEs they choose; the post-16 education they can access; the universities to which they are able to apply; and even the friends they make. Assessment will ultimately determine the route a child will take into adulthood.

Assessment is, of course, more than a series of national tests. In addition to the SATS (as the tests used to be called), the GCSEs and the A-levels, schools have now developed complex systems for measuring progress and ensuring that pupils are on track to meet their targets. These targets are based on prior attainment – in other words, on previous assessments – and, in some secondary schools, they will come to dominate the teachers' view of the students in their classes.

Assessment is either summative or formative. These are sometimes referred to as assessment of learning and assessment for learning, respectively. The National Foundation for Educational Research (NFER) defines the terms as follows:

> Summative assessment sums up what a pupil has achieved at the end of a period of time, relative to the learning aims and the relevant national standards.
>
> Formative assessment takes place on a day-to-day basis during teaching and learning, allowing teachers and pupils to assess attainment and progress more frequently.[1]

Whether it is summative or formative, children will be constantly assessed as they move through the school system. They know they are being assessed and, however confident they may seem, they are anxious about assessment. They want to do well, they want to please their teachers, they want to fulfil their parents' ambitions and they want to retain credibility among their peers. As every teacher knows, the first thing a child looks at when a piece of work is returned to them is the mark or grade. The second thing they do is ask their friends about their marks.

Many children find assessment troubling. It can cause huge anxiety, and the level of anxiety rises as the consequences of failure increase. The more assessment, the greater the anxiety. The child who, at an early age, finds himself disappointed to have scored only four out of 10 in a test, while his best friend delights in her 10 out of 10, soon finds himself wondering whether there is really any point in trying to achieve. If every test defines him as an underachiever, he may think that he is not cut out for education and simply give up. Teachers now go to great lengths to reassure pupils that doing well in tests isn't everything; they encourage them to reach their individual potential, and they work hard to make sure they feel valued and supported. In many schools, assessment is low key, and, in some, work is rarely given a mark or a grade. Ultimately, however, every child has to face national tests and to deal with the results. And however careful their teachers are, all children know where they are in the class and how well they are doing. They may not use the word, but assessment hangs over them like a black cloud almost every day.

Of course, assessment is an inevitable feature of schooling. The problem today, however, is the sheer relentlessness of assessment and the volume of tests children have to undergo. The balance between learning and assessment has tipped; learning is now subservient to assessment. In too many schools, children are taught to pass tests rather than to enjoy their learning; in too many schools, the only things that are taught relate directly to examination syllabuses.

So how did we get here? Very few teachers advocate constant assessment; even fewer pupils rejoice in the constant series of tests they are required to undertake. Parents are probably unaware of the extent of testing which takes place in schools and, after witnessing their child's anxiety on the eve of a test or an examination, would probably agree that things have gone too far. But, as far as politicians are concerned, assessment is essential if we are to compete internationally. For them, the only way we can assess the quality of education is through constant testing. A culture of extreme accountability has developed over the last 20 years or so which has changed the nature of schooling.

The curriculum in schools is now shaped by a succession of interim tests – from the Early Years Foundation Stage profile, through tests at key stages 1 and 2, before we arrive at GCSEs and A-levels. Primary schools are measured by their key stage 2 test results; secondary schools by their GCSE progress scores. A school's success now depends not on the quality of learning offered in the classroom but on its ability to play the system in order to achieve a good progress score. As we shall see, the 2019 Ofsted framework seems to offer a ray of hope, with its deliberate focus on the quality of education rather than the quality of the data, but the tension between learning and accountability will undoubtedly dominate the system for years to come. The classroom will therefore remain a place of anxiety for too many pupils, and too many will lose their appetite for learning at a very young age.

Early years testing

In Chapter 2, the seven areas of learning and the 17 Early Learning Goals (ELGs) of the Early Years Foundation Stage (EYFS) profile were introduced. These are the goals children are expected to reach by the age of 5. At the end of the assessment period, parents are informed about their child's progress. All EYFS providers must give parents a written summary of their child's attainment against the ELGs. For each ELG this must state whether the child is:

- not yet reaching expected levels ('emerging')
- meeting 'expected' levels
- 'exceeding' expected levels

The assessment process is designed to be unobtrusive, but it is comprehensive nevertheless. Throughout their time in Reception, the teacher will watch, listen to and interact with the children in his or her class as they take part not just in formal learning, but also as they play and go about daily activities such as eating their lunch or getting changed for PE. Some observations will be planned – for example, the teacher might spend 10 minutes observing a child completing a set activity – but others will be spontaneous. As the teacher observes a child, evidence of them meeting an ELG will be recorded. This could be by making a brief note on a sticky note, taking a photo or just making a mental note to write down later. They will be looking to see that the child is consistently and independently showing evidence of fulfilling each ELG. Classroom activities have to be planned to make sure children can demonstrate as many of the ELGs as possible.

All this is fantastically time consuming for the teacher, and we are forced to wonder, therefore, how much teaching time is lost while assessments are undertaken. Remember that a teacher may be completing 20 or even 30 profiles, and there is no getting away from the fact that profiles are often large unwieldy documents. Theoretically optional, schools are under considerable pressure to use the EYFS as part of the accountability structure.

Of course, despite the level of assessment involved in the EYFS, politicians are still not convinced that enough assessment takes place. They have therefore proposed the introduction of baseline testing. In response to the 2017 primary assessment consultation, the government announced plans to introduce a statutory reception baseline assessment (RBA) in autumn 2020. According to the government's guidance, the overt aim is to measure the progress primary schools make with their pupils. A brief outline of the new tests is offered:

> Schools will carry out the assessment within the first 6 weeks of children starting school. It will be an activity-based assessment of pupils' ability in:
>
> - language, communication and literacy
> - mathematics
>
> The assessment will be age appropriate, last approximately 20 minutes and teachers will record the results on a laptop, computer or tablet. It will not be used to label or track individual pupils. No numerical score will be shared, and the data will only be used at the end of year 6 to form the school-level progress measure. However, teachers will receive a series of short, narrative statements that tell them how their pupils performed in the assessment at that time. These can be used to inform teaching within the first term.[2]

It is hard not to point out that baseline testing means that children are to be tested as soon as they walk through the doors of the school. The key question, however, concerns the benefit for the child. What exactly is the purpose of the EYFS and who is it for? The union leaders Mary Bousted and Christine Blower were very clear about this:

> Baseline assessment was not introduced, as many think, to support a child's transition into school or to help teachers plan for that child's learning; it is better understood as a measure that would supposedly enable school performance to be accurately evaluated. Yet again the weight of school accountability has been laid on the shoulders of our children.[3]

They also pointed out that when the EYFS was introduced, only 7.7% of teachers agreed that baseline assessment is a fair and accurate way to assess children.

It is, of course, reasonable to make sure that teachers understand the abilities of the children they teach, but is this level of assessment really necessary? It hardly needs pointing out that teachers have always assessed the children in their class, but they have done it informally and without clumsy mechanisms imposed by the DfE. It is also vital that all children make progress and that none are left behind, but teachers know that. Unsurprisingly, they care about that kind of thing. They don't need the government telling them how to measure and record the kind of information they have always understood and used in their teaching every day. Once again, the failure to trust teachers sits at the heart of accountability structures and impacts negatively on the experience of every child in the classroom.

Primary testing

Once they are through the complexities of the foundation stage, pupils immediately find themselves subject to more testing in Year 1. This time it is the phonics test. The phonics screening check is taken individually by all children in Year 1 in England and is usually taken in June. It is designed to give teachers and parents information on how a child is progressing in phonics. It will help to identify whether the child needs additional support so that he or she does not fall behind in reading.

The test comprises a check of 40 words to assess phonics skills and knowledge learned through Reception and Year 1. The child has to read up to four words per page for their teacher in a test which lasts about 10 minutes. It checks that the child can:

- Sound out and blend graphemes in order to read simple words

- Read phonically decodable one-syllable and two-syllable words (e.g. cat, sand, windmill)

- Read a selection of nonsense words which are referred to as pseudo words.

There has been a great deal of debate around the use of made-up words – why use made-up words when real ones are available, as this will only confuse the child – but the importance of sound over meaning is the key here. The test is there to see if a child can break down the sounds of words in order to allow full recognition of the word and thus grasp its meaning.

When it was introduced in 2012, the test proved highly controversial, mainly because it tests children's ability to decode words using a single method, phonics, rather than their ability to read. In a research paper carried out by Oxford and York universities, the authors queried a screening test which had no prescribed course of action for pupils who were struggling. They also measured pupils' phonics check scores against other standardised reading and spelling tests. They concluded that while the government test was accurate in identifying children who were struggling, it offered no information that teacher assessment did not already provide.[4]

The consensus, however, is that the phonics test is both useful and non-threatening. It has also helped to standardise approaches to reading in schools across the country, an approach which the government thinks will lead to higher standards. However, it is nevertheless a test, one given to 5-year-olds, and it still leads to a degree of anxiety. A glance at *Mumsnet* quickly reveals the level of anxiety the test produces in parents, with posts ranging from straightforward questions about the nature and conduct of the tests to more distressing confessions of misery over a child's failure. One mother blames herself because she is a working mum; another says she has failed her daughter because she didn't prepare her for the tests well enough. As always, parental anxiety is passed down to the child. A 10-minute test, no matter how quickly administered, is still a test, and a matter of serious concern for many children and parents. A child who fails the test by not reaching the required standard of around 32 out of 40 has to re-take it in Year 2. This adds to parental concern and elevates its importance in the eyes of both the parent and the child. Perhaps if it were the only test children were obliged to undertake in their first few years of schooling, it would seem less threatening. The fact that it is part of a continual stream of tests raises the stakes.

The next step on the testing conveyor belt comes with the key stage 1 National Curriculum tests. With the introduction of the new baseline tests, those at key stage 1 will become optional, and possibly dropped altogether. The government has announced, however, that schools will be able to choose whether to administer them or not from 2023. Why this delay is unclear. It means, however, that children in schools will still be sitting their key stage 1 tests shortly after completing the phonics screening tests, and not long after the EYFS profiles.

At the end of Year 2, children take SATs, as they used to be called, in:

- Reading

- English grammar, punctuation and spelling (optional paper, schools can decide whether to use it)

- Maths

The reading test for Year 2 pupils is made up of two separate papers:

- Paper 1 consists of a selection of texts totalling 400 to 700 words, with questions interspersed

- Paper 2 comprises a reading booklet of a selection of passages totalling 800 to 1,100 words

They may also sit two separate optional papers in grammar, spelling and punctuation:

- Paper 1: a 20-word spelling test taking approximately 15 minutes and worth 20 marks

- Paper 2: a grammar, punctuation and vocabulary test, in two sections of around 10 minutes each (with a break between, if necessary), worth 20 marks

The key stage 1 maths test is made up of two papers:

- Paper 1: arithmetic, worth 25 marks and taking around 15 minutes

- Paper 2: mathematical fluency, problem-solving and reasoning, worth 35 marks and taking 35 minutes, with a break if necessary

Teacher assessments are also used to build up a picture of a child's learning and achievements. In addition, the child receives an overall result saying whether they have achieved the required standard in the tests, although the actual results are not communicated to parents unless they ask for them. Other National Curriculum subjects, including English writing, speaking and listening, science and computing, are assessed by the teacher based on work throughout the year. By any standard, this is a significant amount of testing.

Until recently, there was something of a gap between the fairly hectic testing regime of the first few years of school and key stage 2 tests taken in Year 6. However, the thought of a three-year gap without a test clearly worried politicians and, as a result, a new test was introduced. The Multiplication Tables Check, to be taken towards the end of Year 4, aims to make sure children are meeting a new times tables benchmark. It is described as an online, on-screen digital assessment, meaning that children take the test on a desktop computer, laptop or tablet. This is the first computerised primary school test to be introduced by the DfE and perhaps a sign of things to come. The program will both test pupils and mark their responses. This should lessen the workload for teachers, although there will still be logistical difficulties to overcome in terms of ensuring that all pupils have access to fully functioning computers – no easy feat in some schools. Teachers will also have to devote a fair amount of time preparing pupils for the tests. They should, of course, already be teaching the times tables, but the introduction of a test is bound to intensify the process.

The test is timed, with the entire assessment lasting approximately five minutes in total. The children are set a handful of practice questions to begin with, mostly from the one-times table. Following the practice questions, the test itself comprises 25 questions. Children are given six seconds to answer each question, with a three-second gap between them. A simple test, yes, but one with the added pressure of a time limit for each question.

Each child's result is passed on to their school, with the DfE creating a report on overall results across all schools in England to measure whether national times tables results improve over the coming years. In other words, yet another accountability measure. The DfE says that the motivation behind the multiplication tables check is purely to allow teachers a chance to identify children who need some more help with their times tables to stop them from falling further behind their peers as they move up to Year 5, but exactly who is being tested here – the child or the school? In a revealing comment in his introduction to the tests, the education minister, Nick Gibb, was keen to stress their importance to the economy:

> Multiplication tables trials will make a positive contribution to the government's commitment through the Industrial Strategy to drive up the study of maths, ensuring that more students leave education at age 18 with a basic level of numeracy, improving the take up of maths qualifications and tackling STEM skills shortages in the economy.[5]

As noted in previous chapters, the government's obsession with STEM subjects, and international comparisons with countries like China and Singapore, is the driver behind a great deal of educational policy. Fear of falling behind our international competitors now reaches down into Year 4. The creation of productive economic units is apparently vital to the economy and key to successful schooling. The happiness and well-being of children is a minor consideration.

The culmination of the primary testing regime is signalled by the key stage 2 tests. This is where the primary curriculum has been heading as these are the tests by which the school is ultimately judged. Much of Year 6 is devoted to preparation for the tests, and it is not unfair to say that the other National Curriculum subjects suffer from an intense period of neglect as a result. Once the tests are out of the way in May, the world opens up again, but by then there is almost a holiday atmosphere in schools as pupils prepare to move on to the next stage of their education. This is the time for trips and visits, musicals and plays, sports days and other fun activities. In many schools, delivery of the curriculum almost grinds to a halt. Is it any wonder that secondary teachers worry that their new Year 7s join them in September having done very little work since May? Winding them back up again is not always easy.

The tests themselves follow a similar pattern to those at key stage 1. At the end of Year 6, children sit tests in:

- Reading

- Maths

- Spelling, punctuation and grammar

The tests are set and marked externally, and the results are used to measure the school's performance. Each pupil's marks are used in conjunction with teacher assessment to give a broader picture of his or her attainment. The reading test is a single paper lasting one hour with questions based on three passages of text. The grammar, punctuation and spelling test is in two parts: a grammar and punctuation paper requiring short answers, lasting 45 minutes, and an aural spelling test of 20 words, lasting around 15 minutes. There are three maths papers: a 30-minute arithmetic paper, and two 40-minute papers based on reasoning skills. In selected years a number of schools (approximately 1,900) are required to take part in science sampling, a test administered to a selected sample of children thought to be representative of the population as a whole.

The purpose of all these tests is simply to measure the performance of the school. It is difficult to see their value beyond that. And yet, these are tests which cause huge anxiety to both children and their parents. Politicians argue that the tests give parents a clear idea of how well their child is doing, and they give secondary schools a definite measure of a child's ability. In fact, they do neither. A child's teacher is able to give his or her parents a much more accurate picture of progress, and not just in in English and maths. As for secondary schools, parents worry that if their child fails to do well in the tests, they will be disadvantaged when they move up to their next school. In fact, most secondary schools take very little notice of the key stage 2 tests when considering a child's ability, and most test them again in Year 7 using assessments which they consider more accurate and reliable. Grammar schools use their own entry tests and ignore key stage 2 tests completely.

Certainly, outcomes at key stage 2 are used in national data sets to record starting points on entry into secondary school, but beyond that they quickly become forgotten. Even as starting points, the tests attract a huge amount of debate, especially since secondary schools are measured according to the progress pupils make from key stage 2 to key stage 4. This means that a secondary school with primary feeder schools where pupils do well in their SATs has to work hard to achieve good progress scores; where the primaries produce weaker results, progress can be demonstrated, though not necessarily made, more easily.

As we have seen, key stage 2 tests narrow the curriculum by encouraging schools to spend more and more time on English and maths at the expense of the other National Curriculum subjects; their sole function is to provide accountability data for the DfE to use to measure the performance of schools; they cause pupils and parents considerable anxiety, and they are quickly forgotten by secondary schools. And yet, as far as the government is concerned, they are a good thing.

Pupils leave their primary schools having been tested when they arrive, tested at the end of their Reception year, tested in Years 1 and 2, tested on their times tables in Year 4 and tested again at the end of Year 6. A toxic diet indeed.

Secondary assessment

When the key stage 3 SATs were discontinued in 2008, it looked as if pupils were to be test-free for their first three years of schooling. De-regulation continued in 2013 when Michael Gove announced that, when the new version of the National Curriculum was introduced to schools from 2014, the system of attainment levels would be removed. As a result, since 2016, the levels used by the old system no longer form part of the statutory assessment.

The hope that teachers would be free to design a curriculum based on learning rather than assessment soon disappeared as tests and teacher assessments quickly filled the gap. Schools were encouraged to introduce their own models in order to track pupils' progress. Some simply stuck to the National Curriculum levels they had been used to; others embarked upon more radical solutions. A whole industry of assessment specialists quickly sprung up, with organisations like Partners in Excellence (PiXL) leading the charge.[6] Probably the most common solution was some form of 'pathway', a system of assessment linking attainment at key stage 2, or baseline tests conducted in Year 7, to outcomes at GCSE. This effectively meant that secondary education became one five-year-long period of preparation for the terminal examinations in Year 11.

Most pathway solutions attempted to link attainment at the end of Year 6 or the start of Year 7 to potential GCSE grades. A pupil achieving a standard score of 100 in a Year 6 test should be expected to achieve a pass grade of a C, under the old system, or a 4 or a 5 under the new. This simple idea resulted in the creation of complex data programmes and sophisticated graphs designed to track pupils as accurately as possible. At the end of each year, the trajectory of each pupil towards his or her GCSE grade would be assiduously checked, and interventions introduced if necessary. It also meant that schools would be able to predict their outcomes five years ahead with a greater degree of accuracy. Large organisations, with access to the results of hundreds of schools, were able to make reasonably convincing predictions, but most schools worked on the shaky assumption that every pupil would make steady progress to a pre-determined goal. Of course, children develop at different rates and the notion of a straight-line course to a particular grade is little more than a mirage. And more to the point, pathways imply that the only purpose of secondary education is the attainment of GCSE grades. School leaders are not surprisingly turning away from these rigid, linear approaches, adopting more flexible teacher assessments based on a more realistic combination of academic attainment and engagement for learning.

Secondary pathways depend upon baseline assessment data. Some schools use the results of the key stage 2 tests, but most regard these as unreliable, especially as they are often the result of months of cramming. Consequently, a plethora of tests is available for 11-year-olds. Virtually all secondary schools use some kind of baseline test, the most common being the Cognitive Abilities Tests (CATs), National Foundation of Educational Research (NFER) KS2 tests, often conducted on transition days, and the Centre for Evaluation and Monitoring (MidYIS) tests. In addition, schools often use reading age assessments and numeracy tests. These are not part of the statutory system; they are conducted to provide the information schools need to make predictions, allocate pupils to sets or tutors groups, and begin tracking. The fact that virtually all secondary schools do this emphasises the strength of the grip assessment has on the English education system. It is also worth pointing out how commercialised all this has become. Once the tests are complete, the majority of schools then use expensive IT packages such as 4Matrix, SISRA, Classroom Monitor, iTrack, SIMS Assessment and so on. These are sophisticated tools which produce mountains of data for beleaguered senior leaders to sort through so they can shower classroom teachers with vast amounts of information which ends up being largely ignored.

GCSEs have come to dominate secondary schooling. With high levels of accountability for schools and school leaders, this is hardly surprising. Poor performance at GCSE can have serious consequences for a school: its reputation will decline locally; it will lose out to competition from other local schools; its roll will decline, leading to financial difficulties; and poor outcomes could result in an Ofsted judgement of Requires Improvement or worse. It could also mean career ending consequences for headteachers and senior leaders.

The discontinuation of the key stage 3 tests meant that schools were free to alter the balance between key stages 3 and 4. Some schools decided to begin formal GCSE teaching in Year 9. This often resulted in a narrowed curriculum in Years 7 and 8, something the new Ofsted framework has sought to address. It also meant that GCSEs gained even greater prominence. As far as pupils are concerned, school is now simply about passing examinations, and the sooner they start preparing for them the better.

GCSEs undergo continual change. They were introduced in 1988 to establish a national qualification for those who decided to leave school at 16 without pursuing further academic study towards qualifications such as A-levels or university degrees. They replaced the former CSE and O-level qualifications, uniting the two to allow access to the full range of grades for more students. Since 1988, there have been frequent changes to the format of the examinations as well as to the regulations. The choice of subjects has increased, and their content altered again and again. The grading system has changed from A to G, A* to G and now 9 to 1. Coursework has been introduced and then withdrawn, and standards have been steadily lowered or raised according to one's point of view.

The most recent overhaul of GCSEs began in 2015 and was introduced over three years. This resulted in changes to syllabus content, new formats and a new grading system. There were to be no interim modular assessments, no coursework and no controlled assessments. A few subjects were able to retain an element of coursework, in the arts for example, and there were to be one or two teacher assessments forming a minor part of the overall qualification, including the spoken language element of GCSE English.

The number of GCSEs taken by pupils varies from school to school, but this too has gradually become more formalised. For some time, the standard diet, prompted by the DfE performance measure, saw pupils aiming for five A*-C grades including English and mathematics. The introduction of the Ebacc, a more sophisticated measure, encouraged schools to enable as many pupils as possible to take English, English Literature, maths, two sciences, a language (ancient or modern), and either history or geography. Progress 8 has added further refinement, with pupils measured according to a complex mix of core, Ebacc and 'open' subjects. In effect, this means that pupils have to study at least eight subjects at GCSE to obtain a good P8 score (although a limited number of non-GCSE Level 2 vocational courses qualify for inclusion in the measure).

Once again, the curriculum is led not by children's needs but by the DfE's accountability measures. This has led to serious dilemmas for school leaders. They know full well that not all pupils will benefit from the academic diet required to ensure a good P8 score, but they are acutely aware of the impact of a poor score on the reputation of the school. Consequently, in far too many schools, too many pupils are following courses that are totally unsuitable for them. The Ebacc curriculum is undoubtedly appropriate for the majority of pupils, even if it does exclude the arts. It is relatively broad and balanced and includes the key academic qualifications they need to equip them for A-level study. However, there are thousands of pupils for whom such a restricted academic diet is unsuitable: they need practical, vocational courses which prepare them to enter the workplace, or courses at levels more appropriate to their abilities. This is particularly true for many pupils with special educational needs for whom the Ebacc is entirely inappropriate.

The change from O-levels to GCSEs, and the gradual evolution of the latter, has led to widespread concerns regarding standards. Grade inflation led to regular howls of outrage in the press, and schools were accused of deliberately dumbing down. It is undoubtedly true that more and more pupils achieved higher grades as the years went by. In 1994 only 2.8% of entries were awarded A*s and this rose to 7% in 2018. However, the number of A grades awarded remained relatively stable, with 12.88% in 1988 and 14.7% in 2018. Similarly, C grades rose from 20.7% in 1988 to 23.4% in 2018.

Whether grade inflation was as serious as the press and politicians maintained – and there was considerable variation in the conclusions reached by the plethora of academic studies on the subject – the result was Michael Gove's determination to make GCSEs more demanding. His reforms were designed to address the problem of grade inflation and return schools to a 'proper academic curriculum'. As a result, pupils now face probably the most demanding qualifications ever attempted by 16-year-olds.

As we saw in Chapter 3, subject specifications are now much more demanding: English language and literature GCSEs are now based on traditional literary texts, with more accessible texts, and American texts in particular, banished to outer darkness; aspects of the AS syllabus now form part of the maths GCSE, and there has been a somewhat absurd stiffening of modern languages specifications. The answer to declining examination entries in languages was, bizarrely, the introduction of much more demanding syllabuses with highly prescriptive mark schemes. Someone, somewhere, clearly thought if we make GCSE French even more difficult, more pupils will want to do it.

The consequence of all this is that the majority of pupils in English secondary schools now follow a demanding curriculum which is closely aligned to the Ebacc – and remember that the government's target is for 75% of pupils to be following the Ebacc by 2022 and 90% by 2025 – and carefully designed to enable the school to achieve a good Progress 8 score. Of course, a significant number of pupils unsurprisingly fail to reach the benchmark achievement figures set by the

DfE. In 2019, 53.3% of pupils achieved five 'good' GCSEs, including English and maths. But what about the 46.7% who failed to achieve the benchmark figure? Doesn't this suggest that the curriculum as it stands is failing to meet the needs of a significant proportion of the school population? We have seen in earlier chapters the difficulties faced by schools in attempting to introduce a more vocational offer, and the hurdles set in their way by accountability measures, but with such a high percentage of pupils failing to reach the DfE's benchmark figure, it is surely time to look again at ways to encourage schools to develop curriculums more suitably adapted to the needs of all pupils, not just the academically capable.

We also need to ask another awkward question: now that pupils are required to stay in full-time education or training until they are 18, how relevant are GCSEs anyway? Is such a complex assessment system really needed at 16 when A-levels and Level 3 qualifications are only two years away? And what is the effect on children's mental health?

There has been a great deal of concern expressed not only in the press but in academic journals and by health organisations regarding the impact of the complex, high stakes testing of 16-year-olds which the new system demands. School leaders are beginning to voice their concerns with increasing passion, and they have been joined by both the National Society for the Prevention of Cruelty to Children (NSPCC) and Childline in attempting to persuade the government to lower the stakes. Pupils nowadays spend more time in examinations than ever before. Whereas a GCSE student in 2016 had an average of 18 examinations for which to prepare, totalling just over 24 hours, a pupil in 2019 sat 22 examinations, the total length of which amounted to 33 hours. Anyone who has worked in school will be aware of the effect of all this on children's well-being. Schools are seeing an unprecedented rise in the number of children with mental health issues, and many now describe the problem as an epidemic. In a system structured on the basis of accountability, rather than the needs of children, it is hard to see how things will change. Once again, we come back to the importance of the teacher's voice. If politicians were able to acknowledge teachers' expertise and listen to what they say about the pressure on children, things might begin to change. If learning is privileged over assessment, we might end up with a very different system.

Assessment post-16

On the face of it, assessment in the sixth form looks fairly straightforward because A-levels have been in place since 1951. After a brief excursion into two-part qualifications, with AS levels and A2s, A-levels have now returned to traditional two-year courses. There have been attempts to broaden the offer, with stand-alone AS levels and other additional qualifications (the latest being Core maths) added at various times. There have also been attempts to create some kind of post-16 English Baccalaureate along the lines of continental equivalents. The basic two-year, three A-level package is once again the norm, however.

Arguments over curriculum narrowing post-16 will doubtless continue, as they have done for years, but for the majority of students, A-levels suit them well. They enjoy the chance to study three subjects (and sometimes four) in depth and they appreciate being able to decide which subjects to pursue and which to drop. This leads to greater engagement and, arguably, greater achievement. There are problems, of course. As we saw in Chapter 3, A-levels are not suitable for every student and, as has happened with GCSEs, they have become more and more demanding as a consequence of the new specifications introduced in 2017. There is also the much more complicated question of university entries.

As we have seen, the school curriculum has been heading towards entry to university virtually since Year 1. It is largely an academic curriculum aimed at preparing students for academic study post A-level. Assessment at the end of the sixth form is therefore vitally important and, more often than not, the key to a young person's future career. Putting aside issues of mental health and grade inflation, as these mirror the discussions taking place at key stage 4, the most pressing issue concerning A-levels, and, indeed, other Level 3 qualifications, is the way they are used by universities to determine offers of places. Oxbridge and most Russell Group institutions now demand the highest grades, with offers of A*AA not uncommon, particularly for the more popular and demanding courses like medicine and law, but in recent years we have seen a rise in unconditional offers. The impact of this trend has been widely discussed, and it is generally seen as a response to the needs of universities that are desperate to fill places for financial reasons, but it is also opening up something of an academic divide. More able students are forced into an ever-more competitive environment in order to secure places at top universities, whereas others are able to get offers, often from well-regarded institutions, without the need to do particularly well in their A-levels. This effect seems only to confirm the impression that the school curriculum is designed for more able, more middle-class students.

At every level, large proportions of the pupil population fall below the various government benchmarks. Children have to repeat the phonics test in Year 2, they fall below expected levels at key stage 2, they fail to achieve five good GCSEs including English and maths at grade 5 or above, and they are denied the chance to study for prestigious A-levels because A-levels are not for them. Even if they do make it into the sixth form, it could be said that universities have become complicit in directing them away from the most reputable institutions via the mechanism of the unconditional offer.

At the end of 14 years of schooling, pupils complete an assessment marathon, only to find that their choices at 18 were virtually predetermined by their performance in tests as early as the Reception class. The students who moved on to FE colleges at 16 were the ones who fell below expected standards at primary school; the same could be said of those who just made it into the sixth form and then found themselves gratefully accepting unconditional offers to follow courses they were not sure about at universities they had never heard of or visited.

All this was predetermined by assessments. Whether they have enjoyed their learning or benefitted from it in other ways than examination scores is rarely considered. Their suitability for the Ebacc, for the sixth form and for university is based solely on assessment. It dominates their lives and determines their future. No wonder the notion of learning as something enriching, character building, and spiritually uplifting has become something of a mystery to pupils sitting in English classrooms today.

Ofsted – a new hope?

The 2019 Ofsted framework seems, at last, to offer a sense of hope as it seeks to play down the importance of data and shifts the focus of inspections away from outcomes towards the effectiveness of the curriculum as a mechanism for learning. Outcomes remain important, of course, but much more attention is to be paid to the aims of the curriculum and the way it is implemented in the classroom. Instead of an outcomes-driven inspection regime we how have one that looks at the intent, the implementation and the impact of curriculum choices on children. It also prioritises the needs of disadvantaged children and those with special educational needs in a way that a purely outcomes-based system fails to do. The inspection handbook puts it like this:

> Inspectors will consider the extent to which the school's curriculum sets out the knowledge and skills that pupils will gain at each stage (we call this 'intent'). They will also consider the way that the curriculum developed or adopted by the school is taught and assessed in order to support pupils to build their knowledge and to apply that knowledge as skills (we call this 'implementation'). Finally, inspectors will consider the outcomes that pupils achieve as a result of the education they have received (we call this the 'impact').[7]

This means that school leaders at every level will be required to think about the curriculum choices they make in much greater depth than they have ever done before. It also means that discussions around pedagogy will be focussed on learning and remembering rather than assessment mechanisms. Inspections judgements are now to be based on a broad range of factors which genuinely do seem to shift the debate away from assessment towards learning:

> The judgement focuses on factors that both research and inspection evidence indicate contribute most strongly to an effective education where pupils achieve highly. These factors are listed below.
>
> - The school's curriculum is rooted in the solid consensus of the school's leaders about the knowledge and skills that pupils need in order to take advantage of opportunities, responsibilities and experiences of later life. In this way, it can powerfully address social disadvantage.
> - It is clear what end points the curriculum is building towards and what pupils need to know and be able to do to reach those end points.

- The school's curriculum is planned and sequenced so that new knowledge and skills build on what has been taught before and towards its clearly defined end points.
- The curriculum reflects the school's local context by addressing typical gaps in pupils' knowledge and skills.
- The curriculum remains as broad as possible for as long as possible. Pupils are able to study a strong academic core of subjects, such as those offered by the EBacc.
- There is high academic/vocational/technical ambition for all pupils, and the school does not offer disadvantaged pupils or pupils with SEND a reduced curriculum.[8]

What can schools do now to put things right?

- **Play down assessments**. It is important for everyone involved in testing in schools to avoid talking up the tests. This is a major cause of stress and anxiety. School leaders need to ensure that tests are conducted professionally but, more importantly, that they are seen as just another part of day-to-day teaching. To achieve this, they will need to train teachers to lessen anxiety around testing, and to work with parents to reassure them that the majority of tests pupils take until the age of 16 will have very little impact on their future prospects.

- **Formative not summative**. When they focus on formative assessment, teachers need to think carefully about how children learn and whether they have learned what has been taught. This leads to significant improvements in teaching and learning. Teachers who focus narrowly on the demands of examination syllabuses restrict learning opportunities and devalue the learning itself.

- **Focus on learning**. Schools should focus intensely on learning as opposed to assessment. Too many school leaders pay lip service to learning but then concentrate on the performance tables. If learning is at the heart of the curriculum, then pupils will inevitably do well in school.

- **Work with Ofsted**. The new inspection guidance regarding the curriculum signalled a dramatic change of direction for Ofsted. School leaders need to recognise the change and adjust the focus of the work they are doing accordingly. The fact that much less emphasis is put on data is surely to be celebrated as it opens the door to genuine discussions of pedagogy.

Of course, schools will still be judged by the DfE on outcomes. League tables will still reflect their key stage 2 scores, or their Progress 8 scores, and it will be interesting to see how the apparent tension between the two systems resolves itself. The important point, however, is that Ofsted, that most reviled of organisations, seems to be leading the way out of the assessment maze in which most of our children find themselves lost. It could be that teachers will once again be able to focus on learning rather than assessment.

What should policymakers do to put things right?

- Dramatically simplify the testing regime by recognising the absurdity of the current system. Testing at 4, 5, 6, 7, 11, 16 and 18 cannot be right.
- Trust teachers to assess pupils.
- Recognise that schools are about learning not testing.
- Review the purpose, relevance and impact of school performance tables.

Notes

1 National Foundation for Educational Research, *An Introduction to Formative and Summative Assessment.* www.nfer.ac.uk/for-schools/free-resources-advice/assessment-hub/introduction-to-assessment/an-introduction-to-formative-and-summative-assessment/
2 Guidance. 2019. *Reception Baseline Assessment*, February. www.gov.uk/guidance/reception-baseline-assessment
3 From the introduction to: A. Bradbury & G. Roberts-Homes. *'They Are Children . . . Not Robots, Not Machines': The Introduction of Reception Baseline Assessment*, London, UCL, Institute of Education. www.teachers.org.uk/files/baseline-assessment-final-10404.pdf
4 M.J. Snowling et al. 2015. Validity and Sensitivity of the Phonics Screening Check: Implications for Practice, *Journal of Research in Reading, UKLA*, Volume 38, Issue 2.
5 N. Gibb. 2018. *Department for Education*, 14 February. www.gov.uk/government/news/multiplication-tables-check-trials-to-begin-in-schools
6 Founded by Sir John Rowling, PiXL emerged in 2008 from the school improvement programme, the London Challenge. When government funding for the initiative ceased, the 50 member schools at that time decided voluntarily to continue with their model of collaboration around leadership and shared resources. PiXL has since grown to become the largest network of schools in England and Wales.
7 Ofsted. 2019. *School Inspection Handbook*, May, Updated September 2019, p. 41.
8 Ibid. p. 41.

6 Structures

As we have seen, the extent to which politicians are able to influence what happens in the classroom is really quite shocking. Accountability requirements shape the nature and frequency of assessment in schools, and political control of the curriculum impacts directly on what children are taught in almost every lesson. However, despite the fact that teachers and school leaders are often marginalised when key educational decisions are made, they are usually able to ameliorate the impact of the more extreme political diktats. The introduction of the Ebacc is a good example: the government's target for take-up of the Ebacc is unlikely to be met simply because school leaders know that it is both inappropriate and ultimately unworkable. The structure of the school system itself is another matter, and here teachers have very little influence.

There was a time when it was fairly easy to describe the educational landscape in England. There were grammar schools, secondary moderns and independent schools. When the majority of local authorities abandoned selection, we were left with comprehensive schools and around 150 grammar schools in pockets of affluence around the country. Since then, however, a bewildering variety of schools has been introduced, and parents are now left scratching their heads as they try to work out the differences between them. The nomenclature is often baffling: why has the local school suddenly become a college? What is the difference between a school and an academy? What exactly is a free school? Is there any difference between a city technology college and a studio school? And why on earth does the village primary have an executive headteacher and a CEO?

At the heart of what has effectively been a revolution in educational provision is the steady withdrawal of local authorities (LAs). LAs were once responsible for all the maintained schools in the local area, but this is no longer the case. Schools have gradually moved away, first via grant-maintained status (GMS), then foundation status and then via academisation. Grant-maintained schools, or GM schools, were state schools that, between 1988 and 1998, were able to opt out of local government control, and they were funded directly by a grant from central government. In other words, they were given direct control over their own finances and thus over a wide range of decisions affecting the way they worked. This was seen as something of a liberation by the headteachers who took advantage of the opportunity. Next came foundation schools, state-funded schools in which the governing body had much greater freedom in the running of the school. Foundation schools were set up under the School Standards and Framework Act 1998 to replace grant-maintained schools and were also funded directly by central government. The most significant change, however, came with the academy programme.

Academies

The Labour government led by Tony Blair established academies in the Learning and Skills Act 2000 with the aim of transforming the life chances of children in areas of the country where educational provision was poor, school buildings crumbling and expectations low. Academies originally needed a private sponsor who could be an individual, an educational organisation or simply a profit-driven business. These sponsors were expected to bring best practice and innovative private-sector management to academies. They were originally required to contribute 10% of the academy's capital costs, with the remainder of the costs met by the state through grants funded by the local authority. The government later removed the requirement for financial investment by a private sponsor in a move to encourage successful existing schools and charities to become sponsors. The Academies Act 2010 sought to increase the number of academies. It enabled all maintained schools to convert to academy status, known as converter academies, and encouraged new academies to be created via the free school programme. Whether academies were more effective than maintained schools was never seriously discussed; the decision was essentially ideological. Schools classed as academies today are very different from the original 2000 blueprint.

With the introduction of academies, schools had effectively become privatised, while nominally remaining under state control. Headteachers and governors were attracted to academisation by the promise of greater financial freedom and the chance to make better use of their funding allocations which were paid directly to the school. The lure was the thought that schools would receive funds normally top-sliced by the LA and thus be better off. Indeed, initially the government offered substantial grants to encourage schools to convert. Sadly, but not surprisingly, the savings promised by academisation never really materialised; large numbers of academies are now experiencing serious financial difficulties and running significant deficits, without the support of the LA to help them out. There was also another strong appeal to headteachers who were promised freedom from the constraints of the National Curriculum and the chance to innovate. However, due to national accountability structures, virtually all academies deliver a curriculum very similar to the one on offer in maintained schools. The freedom to innovate also turned out to be something of an illusion.

Academies are now managed by the office of the Regional Schools Commissioner (RSC). Their responsibilities are to:

- Take action where academies and free schools are underperforming
- Intervene in academies where governance is inadequate
- Decide on applications from local authority-maintained schools to convert to academy status
- Improve underperforming-maintained schools by providing them with support from a strong sponsor
- Take action to improve poorly performing sponsors
- Advise on proposals for new free schools
- Advise on whether to cancel, defer or enter into funding agreements with free school projects

In other words, they perform many of the functions previously carried out by local authorities but at arm's length, and because of the sheer numbers of academies involved, they are struggling to carry them out effectively. RSCs are now beginning to create sub-regional groups to enable them to keep in touch with schools more closely. Cynics might point out that these are not wildly different from local authorities. Once all schools are academies and grouped in sub-regions, will these sub-regional groups really be any different from the old LAs? It is hard to think of a better example of a major change to the educational system which simply wasn't thought through.

Free schools

There are, of course, various types of academies, the most well-known of which is the free school. A free school is a non-profitmaking, independent, state-funded school which is free to attend but which is not wholly controlled by a local authority, meaning they have greater control over how they operate. Free schools can set their own pay and conditions for staff, change the length of school terms and the school day, and they do not have to follow the National Curriculum. The most unusual feature of these schools is that they can be set up by parents, teachers, community and faith groups, universities and businesses. Unsurprisingly, they have attracted huge controversy, and for lots of reasons.

Since free schools can be established almost anywhere, without any real consideration of the need for school places in the local area, many have been heavily criticised for diverting money from other schools, depleting the rolls of nearby schools, increasing segregation by attracting middle-class children or children of a particular faith, and generally disrupting well-planned and effective local educational provision. Many had millions of pounds of set-up funding allocated only to attract a handful of pupils. In 2017, the National Audit Office warned that the programme had run up a bill of billions of pounds due to staggering procurement and construction costs, while existing schools were falling into disrepair. There have also been numerous examples of free schools closing shortly after opening and many never opening at all.

Advocates of the scheme, including the former director of the New Schools Network and co-founder of the West London Free School, Toby Young, insist that the money is well spent. Free schools, he argues, are a cost-effective way of creating much-needed new places with enough money left over to refurbish and maintain existing schools. Others argue that this view is naïve and unrealistic. As for performance, the New Schools Network stresses the fact that more free schools are accorded outstanding status by Ofsted than their maintained sector counterparts, and their results are often the best in the area. It doesn't take a genius to work out, however, that if one teaches a select group of highly motivated middle-class children, then the outcomes are bound to be strong. Free schools are not, of course, intended to be selective, but, like independent schools, they inevitably are. They rarely attract disadvantaged pupils, or those with special educational needs, and their appeal is largely to parents who would go private if they could afford it. Very few serious educational professionals support free schools and regard them as misguided ideological experiments which are almost certain to fail. Some will eventually become absorbed into the system; others will decline and disappear. It is difficult not to regard free schools as an extreme example of the way in which politicians unthinkingly play with children's lives.

If choosing between a maintained school, an academy or a free school wasn't hard enough for parents, there are other choices to be made. For example, there are two distinct types of academy: studio schools and university technical colleges (UTCs). A studio school is a small free school, usually with around 300 pupils, designed to give students practical skills in workplace environments as well as traditional academic and vocational courses of study. A UTC is a free school for the 14- to 18-year-old age group similarly specialising in practical, employment-focussed subjects, sponsored by a university, employer or an FE college. In both cases, these schools have struggled to attract pupils, and their future is unclear. Pupils likely to benefit from a more vocational curriculum still find themselves bound by the National Curriculum and disappointed by the lack of time spent on practical activities. UTCs also find it difficult to attract pupils in Year 9 – pupils who are often already well established in mainstream schools with networks of friends and teachers who know them. There is also the problem that these schools inevitably attract lower ability pupils who find mainstream schooling difficult, and this can sometimes lead to behavioural issues.

The most recent addition to the free school roster is the mathematics school. Mathematics schools are university-sponsored specialist 16–19 free schools for pupils who are mathematically able. They are supported by universities which offer highly selective, high-tariff undergraduate maths courses. There are two maths schools already open, King's College London Mathematics School and Exeter Mathematics School, both of which are rated outstanding by Ofsted, and several more are planned. These schools are to have 'a vital role to play in addressing shortages of skilled graduates in science, technology, engineering and maths (STEM)'.[1] They are also tasked with attracting students from disadvantaged backgrounds and recruiting a higher proportion of girls to study maths and physics than national averages.

On the face of it, there seems little to object to here but, of course, there are problems. Putting aside the half-humorous fear that these places will become ghettoes for nerds and geeks, there is the impact on other schools to consider. The Exeter Mathematics School is a case in point. It attracts students not only from the city of Exeter but also from across Devon and, in doing so, it endangers the very existence of A-level maths courses in many of the secondary schools in the area. Many Devon schools have sixth forms of around 200 students and run one mathematics A-level class; if they can, they also offer further mathematics. The loss of only a few students can make a class financially unviable and, as a result, further maths has now disappeared from a number of school sixth forms in the area. Headteachers also question the real need for such schools. Virtually all school sixth forms and sixth form colleges offer maths and physics, with the majority offering further mathematics in addition. They have strong links with local universities, and their results are often as good as the mathematics schools. It is also true to say that their pupils have far greater opportunities in terms of subject choice, pastoral support and social activities. Mathematics schools may do well, but are they really necessary? Once again, the political focus on STEM subjects is the driver here, not the needs of the child.

Multi-academy trusts

Academies are increasingly joining together in groups known as multi-academy trusts (MATs). This is partly due to the need to seek the support formally provided by local authorities and partly due to the supposed financial advantages such arrangements are able to supply. Originally, the multi-academy trust model of governance was imposed upon schools deemed to be failing by central government, and they were forced to seek sponsorship. Since then, more and more schools have become part of MATs, often at the behest of the RSCs. MATs vary in size from two or three small primary schools to national chains with over 50 schools. The largest chains, including the Academies Enterprise Trust (AET), Reach 2, Oasis, the School Partnership Trust Academies and United Learning, have considerable influence and political power.

MATS are promoted as being more effective than stand-alone schools in terms of both financial efficiency and pupil performance, but exactly how effective they actually are is unclear. It seems likely that the larger MATs can provide examples of significant savings with regard to services such as payroll, catering and grounds maintenance; in other words, the services previously managed by local authorities. However, NFER analysis of DfE data suggests that the larger the trust, the more likely it is to be in a deficit position.[2] When it comes to outcomes for pupils, there is very little evidence either way and accurate data is hard to come by. Experimental statistics analysing MAT performance measures released by the DfE in January 2017 revealed a varied picture.[3] At key stage 2, more than half of MATs had above average progress in writing and maths, but in reading progress over half had below average scores. At key stage 4, two-thirds of MATs had below average Progress 8 scores. According to NFER research, if one compares MATs to Local Authorities, there is also a very varied picture. At primary level, MATs are over-represented among both the best and worst performers, while at secondary level MATs make up a disproportionate number of the lowest-performing school groups. If the focus is placed on disadvantaged pupils, very significant variation in outcomes is seen, both within MATs and between MATS and other schools.[4] Put simply, there is no real evidence that MATs produce improved outcomes for pupils.

The key question, of course, is what is it like for a child in a multi-academy trust? Since MATs are essentially organisational structures, the hope would be that the impact on the child would be fairly minimal but that is often not the case. When a school joins a trust, the pupil may see some immediate changes, especially if it is a large trust: a new corporate image, new staff, and, almost certainly, the appointment of a CEO and an executive headteacher. Surely one of the least convincing financial savings relates to the introduction of new leadership structures. When two schools combine, one headteacher is likely to become the executive head, usually with a headteacher or head of school in each one. This doesn't strike me as a saving. It is also hard to see exactly what an executive head in a small MAT actually does to earn his or her salary, other than attend trust meetings and monitor the headteachers.

Schools often combine, especially if they do so at the behest of the RSC, in order to bring about improvements in one particular school. When this is the case, pupils may find that their class teacher is transferred in order to help raise standards. It is assumed that the donor school will be able to maintain its high standards, and that an equally good teacher will be found for the class, but this isn't always the case. There are too many examples of good or outstanding schools which take on failing schools only to end up with falling standards themselves. When things work well, standards are maintained but there is always a risk of things going the wrong way. Of course, for pupils in the failing school, the sudden arrival of an excellent teacher is a positive development, although we must remember that an outstanding teacher in one school isn't always outstanding in another, especially if the social and behavioural context is significantly different.

Pupils may also experience a change of culture as new rules and regulations are imposed, and the corporate image is enforced. Most academy chains adopt common policies and, in the most restrictive, they go as far as imposing common schemes of work. A school's unique culture, its sense of individuality, and its community feel, can easily be replaced by a one size fits all approach. Pupils are encouraged to regard themselves as members of a multi-academy trust rather than an individual school.

There are changes for staff and parents, too. Staff are given new contracts which may differ significantly from those in maintained schools. Often the changes go unnoticed until it is pointed out, for example, that they are expected to stay on site until 5:30 every day or find themselves with extra lunchtime duties. If they want to retain their posts, however, they often have very little choice but to accept the new contract. They may also be asked to transfer to another school in the trust, especially if they have skills that are in demand elsewhere. Having worked contentedly in one school for years, where they know their pupils and they are well respected, they find themselves dealing with challenging classes in a completely alien environment. Parents will notice less of a difference, but they may find that school leaders and governors become increasingly distant. Most MATs have a local governing board, but the real power lies with the trust, and the trust could well be based in a city many miles away. They may also notice that the headteacher they used to chat to regularly in the playground doesn't seem to be around anymore and that concerns are dealt with by an anonymous executive head who they barely know.

In the most unfortunate cases, some schools find themselves moving from one trust to another. If the MAT fails to bring about sufficient improvement, it is up to the RSC to re-broker the school and find another MAT willing to take it on. When that happens, everything changes again: a new CEO, a new executive head, new uniforms, new rules, and so on.

There are, of course, some highly effective multi-academy trusts where schools work together to bring about genuine change, change which in some cases can be transformative. These MATs encourage schools to retain their individuality, they focus relentlessly on teaching and learning, they offer high-quality professional development for their staff and they put pupils first. I suspect, however, that these are few and far between. The majority of MATs struggle to live up to the ambitious aims they set out to achieve, and many have little or no impact on school improvement or pupil performance. It is also worrying to see more and more governing bodies joining MATs out of sheer panic: they see schools all round them joining up and they feel obliged to do the same. High-performing secondary schools, in particular, come under great pressure from the RSCs to create MATs, and they are told that it is their moral imperative to help other schools. A more convincing imperative could be to focus on their own pupils and continue doing what works for them.

Grammar schools

Most grammar schools became academies in the hope that it would offer further protection from the threat of non-selective status. They are, of course, something of an anomaly in the system, but even though most of them went comprehensive in the 1970s, those that remain are fairly secure. It would be a foolhardy politician indeed who stood for election promising to abolish the local grammar schools, especially when grammar schools are often held up by right-wing politicians as the solution to social inequality. There are only 163 grammar schools in England, out of some 3,000 state secondaries, and a further 69 grammar schools in Northern Ireland. When they were more common, grammar schools were part of a simple system: pupils who passed the 11 plus examination went to the grammar school; those who failed went to the local secondary modern school. The introduction of comprehensives led to a dramatic reduction in the number of grammar schools, but those that remain exercise a strong grip on the public imagination. There are frequent calls for their reintroduction and, although this has long seemed unlikely, recent legislation has allowed existing schools to expand and many have done so.

Grammar schools achieve excellent results, but they should. If only the very brightest pupils in the local area are selected, it is hardly surprising that they go on to achieve dazzling sets of GCSEs, or high grades at A-level. It is easy for grammar schools to publicise their success, but they rarely acknowledge that their success is almost inevitable. Teaching is no better than in comprehensive schools, and in some where tradition reigns, it is worse. When a parent sends their child to a grammar school, they are not choosing better teaching – though many doubtless think they are – they are choosing segregation. They want their children to spend the day with bright middle-class peers – children just like them. Although they would never admit it, they also want to shield their children from the influence of less desirable company. To put it bluntly, they don't want their children mixing with hooligans from the council estate. They want their child to learn the violin and take part in public speaking competitions; they certainly don't want them hanging round with the youths they see smoking in bus shelters in the summer holidays.

Despite the fact that bright pupils will achieve equal success in comprehensive schools, parents still subject their children to the incredibly stressful experience of the 11 plus examination. There is a whole industry based around preparing them for the exams, and some parents sign up their children to a year's worth of extra lessons and examination coaching in the run up to the tests. Even if they are successful, one wonders whether it is worth the inevitable anxiety generated by the 11 plus. As for the impact on those who fail, this can last a lifetime.

Independent schools

Independent schools are still widely venerated in society today. Their pre-eminence in the English imagination is reinforced almost daily and in dozens of ways. Whenever headteachers of state schools are interviewed by the BBC, for example, they are introduced simply as the headteacher of a particular school; when the head of a public school appears, he or she is described as 'a leading headteacher' or, more commonly, as 'a leading headmaster'. This is a subtle difference, but it says everything about the way independent schools are regarded. Their influence seeps into every aspect of society: this is partly due to the fact that the professions and the political classes are dominated by ex-public school pupils and partly due to the ideological underpinnings of English society which posit the wealthy as the natural rulers. Consequently, even though independently educated pupils make up only 7% of the school population, they exert a profound influence on the English psyche.

Sending their child to a public school is still the dream of parents from all walks of life, but are they really any better than state schools? Of course, in lots of ways they are. The most successful public schools have superb facilities which no state school can match. Indeed, the disparity between the facilities on offer at the local comprehensive school and those available at the nearby independent offer a striking illustration of just how divided our society remains. A well-equipped comprehensive may have modern buildings, purpose-built sports facilities, a theatre, a large dining area and bright modern classrooms, but the local independent will have all that and more. It is not uncommon for independents to have separate music blocks, several large assembly halls, one or two professional standard theatres, extensive grounds with boating and equine facilities, a chapel and a wide range of sports facilities including fully equipped fitness centres, gymnasiums, pitches for every sport and even golf courses. Some public schools look more like holiday leisure centres than schools.

They also offer smaller classes. There is no evidence to suggest that class size has any impact on attainment, but the assumption is always that it will. Fifteen students in a class will always seem more comfortable than 30, and those students will undoubtedly receive more individual attention. The real value of a public school education, however, has nothing to do with facilities or class sizes, it is all to do with how pupils from independent schools are perceived and the networks to which they are granted access. Independent schools prepare pupils for public life; they equip them with the confidence and the contacts they need to advance much more quickly and easily than their state school counterparts. This is the kind of advantage that is impossible to replicate in state schools, and it is what makes independent schools so successful and sought after.

What about attainment? Do pupils at independent schools do better than those in comprehensive schools? Generally, the answer is yes, but how can it be otherwise? Despite energetic denials from leading headteachers, the majority of independent schools are highly selective. They are not only selective in terms of academic ability but selective in the sense that their intake is drawn from highly motivated middle- and upper-class families with the ability to pay substantial fees. Most independents offer bursaries of some kind or another to attract disadvantaged children, but those that attract more than a handful are few and far between. Consequently, they are almost bound to achieve good results. It would be unfair, of course, to ignore the fact that some outstanding teaching takes place in independent schools but nonsense to assert that it is any better than the excellent teaching taking place in state schools.

We also need to acknowledge that there are some dreadful private schools which survive on reputation alone. As the headteacher of a rural secondary school surrounded by outstanding primaries, I was often baffled by the numbers of parents who chose to pay to send their children to dramatically inferior schools. I suppose the assumption was that because it had to be paid for, it was therefore better. I must confess to enjoying pointing out to some of them one of the hidden secrets of the profession, that the failing teachers moved out of state schools, and the weakest trainee teachers almost invariably end up working in the private sector.

Finally, there is the matter of boarding. I am sure there are many benefits to boarding, but I find it almost impossible to understand how a parent can send a 7-year-old child away from home. It strikes me as both cruel and unnatural. Because it is part of the public school ethos, however, it is rarely seriously questioned. Perhaps it is time that society took a long look at the potential damage such early separations inflict on children. It could well be that the independent school classroom is the most toxic of all.

Faith schools

Faith schools are equally contentious. Among the accusations levelled against them are concerns regarding admissions, segregation, extremism and failure to deliver the National Curriculum. In addition, faith schools encourage us to ask a particularly challenging question: at what point does education becomes indoctrination? Nor are they an insignificant part of the education system: around 25% of primary-age children attend faith schools, the vast majority of which are controlled by the Church of England, although there are significant numbers of Catholic as well as a handful of Jewish, Muslim and Sikh schools. In addition, there are large numbers of independent schools with a religious ethos.

State-funded faith schools are usually voluntary aided (VA) or voluntary controlled (VC). This means that they get some of their funding from a religious organisation, which also usually owns the school buildings and the land. They are run in roughly the same way as other maintained schools, although often the governing body rather than the local authority is responsible for matters such as deciding the admissions policy and appointing staff. Many have now joined multi-academy trusts, and there are several large faith-based MATs in operation. In many ways, however, apart from the sign over the gate, it is hard to tell the difference between a faith school and a non-faith school. This is particularly the case with Church of England schools which attract large numbers of parents of very little faith due to the fact that faith schools tend to achieve better results. As with grammars and independents, of course, there is a degree of natural selection here which means that faith schools tend to attract the more motivated and thus higher attaining middle classes.

In addition to the standard Ofsted inspections, faith schools are expected to organise Section 48 inspections. Each faith and denomination have their own inspection frameworks and their own inspectors. Church of England and Catholic school inspection is undertaken by the relevant diocese whose inspectors work with either the Framework for the Statutory Inspection of Anglican and Methodist Schools (SIAMS) or the appropriate diocesan version of the Catholic Education Service's framework. Jewish schools are inspected by Pikuach ('inspection' in Hebrew), the Jewish Studies Education Inspection Service. Muslim schools are inspected by the Association of Muslim Schools (AMS) and most Sikh schools by the Network of Sikh Organisations. How demanding these inspections are in practice is a matter of opinion. They tend to focus on the religious aspects of schools, leaving the more detailed analysis of performance and pedagogy to Ofsted.

It is hard to avoid the fact that faith schools segregate pupils. When the religion in question is the religion of the state, even if nowadays this is really in name only, the question of segregation doesn't seem particularly pressing, as so many pupils attend these schools. Issues arise, however, when a so-called minority faith is involved, and the schools are then open to the accusation that they are cutting themselves off from wider society. What chance do children have to integrate with those of other faiths, critics argue, and how will they learn to be tolerant of others if they spend all day long only with children of their own faith? Faith-based schools are often regarded as religious ghettoes where children are taught to set themselves apart from the communities in which they live. This is clearly rarely the case, and most faith schools work hard to ensure that they interact with all members of the local community. The Church of England and the Roman Catholic Church both point out that their schools provide education for all children and that significant numbers of pupils, around 30% in the case of Catholic schools, are of other faiths or none.

There is also the question of whether it is appropriate for religion to be taught in schools. Isn't this a family matter? The Secular Society argues that faith schools are harmful to society and should not receive public funding:

> Parents are entitled to raise their children within a faith tradition, but they are not entitled to enlist the help of the state to do so. The state should not fund proselytization or allow the schools it funds to inculcate children into a particular religion.
>
> There are other reasons why organising children's education around religious identities is a bad idea. Separating children along such fundamental lines of difference is divisive and leads to religious, ethnic and socio-economic segregation.
>
> To make matters worse, many faith schools can discriminate against pupils and teachers who do not share the faith of the school.[5]

Much of the debate around faith schools, however, centres on the fairness or otherwise of the admissions system. In particular, Church of England schools are often criticised for prioritising children whose families worship at a designated church, sometimes as little as once a month for a year. This has led to people going to church simply to gain a place, to the detriment of other children who live nearer the school, or who live further away but come from genuinely religious families.

Religious extremism is also a concern. In a speech delivered at the Church of England Foundation for Educational Leadership in 2018, Ofsted's Chief Inspector, Amanda Spielman, said that schools were being used by individuals who want to narrow youngsters' horizons, and in the worst cases 'indoctrinate impressionable minds' under the guise of religious belief. She pointed out that inspectors were increasingly coming across those who want to 'actively pervert' the purpose of education. This is a brave stance, and she is aware that tackling religious extremism is far from easy:

> Occasionally that will mean taking uncomfortable decisions or having tough conversations. It means not assuming that the most conservative voices in a particular faith speak for everyone – imagine if people thought the Christian Institute were the sole voice of Anglicanism. And it means schools must not be afraid, to call out practices, whatever their justification, that limit young people's experiences and learning in school. In that regard schools must not, in their entirely correct goal of promoting tolerance, shy away from challenging fundamentalist practice where it appears in their schools or communities.[6]

Pupils caught up in arguments over extremism are very vulnerable. They are open to attacks from protestors, bullying by pupils from other schools and rejection by the community. In almost every chapter of this book we are forced to wonder whether politicians ever think about the impact of their decisions on the children in the classroom; in the case of faith schools, we might well ask the same question of religious leaders.

Beyond the mainstream

Around 2% of the school population attend special schools. These are schools for children with a special educational need or a disability. The majority of pupils in these schools have a statement or, its replacement, an educational health care plan (EHC). An EHC is a plan for children and young people who need more support than the SEN department of a school can offer, and it usually involves external professionals. Obtaining an EHC is far from straightforward: it is a lengthy bureaucratic process which both schools and parents find immensely frustrating.

Special schools can be maintained schools, academies or independents, and, although some cater for a wide range of needs, many tend to specialise. The DfE lists four broad types of specialism:

- Communication and interaction
- Cognition and learning

- Social, emotional and mental health

- Sensory and physical needs

Some mainstream schools have their own special units or resources bases, as they are known, and these are often preferred by parents who want their children to receive specialist support and still be able to mix with a wider peer group. All maintained special schools have to follow the National Curriculum, but they have the freedom to make reasonable adjustments in line with pupils' specific needs. They are also subject to the normal round of Ofsted inspections.

Special needs education is undoubtedly the most complex and sensitive part of the system, and yet it is, in many ways, the most neglected and underfunded. Choosing a mainstream school is hard enough for parents, but choosing and then gaining access to specialist support is currently something of a nightmare. In October 2019 the Commons Education Select Committee published a fairly damning report on the state of SEND provision in England and Wales today. Its conclusions were stark:

> A generation of children and young people with special educational needs and disabilities is failing to receive the support it deserves, with poorly implemented legislation leaving families facing a nightmare of bureaucracy, buck-passing and confusion. . . .
>
> The Committee concludes that while the reforms to the support for children and young people contained in the Children and Families Act 2014 were the right ones, poor implementation has put local authorities under pressure, left schools struggling to cope and, ultimately, thrown families into crisis.[7]

For the child in the classroom, this is something of a disaster, as the report makes clear:

> The Committee heard overwhelming evidence that the reforms were letting down young people who need additional support with their education. It heard from young people that poor support can result in them being isolated in school, unable to access the curriculum and find it hard to make friends. As adults, the training and employment opportunities were found to be poor, deriving from a fundamental lack of ambition for young people with SEND across the country.[8]

Such is the complexity of special needs provision; there will always be debates around its nature and the way it is implemented in both mainstream and special schools. The prevailing view is that, where possible, children should be integrated into mainstream classrooms, but this is not as easy as it sounds. The lack of funding in schools means that headteachers simply cannot afford the specialist support required or, indeed, make the adaptations that some pupils need simply to make their way around the site. Nor is it simply a matter of providing access to mainstream classrooms for SEND pupils: many require a level of specialist teaching expertise which teachers are not trained to deliver. Effective SEND support depends upon high levels of pedagogical and, sometimes, medical expertise, high levels of staffing and strong support from external agencies.

There is also the problematic issue of the impact of SEND pupils in the classroom on the other pupils. This is a discussion which is often avoided due to its sensitivity, but it cannot be avoided. Clearly, a teacher's role is to teach the 30 children in his or her class; a child with complex needs, no matter how much support is available, inevitably alters the dynamic in the classroom and makes teaching much more demanding. It would be dreadful to say that a child with SEND should not be part of a mainstream classroom because his or her teachers won't be able to cope, but naïve to ignore the impact such a decision will have on the education of everyone in the class. This takes us to the heart of the inclusion debate: where is the best place for a child with special needs to be educated? For the majority of pupils with SEND, the mainstream classroom will undoubtedly be the right place, provided the support and the funding is there, but for those with more complex needs, a special school may well be more appropriate. This is a complex decision which can only be made after lengthy discussions with parents, professionals, schools and, of course, the child. As the select committee report pointed out, however, the system is currently failing to make this possible.

Children with behavioural difficulties are often overlooked, but they are clearly part of the special needs debate. If they cannot cope with mainstream schooling, they often end up in Pupil Referral Units (PRUs). PRUs are a type of school that caters for children who aren't able to attend a mainstream school. Pupils are often referred to them if they need greater care and support than their school can provide. It is often assumed that every child in a PRU is there because his or her behaviour is too challenging for them to be in a mainstream classroom, but this is not always the case. PRUs cater for a much wider range of pupils than many parents, and indeed, some teachers realise. They do, of course, provide education for pupils permanently excluded from mainstream schools, as well as those with anger issues, but they also support children who have been bullied, those who have special educational needs who are awaiting diagnosis, children without school places, pregnant teenagers or young mothers and those suffering long-term illnesses which mean they cannot attend school every day. PRUs are therefore complex institutions which are often wrongly written off as the nightmare establishments where only the permanently excluded go.

PRUs don't have to teach the full National Curriculum, but they must provide a broad and balanced education. Although attending a PRU is often seen as a last resort, it can be exactly what pupils who are having difficulties at school need to get them back on track. PRUs are often staffed by highly qualified and experienced teachers who have expertise in dealing with special needs, and emotional and behavioural difficulties. In addition, pupils have access to support from social workers, educational psychologists and counsellors. Class sizes are typically small, allowing pupils one-to-one attention, and they usually have timetables tailored precisely to their needs.

Like special schools, however, PRUs are dramatically underfunded. Many are closing, forcing pupils back into mainstream schools, or, more often, out of education altogether. As we have seen, the mainstream classroom is hardly a comfortable environment for children, with constant change, high levels of accountability, political interference, underfunding and real confusion over the purpose of schooling, but how much worse must it be for pupils with special educational needs or behavioural difficulties. What does it say about our nation when its most vulnerable children are neglected in this way?

Admissions

The chaos and complexity of the current education landscape is mirrored by the admissions system. Having struggled to understand the difference between maintained schools and academies, free schools and independents, UTCs and studio schools, parents then have to subject themselves to a wildly complicated admissions system. There is perhaps no stronger argument for a system in which every child is compelled to attend his or her local school than the current admissions set-up. Although local authorities coordinate the admissions system, most schools have their own admissions criteria, and these can be complicated to say the least. LAs are now legally required to operate what is known as an equal preference system, which means that places are offered purely on the strength of how well children fit the admissions criteria. Schools can't favour children whose parents list the school as their first choice, nor rule out those who placed it lower down the list.

That said, schools still retain considerable control over which children they admit. As we have seen, faith schools are able to favour children of a particular faith, and grammar schools are still able to set entry tests. Most mainstream schools include basic criteria such as catchment areas, distance from the school, siblings, children of staff and so on. Children with EHCs and children who are looked after are supposed to receive priority. A parent who chooses a popular local school may find they miss out on a place because they are a few hundred metres too far away. In some cases, they don't actually gain access to the nearest school. If a child lives in an area where there is a grammar school, two or three outstanding schools and perhaps a free school, they may well end up caught in a maze of possibilities as their parents attempt to successfully navigate the system. Such is the complexity of the system that it inevitably favours the sharp elbowed.

If a parent fails to gain a place in their first-choice school, they can always appeal. This is an even more complicated and intimidating process, again designed to exclude anyone beyond the professional classes. It is also open to widespread abuse. Even though appeals panels are independent and chaired by volunteers who have no connection with the school, it is easy enough for headteachers to manipulate the outcomes in favour of the most desirable pupils, even if none of them would ever admit doing so. A smile in the right place and the lack of an objection could easily encourage the panel to admit a child; a stern rebuttal of an application and a detailed defence of the school's case can ensure that a difficult child is kept out.

There are frequent calls for an overhaul of the admissions system. The Comprehensive Future campaign group insists that local authorities now have little say on how pupils are admitted to schools in their area because more than 70% of schools, including academies and faith schools, now act as their own admission authorities.[9] In a report of the Office of the Schools Adjudicator (OSA), published in January 2019, the chief adjudicator, Shan Scott, expressed concerns that admissions are becoming harder to police. She said there were 'less and less justifiable reasons' for schools turning away pupils with special needs, and she was concerned that some local authorities reported difficulty in establishing whether a child had or had not been previously looked after (which should give them priority admissions). She also noted that the proportion of children eligible for the pupil premium securing places at grammar schools had not increased in the ways for which she had hoped.[10]

In 2019, nearly one in five children did not get their first choice of secondary school. The much-publicised notion of parental choice, which has driven the academy and free school programme, turns out to be little more than a myth. According to DfE statistics, the proportion of children denied their preferred secondary school reached a 10-year high in 2019. As we have seen, the anxiety of parents desperate to secure a place at a good school is inevitably passed on to the child. The toxicity of the system, therefore, affects children before they have even walked through the school gates.

Departures

At the other end of the spectrum we have exclusions from school. These can be fixed term or permanent. Fixed-term exclusions are used by schools for a wide variety of reasons, usually to punish a child for a particular example of poor behaviour, or to allow them time to cool down before returning to the classroom, and they generally last only a few days. A permanent exclusion is much more serious and means that the child will not be allowed to return to the school at all. This means that he or she will either be transferred to another school, often some distance away, or placed in a pupil referral unit. When a pupil is permanently excluded, it sends a shock wave through the school which undoubtedly makes other pupils think about their behaviour; and the shock is all the more profound because permanent exclusions are seen as something of a rarity, only used by schools in extreme cases.

The reality is very different, however, and there are far more permanent exclusions than many of us realise. According to the DfE, the increase in permanent exclusions seen in recent years has slowed, with the number across all state-funded primary, secondary and special schools increasing slightly from 7,700 in 2016/17 to 7,900 in 2017/18. The rate may have slowed, but the numbers involved are eye-watering. Nearly 8,000 pupils are permanently excluded from mainstream schools every year.[11]

The reasons for permanent exclusion are fairly predictable: physical assault, threatening behaviour, bullying, racist abuse, sexual misconduct, drug or alcohol issues, damage, theft and persistent disruptive behaviour. With so many pupils permanently excluded, does this suggest that behaviour in schools is poor? In some schools, undoubtedly, but when one considers that 8,000 exclusions nationally equate to 10 pupils per 10,000, then things don't seem quite so bad. In fact, as Ofsted data confirms, standards of behaviour in English schools are remarkably good, despite the regular tabloid portraits of schools as dangerous hellholes. The vast majority of pupils in schools today are well behaved, polite, courteous to adults and engaged in their learning.

A great deal of pressure is exerted on schools not to exclude. This seems reasonable when one considers the damage such an exclusion can do to the education and life chances of the pupils involved. More often than not, these pupils need help and support: far too many are from disadvantaged backgrounds and many have special educational needs. On the other hand, it is important to remember that school leaders are tasked with providing good quality education to all pupils, and a child who poses a threat to others, or is constantly disruptive, is likely to have a negative impact on the rest of the class. This is something that is often overlooked in debates about permanent exclusion; the ordinary child who behaves well in class needs protecting from disruptive students, however extreme their needs.

The real problem with permanent exclusion, however, is not the numbers involved but the lack of provision. As described earlier, PRUs are bursting at the seams, and many are closing down due to a lack of funds. More and more permanently excluded pupils are being placed in schools where they are likely to repeat the same patterns of behaviour that led to their exclusion in the first place. It is also clear that schools are not equipped to cope with these pupils and, far too often, they are excluded again. At that point, the LA has to provide them with an education, but this often means a part-time place in an over-crowded PRU. Consequently, many simply drop out and do not attend.

The provision of education for permanently excluded pupils is a complex and sophisticated undertaking which must be properly funded. PRUs are the Cinderellas of the educational landscape, however, and MPs and councillors looking for budget cuts know full well that there will be fewer objections to cuts to PRUs than to mainstream schools. The education of disaffected youths who find school too challenging is one of the most neglected aspects of the entire system. It may not be a vote winner but, if we were to get it right, it could have a profound effect on both the children involved and society in general.

Under pressure not to exclude, schools began to suggest to parents that home education might be a good idea. Ofsted has begun to look more closely at this with a stronger focus on 'off-rolling' now part of the new inspection framework. It undoubtedly still happens, however, and it isn't always the school's fault. Many parents see home education as the best way of avoiding the stain of a permanent exclusion on a child's records, and far too many have simply given up on the education system altogether.

Home education is not just about excluded children, of course; it has been a long-established practice preferred by parents who choose to educate their children in their own way. It can be very successful, and there are extensive support networks which assist parents in educating children at home. The law is very accommodating: parents are fully entitled to home educate provided they make sure their children receive a full-time education from the age of 5. They don't have to follow the National Curriculum, though many of course do, and they are monitored with an extremely light touch. The council may make an informal enquiry to check that a child is getting a suitable education, but that is probably all that will happen. A school attendance order can be issued if the council feels that the child is not being educated appropriately, but these are rare and difficult to enforce.

The issue comes with the sheer numbers of children who have been withdrawn from school, estimated in 2019 to be around 60,000. The government is consulting on introducing a register of home-educated children, but this is likely to be resisted by the parents involved. Meanwhile, it is highly likely that thousands of children are not receiving any kind of genuine education at all.

Parents opt to home educate for all sorts of reasons, but more and more are choosing to do so because they regard schools today as oppressive, overly regimented and more interested in data than people. They see the anxiety that constant testing causes, and they worry about their children's mental health. The rise in the numbers of home-educated children may say more about the toxic classroom than the advantages of home education itself.

A final thought on age

The current structure of the education system in England is undoubtedly complicated and confused, thanks both to the academisation programme and the variety of schools already in existence. There is, however, one more complication with which parents have to deal: age on entry. We have already seen that children in England start school at a much younger age than children in most other parts of the world, but at each step of a child's career there are choices to be made. The old distinction between nursery, infant and junior schools is gradually disappearing as more and more primary schools establish pre-schools. This means that most children stay in the same school from the age of 2 or 3 until they are 11. However, infant and junior schools still survive in several parts of the country, meaning that parents have the chance to move their children to other schools at the various transition points.

As we approach secondary education, things become more complicated. Most children move up to secondary school when they are age 11, but there are still some secondary schools where the first year of entry is Year 8. Middle schools, where transition takes place at age 13, following the public school model of preparatory and senior schools, are also available. Indeed, the recent introduction of studio schools has reinforced age 13 as a transition point. At 16, pupils can choose to stay in the school's sixth form, if it has one, or move on to colleges of further education. Nor should we forget that children now have to stay in school longer than ever before. On 1 September 1972, the school leaving age was raised from 15 to 16, after preparations which had begun in 1964. From 2015, this was effectively raised to 18. Pupils can leave school at 16, but they must stay in some form of full-time education. They can join the sixth form, move to the local FE college, take up an apprenticeship or traineeship, or spend 20 hours or more a week working or volunteering while in part-time education or training.

Parents, already bewildered by the choice of schools available, also have to re-think their choices again and again as their children grow up. Parental choice can lead to frequent changes of school for their children. If they are lucky, children move from primary school to a secondary school with a sixth form; they could, however, move from nursery to infants school, to a primary or junior school, then on to a middle school, then to a senior school or studio school, and then on to FE college. For children already working under the considerable stress of the current accountability culture, frequent changes of school add yet another layer of unnecessary anxiety.

There is a significant body of research which suggests that changing school too often leads not only to poorer academic performance but, more worryingly, to feelings of low self-esteem and a sense of social defeat. A well-known study, published in the *American Academy of Child and Adolescent Psychiatry*, but based on data from the southwest of England, found that children who have moved school three times or more before the age of 12 are 60% more likely to display at least one psychotic symptom.[12] Feelings of being excluded, which often come with moving school frequently, can heighten the risk of psychotic-like symptoms in vulnerable individuals. Students who move school regularly could also be more prone to being involved with bullying, another factor that is linked to these symptoms.

Perhaps, therefore, all-through schools are the solution: one school where children stay put from the age of 4 until they are 18. In other words, from Year 1 to year 13. In 2009 there were only 13 of these schools in the country, but the free school programme has seen their numbers rise rapidly in recent years. Advocates of all-through schools say that they have significant advantages over more traditional structures. Pupils in all-through schools have access to specialist subject tuition in the early stages of their education, and this means that they are able to progress at a quicker pace. The problem of the dip in performance between primary and secondary level is also avoided. Above all, pupils stay put, and this has an important impact on their well-being and their mental health.

Whether it is the type of school or age on entry, it is clear that reform of the English system is desperately needed. It too complicated and too susceptible to political interference. Above all, the needs of the child get left behind in the rush to innovate.

What can schools do now to put things right?

- **Assert independence.** Whether a school is maintained by the LA, or part of an academy chain, school leaders must ensure that the school retains its own individuality and ethos. This many involve fighting hard against local or national pressure to conform, but the best schools develop their own identities.

- **Work with others.** The most successful schools are those that work with the schools around them to achieve the best outcomes for pupils.

- **Think it through.** Academisation may well be the right choice for some schools, but it can be a disaster for others. A major change such as the switch from LA control to an academy chain can have long-lasting consequences and therefore needs to be considered with the utmost care. Governing bodies should be encouraged to take fully impartial advice before committing to a change. The change is, after all, irreversible.

- **Take care with admissions and exclusions.** The admission system is deeply flawed, and exclusions are becoming increasingly contentious. Schools therefore need to ensure that they follow the admissions code to the letter and the school's exclusion policy as closely as possible.

- **Take care with home education.** Great care needs to be taken when discussing home education with parents. It is important to keep careful records at every stage, particularly those which demonstrate what the school has done to address any concerns about the quality of education provided which may have led to the decision to home educate. Although the headteacher may well want to suggest home education as a potential solution, this needs to be done with great care.

What should policymakers do to put things right?

- The current system of education in England is confused and chaotic. There are too many types of schools, too many layers of governance and too much ideological experimentation. The system is in urgent need of review.

- Provide appropriate funding for special schools and PRUs.

- Review the admissions process in the light of increasing complexity in the system.

- Reconsider the role of grammar and faith schools.

- Create a national register of home-educated pupils and ensure that regular checks are put in place to make sure that they are actually receiving an education.

Notes

1. New Schools Network. 2018. *DfE Invites Top Universities to Open Specialist Maths Free Schools*, 26 March. www.newschoolsnetwork.org/what-are-free-schools/free-school-news/dfe-invites-top-universities-to-open-specialist-maths-free
2. NFER Systems and Structures. www.nfer.ac.uk/key-topics-expertise/systems-structures/
3. DfE. 2017. *Multi-Academy Trust Performance Measures: 2015 to 2016*, January. www.gov.uk/government/statistics/multi-academy-trust-performance-measures-2015-to-2016
4. K. Wespiester. 2018. NFER, *Spotlight on Multi-Academy Trusts: Pupil Outcomes*, January. www.nfer.ac.uk/news-events/nfer-blogs/spotlight-on-multi-academy-trusts-pupil-outcomes/
5. The Secular Society. 2019. *No More Faith Schools*, October. www.secularism.org.uk/faith-schools/
6. A. Speilman. Speech Delivered 1 February 2018. *Transcript*. www.gov.uk/government/speeches/amanda-spielmans-speech-at-the-church-of-england-foundation-for-education-leadership
7. Commons select committee summary article: *Government's Special Educational Needs Reforms Failing Young People and Parents*. www.parliament.uk/business/committees/committees-a-z/commons-select/education-committee/news-parliament-2017/send-report-published-19-20/
8. Ibid.
9. The Comprehensive Future website. https://comprehensivefuture.org.uk
10. Office of the Schools Adjudicator Annual Report, December 2018. https://assets.publishing.service.gov.uk/government/uploads/system/uploads/attachment_data/file/771529/OSA_annual_report_September_2017_to_August_2018.pdf
11. DfE. 2019. *Permanent and Fixed Period Exclusions in England: 2017 to 2018*, July. https://assets.publishing.service.gov.uk/government/uploads/system/uploads/attachment_data/file/820773/Permanent_and_fixed_period_exclusions_2017_to_2018_-_main_text.pdf
12. S.P. Singh, C. Winsper, D. Wolke & A. Bryson. 2014. *School Mobility and Prospective Pathways to Psychotic-Like Symptoms in Early Adolescence: A Prospective Birth Cohort Study*. www.jaacap.org/article/S0890-8567(14)00095-1/fulltext

7 A wider view

It should be clear by now that children in schools pursue their education in a vortex of change. Teachers and school leaders have long been accustomed to protecting pupils from external influences, but there comes a point when it is simply impossible to shield them completely. As we have seen, the rate of change in schools has accelerated in recent years, and it is undoubtedly accurate to describe the current rate as extreme. In the last 10 years, pupils have been subject to significant curriculum change, including the introduction of the Ebacc; new examination specifications; a new Ofsted framework; new accountability measures which impact directly on what they learn in the classroom; radical new school structures; the raising of the school leaving age to 18; frequent pedagogical experimentation; and the complexities of a new world of instant communication and social media. Is it any wonder, therefore, that the mental health of young people is often described as reaching a crisis point? But how did it get like this, and is there anything that can be done about it?

This chapter explores some of the broader issues underlying the pace of change in schools before we move on in the next chapter to consider what a new, more stable education system might look like. Beginning with a consideration of the erosion of the learning culture in schools today and, indeed, society in general, it explores the impact of social care provision in the classroom before examining the often-overlooked effects of nationalism on the education system. This may seem to be an exceptionally broad agenda, but education sits at the heart of society and, in many ways, society's attitudes to education say a huge amount about how a country sees itself and how it cares for its children.

What happened to the learning culture?

A few years ago, I interviewed a group of very bright 17-year-olds in a school in Finland, and I asked them about their career plans. 'A lot depends on how well I do this year', said one of them. 'If I do well, I might think about medicine or the law. If I do really well, I might train to become a teacher'. The fact that teaching was considered to be such a high-status profession was something of a surprise, to say the least. I cannot imagine a sixth former in an English school answering in the same way. I asked the student to expand on her answer, and it became clear that teachers were held in high regard in Finish society. Consequently, there is very little government interference in Finish schools, very little public testing, no league tables and no equivalent of Ofsted. Teachers are trusted to get on with the job, and the brightest graduates see teaching as a natural career choice.

Things are very different in the UK. Although parents and politicians pay lip service to the valuable work of teachers, in practice, teaching is increasingly regarded as a low status profession. Teachers are regularly reviled in the tabloid press; their views are rarely taken into account when key educational decisions are being made; and schools are dramatically underfunded. Teachers regularly complain about the excessive workload and pay that simply doesn't compare with other professions, and the rise of social media has meant that hyper-vigilant parents are ready to complain at the drop of a hat. It is hardly surprising, therefore, that fewer and fewer graduates choose teaching as a career, and the numbers of teachers who leave the profession within their first few years continues to rise year on year.

If teachers are undervalued, can the same be said about education generally? Part of the problem here is the increasingly dysfunctional relationship between learning and qualifications. Such is the significance accorded to examination results at all stages – from key stage 2 tests to GCSEs and A-levels – the purpose of schooling has shifted from learning about the world, whether through literature, science, languages or the arts, to learning to pass examinations. In many schools, teachers feel compelled to start thinking about addressing the demands of examination specifications as soon as children walk through the door. The notion that things can be learned simply for the love of learning has been banished from the classroom; the only things that need to be learned are those that meet the requirements of the examination boards. Once the examination has been passed, the learning becomes irrelevant. In a system where teachers are held accountable at almost every stage – from the early learning goals, via the phonics test, the multiplication test, tests at key stages 1 and 2, through to GCSEs and A-levels – an intense focus on examination outcomes is inevitable. From the moment they enter the classroom, children are taught to prepare for examinations. It is hardly surprising therefore that they quickly begin to regard examination preparation as the sole purpose of education. Parents too, worried about how well their children will do at every stage, are encouraged to see examination success as the only criterion by which to judge schools and teachers.

As we have seen, current accountability measures impact directly on children's learning as they shape what is taught in the classroom. The introduction of the Ebacc and Progress 8 measures have driven down the numbers of children following courses in the arts, for example, and, indeed, driven out vocational courses from many schools almost entirely. Furthermore, the intense focus on

STEM subjects has served to devalue large areas of the curriculum, meaning that not only is examination success vital to a child's life chances, but it is success in a very particular subset of examinations that is now required.

School leaders and teachers who cannot deliver in terms of examination success are regarded as having failed, and the fact that not all children achieve 'expected standards' in primary schools or 'good passes' in their GCSEs provides the evidence. Thanks to the current accountability measures, politicians have convinced parents that schools are not good enough and that teachers are failing. The fact that teachers are better trained, more qualified, more committed and harder working than ever before is rarely acknowledged. Parents have become snow blind in a blizzard of examination statistics.

Social media, which offers instant communication coupled with a cloak of anonymity, has made complaining endemic in contemporary society and, unsurprisingly, teachers and school leaders now find themselves subject to a constant stream of complaints. The image of the class teacher as a highly respected figure in the local community is long gone, and many parents now feel empowered to complain about the service offered in schools in the same way that they might complain to a retail store about a faulty washing machine. Similarly, headteachers were once regarded as high-status professionals, with a secure place in the local community alongside doctors and magistrates. This is far from the case now. As a headteacher, I regularly had to deal with parents arriving at school and demanding to see me straightaway, and I often wondered whether they would burst in upon their GP, their bank manager or their solicitor in the same way. Headteachers who are new in post are often surprised by how little respect they are accorded not only by parents who hurl abuse at them but by the local community where the image of feckless teachers who are always on holiday has firmly taken hold, thanks largely to the portrayal of teaching in the press.

Some factors contributing to the loss of the learning culture in schools are attributable neither to schools nor politicians but rather to changes in society generally. The value of reading is a good example. A huge amount of work has gone into making sure children learn to read. Reading is a key feature of testing in primary schools, and the new Ofsted framework insists that every primary school inspection will involve a 'deep dive' into the teaching of reading. And yet, fewer and fewer children read for pleasure. It is not difficult to see why: books face stiff competition from social media, video streaming and computer games. Even the most bookish children still spend huge amounts of time online. Teachers encourage children to read and to read more widely, but in primary schools they are reading to be tested and in secondary schools the only reading they feel they need to do is based on the set texts and textbooks required for the examinations.

Of course, children read a great deal online, and many read via kindle or listen to audiobooks, but the act of sitting quietly in a room reading a whole text is seen by most children as something desperately old fashioned and almost quaint. Why would they do it when so much is available online? Why would they read so much when much shorter texts are available? Young people are growing up in a world of soundbites and instant messaging. Longer texts have become a challenge. A student might tackle one if there is an examination involved, but why would he or she do it for pleasure? It is, of course, possible to argue that children are still reading but in different ways, and that they are learning a whole new skill set enabling them to thrive in the online world, but the loss of reading for pleasure, and reading in depth over time, is bound to have an impact on the way children learn. The contemplative hour with a book, where the reader has to use his or her imagination to construct the writer's world, has been replaced by the instant dazzle of an online fantasy world which appears at the touch of a button.

It is hardly the child's fault, therefore, that reading has lost some of its appeal, but we must acknowledge the fact that the education system has not yet adapted to take account of the new ways young people interact with the world. The digital revolution has undoubtedly had a profound effect on our learning culture, and it has happened incredibly quickly. It should therefore be a priority for educators to learn to adapt in order to preserve a genuine culture of learning in schools. The learning will be different, but it should be at the heart of the education system. And learning, however it is done, should always take precedence over examinations.

Another factor influencing the loss of the learning culture is the intensity of the focus on education for industry. For many, the purpose of the school system is to prepare children for employment. This is surely an intensely regressive view of education. Whenever politicians announce a consultation period for a new educational initiative, the involvement of industry is always stressed. It is up to industrialists to determine the skills commercial businesses require to become more successful and more profitable, the skills needed to compete in global markets. Occasionally, initiatives emerge which suggest a wider view – the recent promotion of character education is a good example – but it is hard not to conclude that most politicians see education in stark economic terms.

As we have seen, the curriculum in schools points relentlessly to a university education, with an increasing emphasis on STEM subjects. The teleology of education is therefore economic success. The idea that education should be about imparting knowledge to develop character has been subsumed by economic imperatives. Of course, the tension between these competing objectives is hardly new. Socrates argued that the purpose of education was to draw out what was already in the student: 'I cannot teach anybody anything, I can only make them think', he declared. This idea is, of course, captured in the Latin 'educere', to lead out. The Sophists, however, promised to give students the necessary knowledge and skills they would need to gain positions in the city-state. This is a tension that will always be with us, but it is not hard to see that current policy favours the Sophists' view of education as a means of shaping young people to play their part in the nation's economy.

Ironically, the skills demanded by industrialists are rarely the skills they look for when interviewing for new recruits. The great finance houses, for example, still favour classicists and PPE graduates over students who have studied business and finance. Most employers look for candidates who are bright, articulate, hard-working and ready to learn. Certain professions obviously require degrees in relevant disciplines – law, medicine and so on – but the majority of employers look for employees prepared to learn the skills they will need to contribute to the company in question. In a sense, degree subjects are often irrelevant. The young people they appoint are fully rounded individuals, not economic units. It might therefore be true to say that employability is not really about proven ability in a particular STEM-based skill set but more to do with enthusiasm for learning and the ability to learn. These are attributes which will equip young people to deal with life in general, not just employment. Ayn Rand put it succinctly:

> The only purpose of education is to teach a student how to live his life – by developing his mind and equipping him to deal with reality. The training he needs is theoretical, i.e., conceptual. He has to be taught to think, to understand, to integrate, to prove. He has to be taught the essentials of the knowledge discovered in the past – and he has to be equipped to acquire further knowledge by his own effort.[1]

Education, childcare or social service?

An increasingly important factor contributing to the diminution of the learning culture in schools pertains to the enormous range of additional functions schools are now expected to perform. Education is no longer simply a matter of teaching children the subjects specified in the National Curriculum; education now encompasses safeguarding, pastoral support, citizenship, health education, social care and, cynics might add, child-minding. The information which the Ofsted handbook insists that school leaders must provide before an inspection exemplifies the range and complexity of the services schools are now required to perform. Headteachers are asked to provide:

- records and analysis of exclusions, pupils taken off roll, incidents of poor behaviour and any use of internal isolation

- the single central record for the school

- records and analysis of sexual harassment or sexual violence

- records and analysis of bullying, discriminatory and prejudiced behaviour, either directly or indirectly, including racist, sexist, disability and homophobic/biphobic/transphobic bullying, use of derogatory language and racist incidents

- a list of referrals made to the designated person for safeguarding in the school and those who were subsequently referred to the local authority, along with brief details of the resolution

- a list of all pupils who have open cases with children's services/social care and for whom there is a multi-agency plan
- up-to-date attendance analysis for all groups of pupils[2]

This is a fairly comprehensive list, but it is, of course, only part of the story. Schools have become responsible for the care of the child, not just his or her education.

Teachers in schools today are expected not only to deal with but be experts in a wide range of personal and social issues. To be a good subject or class teacher is no longer enough; teaching is now as much about care as it is about imparting knowledge. New entrants to the profession are often surprised, and sometimes overwhelmed, by the range of tasks expected of them and, indeed, the levels of responsibility thrust upon them in the classroom. The naïve graduate who joins the profession to pass on his or her love of history or English literature finds that a huge amount of time is spent on activities once considered the realm of parents, social services or health professionals.

Early years teachers have always been aware of their duty as carers, but they are increasingly being asked to deal with children who enter school not yet potty trained, for example. More and more frequently, schools are expected not only to parent children, but to provide the intimate care formerly the preserve of health workers. Moreover, the increase in the number of students with severe special needs admitted to mainstream schools has meant that intimate care can be required of school staff at all levels of education.

Intimate care may be an extreme example, but the role of teachers as carers takes many forms. First, there are the duties surrounding safeguarding. It is fairly obvious that teachers and school leaders need to ensure that children are safe in school, but the extent of teachers' safeguarding responsibilities seems to grow year on year. Pupils can expect to be provided with a safe environment, where behaviour is good and bullying is rare, but teachers are now required to ensure that they are kept safe in dozens of other ways. Teachers are now trained to identify children who may be showing signs of mental health problems; they have to look out for those who are self-harming or at risk of anorexia; they have to report any signs that a child may be being abused or groomed; they are expected to be aware of children who may have been victims of female genital mutilation, or have been forced into arranged marriages; they are alert for signs of radicalisation; and they are constantly vigilant about the effects of drugs on students' behaviour in class. In addition, knife crime and county lines' drug gangs are hot topics in more and more schools.

In addition to teaching his or her specialism, teachers are expected to deliver lessons in subjects such as Personal, Social and Health Education (PSHE) and citizenship. Sex and Relationship Education (SRE) is also a compulsory part of the school curriculum, and Ofsted inspections always involve a consideration of pupils' spiritual, moral, social and cultural development (SMSC). In many schools, PSHE is a timetabled subject, though it is rarely taught by specialists. Teachers often find that they have to teach PSHE as part of their role as form tutors. In addition, many schools have detailed tutorial programmes which classroom teachers are expected to deliver, and school leaders work hard to ensure that key aspects of safeguarding are delivered via assemblies and on days when the timetable is suspended. For a school to cover all aspects of safeguarding, citizenship and PSHE careful planning is required and classroom teachers are expected to play a key part in delivering the wrap around care which society now demands of its schools.

As we saw in the chapters on curriculum, some aspects of the wider role of schools are particularly controversial, with critics arguing that teachers are forced to move beyond education to indoctrination. Religious education is a key area of contention, but recent initiatives, such as the teaching of fundamental British values (FBV), seem to suggest that the role of teachers is not only to protect the safety of children but to encourage them to adopt particular political ideologies. For many, FBV takes citizenship a step too far, arguing that it is not the job of the school to promote a particular version of Britishness.

In addition to their safeguarding responsibilities, and the teaching of PSHE and citizenship, teachers are expected to get involved with a wide range of extra-curricular activities. Such involvement is not, of course, compulsory, but it is undoubtedly expected. A teacher who refuses to run lunchtime clubs or go on trips is unlikely to progress far in the profession. Consequently, on top of a full teaching load, most teachers take responsibility for lunchtime or after-school activities, they plan visits, and they often give up their holidays to take children on residential trips both in the UK and abroad. Of course, parents often characterise such trips as holidays for the teacher, but anyone who has supervised a school trip will know how far from the truth this actually is. Most teachers accompany trips because they want to support the school and help their pupils learn.

Schools also offer additional services such as nurseries, breakfast clubs, nurture rooms and summer schools. Schools which offer childcare in the mornings and the evenings are increasingly popular with parents, and most schools now offer such services if they possibly can.

Of course, all of this is enormously positive. Children are safer in schools than they have ever been before; they are offered more opportunities than ever before; and parents benefit hugely from the care schools provide. But the development of the caring and social responsibilities of schools has undoubtedly led to a change in the culture of education. Asserting the pre-eminence of learning is therefore becoming increasingly difficult, especially when schools begin to look more like health and social centres than centres of learning.

Educating for global citizenship

There has also been a change in the way schools are encouraged to see themselves in relation to the rest of the world and this, too, has had an impact on what happens in the classroom. Education often reflects the way a nation sees itself and, as we have seen, schools are often regarded as part of the solution to national problems. There is no doubt that in recent years the UK, and England in particular, has begun to struggle with its place in the world. With many wedded to the belief that England is still an international superpower, there is clearly a need for the country to assert itself on the global stage. The political chaos engendered by the vote to leave the European Union is symptomatic of this uncertainty, but more worrying for many is the threat posed by China and the east. Although it would be easy to disregard the effect of international politics on schools, there is undoubtedly a strong link between high-level political concerns and the curriculum shaping learning in the classroom.

The legacy of empire, when Britain was supposedly a great nation, has a powerful effect on a society which clings to its monarchy, admires its aristocracy, ensures that it is led by public school boys and is deeply suspicious of potential rivals. Distrust of the French, for example, is something of a national hobby, and the French are often portrayed in the tabloid press as the untrustworthy scoundrels depicted by Shakespeare in *Henry V*. Similarly, although the Second World War ended nearly 80 years ago, and our enemies are now our closest allies, we hang on to the view of Germany as an enemy state. The result of this confused mix of patriotism and jingoism is a National Curriculum that specifies a combination of subjects that wouldn't be out of place in a 19th-century public school.

As we have seen, the most recent curriculum changes have reasserted the value of pre-20th-century literature in the English GCSE specifications, and the history curriculum has been redesigned to focus on key historical events which emphasise Britain's role as a great nation. Moreover, increasing national uncertainty about what it means to be British has led directly to the introduction of (FBV, a crude attempt to reassert British values and, by implication, British greatness. Although FBV was undoubtedly driven by changes in society as a result of immigration, the values to be asserted have more than a tinge of empire. In effect, they are a gentleman's code of conduct dressed up in contemporary liberal terminology.

Many still regard Westminster as the beating heart of empire, despite the fact that the British empire no longer exists. The political and social structures that enabled Britain to hold sway over a quarter of the world still exist, and, for many, the mindset remains the same. Consequently, the image of Britain's greatness is firmly embedded in the national psyche, making it difficult for many to regard our European allies as equals. The introduction of the Ebacc, FBV, and the heavily revised GCSE syllabuses can therefore be seen as an attempt to reassert Britain's greatness in the minds of young people growing up in a world where that greatness is far from self-evident.

If historical confusion over our relationship with Europe is not worrying enough, recent years have seen the appearance of a more serious threat. The rise of Asian nations, and in particular China, has had a huge impact not only on the British economy but on the way Britain understands its place in the world. The rivalry over global supremacy, which was once played out amongst European nations, has now widened to involve the mysterious east, a part of the world which the west has always regarded as distinctly other and definitely irrelevant. The increasing dominance of Asia is clearly apparent both economically and politically, and this dominance is reflected in the success of Asian youngsters in international test results. For British politicians, the PISA tests symbolise both the intellectual and the economic threat posed by Asian nations, and just as the legacy of empire led to the introduction of FBV, concerns over our youngsters' performance in the tests has led to an intense focus on STEM subjects, and mathematics in particular. It is almost as if success in the PISA tests will enable Britain to reassert itself on the national stage.

Although seemingly distant from international politics, schools are directly influenced by national concerns. Confusion over national identity has had a profound impact not only on the curriculum but on the culture and ambition of school communities. The attitude of young people to learning languages is a good example. Despite the introduction of the Ebacc, fewer and fewer students are choosing to study languages, a decline which is stark at A-level. School sixth forms are finding it harder and harder to offer language A-levels, and equally difficult to recruit language teachers. The perceived difficulty of language learning is a factor here – and this has not been helped by the examination boards making it harder and harder for students to achieve the top grades – but the real problem, of course, is the British, or more correctly, the English attitude to other nations. As politicians insist on re-asserting Britain's greatness, it seems obvious that the only language students need to learn is English. This view is, of course, reinforced by the dominance of English as the international language of commerce and diplomacy, even though the version of English spoken most widely in international meetings is closer to American English, and the lack of appeal of foreign languages in terms of their role in the media. A student in a French school will be keen to learn English in order to appreciate American movies and American pop culture; a student in England has no such incentive. Nevertheless, the most powerful influence here is the notion that England is the most important country in the world, and English the dominant language. In turn, despite the efforts of teachers and leaders, this has led to the rise of an unpleasant jingoism in schools, an approach undoubtedly bolstered by the current political focus of the National Curriculum and FBV.

There is, of course, a huge irony in young people's rejection of language study since most youngsters regard themselves as global citizens. They have grown up in a digitally connected world, they make friends and play online games with people from dozens of other countries, many travel abroad regularly, and they are intensely aware that Britain is now a multi-cultural society. They are also deeply concerned about climate change and the impact of global warming. Most would undoubtedly regard themselves as global citizens and yet, such is the power of political ideology and its reach into the classroom, their thinking, often subconsciously, is still underpinned by traditional notions of Englishness. The confluence of contemporary political ideology and globalism in English classrooms has led to a strange hybrid: small island globalism.

What can schools do now to put things right?

- **Establish a learning culture.** Is there a genuine learning culture in the school, or is it dominated by testing and assessment? Putting examination performance aside, it is important to consider exactly what constitutes a learning culture and to what extent it can be enhanced. What do leaders, teachers and pupils do to celebrate learning?

- **Develop a social media policy.** Managing social media is becoming more and more important in today's society. Schools should regularly review their social media policies. It is also important to make sure that skilled staff are in place to help create a positive digital footprint for the school and to deal with negative feedback effectively.

- **Insist on support.** Schools are being asked to do more and more social work nowadays. School leaders must insist that adequate support is provided, and they must fight hard to ensure that their demands are taken seriously. School leaders must protect staff from having to provide unreasonable levels of support.

- **Promote global citizenship.** The current DfE model is distinctly biased towards Englishness. Schools should balance this model by promoting global citizenship wherever possible. Young people today see themselves as citizens of the world, and education must respond accordingly. In a multi-cultural society, a global perspective is surely vital.

What should policymakers do to put things right?

- Politicians need to recognise that the role of teachers is to teach. They are not carers. Funding must be put in place to ensure that social services are available to support schools in dealing with children who need help which goes beyond day-to-day pastoral care.

- The knee-jerk reaction of politicians who, when asked for a solution to a particular social problem reply that schools will be directed to amend their curriculums to deal with it, should be avoided. Schools are not always the answer.

Notes

1. A. Rand & P. Schwartz. 2019. *Return of the Primitive: The Anti-Industrial Revolution*, London, Penguin, Putnam Inc., p. 88.
2. Ofsted. 2019. *School Inspection Handbook*, May, Updated November 2019, p. 16.

8 A vision for the future

There is a certain irony in the fact that a book about the damaging effects of change must inevitably suggest more change, but I think it is clear that things cannot carry on as they are. Change is necessary to bring about stability, and stability is what the education system desperately needs. Some changes need to be radical; others less so. Much can be achieved, however, by simply putting an end to the unnecessary practices which divert teachers' attention away from teaching and learning. Similarly, if education could be distanced and protected from political interference, a huge amount could be achieved.

Of course, looking to the future is no easy task. As we have seen, education is a complex and sophisticated undertaking, and any vision for the future needs to take this into account. If we construct a system from scratch, we still need to think about the nature and purpose of schools, types of schools, school structures, the aims of the curriculum and its contents, the age at which children start and leave school, governance structures, the role of parents, the timings of the school day, how teachers are trained, their workload and the extent of their responsibilities. The list is nearly endless. However, we would also need to start with a fundamental vision: schools are about learning and the development of a love of learning. With that in mind, what might a re-imagined system of schooling in the UK look like?

Independent, grammar and faith schools

In an ideal system, there should be a good local school for every child. This is something that all parents and most politicians would agree about, and many of the changes introduced over the last half a century have used this mantra to initiate change. However, as always, some of the fundamental issues are often swept under the carpet as they carry too much political baggage. The role of independent schools is a good example.

Independent schools fundamentally distort the education system in this country. Although only around 7% of the population attend independent schools, the effect on the system is profound. As soon as a child is moved away from his or her local school, the dynamic and the social mix of that school changes; if the child is then granted privileges unavailable to other children, then the effects are magnified. The result is obvious: the creation of a superior social elite which goes on to occupy key roles in society, top jobs in the professions, and to have an influence on the political life of the country which cannot be underestimated. It is a superiority, however, not based solely on better educational provision – superb facilities, small classes, intense individual support – but on the effective creation of a club where access is granted only to the privileged few. In their heart of hearts, the parents of children at independent schools know this, and that's why they are prepared to pay for something which is free for all. They also know, though they are unlikely to admit it, that they are not paying for better teaching, or a better educational experience, they are paying for exclusivity, protection from less affluent families and an entrée into a social milieu beyond the reach of most of us.

In many of the more sophisticated international school systems, independent education is rare, and the quality of education in mainstream schools is all the better as a result. In Britain, and England in particular, public schools have a protected status equivalent to that of the monarchy or National Trust properties. Logical arguments regarding their damaging effects on society as a whole therefore fall at the first hurdle confronted by nostalgia and Englishness. If politicians genuinely want to improve education for all, then independent schools must be abolished. How much better would state-maintained schools be if political and business elites had to send their children to the local school?

Grammar schools have a similarly corrosive effect on the educational system. There may be no payment involved, but charges of exclusivity and privilege still apply. The principle of selection may seem fair to some, but selection also means rejection. The 10% or so of local children who successfully achieve grammar school places immediately define themselves against those who were unsuccessful. They are assumed to have gained places at 'better' schools even though, as we have seen, many grammar schools offer particularly poor standards of education. They are better simply because they have brighter students who are much more likely to do well. Although in a diluted form compared to independent schools, social privilege is also a factor here. What most delights parents is the thought that their children will be with other bright children – and for bright, read middle class – and protected against the rougher elements of society.

No doubt convincing arguments can be put forward for the retention of both grammar and independent schools, but it is impossible to ignore the impact they have on the maintained schools around them. A comprehensive school which loses a proportion of its intake, no matter how small, to independent and grammar schools is no longer comprehensive. In some parts of the country, where the middle classes have deserted their local schools en masse, comprehensive schools have become *ipso facto* secondary moderns. In order to create a fair and equitable education system, therefore, the principle of a local school for every child must be paramount, even if this means the abolition of both independent and grammar schools.

But what about faith schools? The issues undoubtedly become more sensitive here, but surely the same principle applies. If children are removed from the mainstream system, then that system is distorted. Religious groups argue that they have the right to practise their faith and to bring their children up in that faith, but it does not mean that they have the right to segregation, which is what, after all, faith-based education means. Many argue, of course, that religion should play no part in schools; schools should be secular organisations where children are taught about faith but not a particular faith. In a multi-cultural society, surely the overriding consideration should be integration? In communities where pupils of all faiths and cultures spend time together in the classroom on a day-to-day basis integration is much more likely; where children of particular faiths are segregated in religious schools, they are regarded with suspicion and, sometimes, fear.

Structural confusion

If the first step towards a fairer system is the abolition of independent, grammar and faith schools, the next is surely to iron out some of the structural confusion built into mainstream education. As we saw in Chapter 6, there is a bewildering variety of non-selective school types from which parents can choose. Depending upon where they live, they may have access to comprehensive schools, secondary moderns, city technology colleges, studio schools and so on. They may also have a choice of schools catering for widely differing age ranges: nursery schools, infant schools, primaries, juniors, middle schools, age 11 to 16 schools, age 11 to 18 schools, sixth form colleges, and, of course, all-through schools. The nature of governance can also vary from school to school. Although the majority of secondary schools are now academies and therefore run by trusts, there is a wide variety of other forms of governance available: community schools, co-operatives, foundation schools, voluntary aided schools, and free schools. Some schools retain close links with their local authorities; others are more independent. Some academies are stand-alone schools, or orphan academies (as they are entertainingly named in some quarters), and some are linked to large multi-academy trusts.

Logic suggests that this chaotic system is in desperate need of rationalisation. There are clearly too many different types of school in existence. The obvious answer, therefore, is a move towards one type of school. Is there really any need for such complexity in the system? Do children really benefit from access to free schools, or studio schools, for example? The aim should surely be a good school for every child based on a standard pattern. This does not necessarily mean suffocating uniformity – a school would be able to adapt to the local context and thus develop a distinctive ethos – but in terms of their design, governance and educational ambitions, schools should surely be constituted according to a basic pattern which is understood by all. More to the point, that pattern should be based on the educational needs of the child and not the ideological whims of politicians.

If the aim, therefore, is a good local school for every child, then the way to achieve it is to create one type of school that caters for everyone. A simple thought, certainly, but one that is far from easy to achieve. First, we have to ask the question, what do we mean by every child? Can a local, mainstream school really cater for children of all abilities, from those with severe learning difficulties to the very brightest; from children who are happy to conform and ready to socialise to those with behavioural and social issues? And what about children with specific medical needs?

For the purposes of our argument, let us consider one potential solution: the school campus model. This is a model that assumes a large site with either an all-through school or closely linked primary and secondary schools at the centre, with specialist satellite schools equipped to cater for a wide range of needs. However, though an excellent idea, and a splendid vision, campus schools raise all sorts of difficult questions which local communities would need to resolve. For a campus structure to work, the school must be located at the centre of a large population, so that economies of scale are possible, and to ensure that specialist support is both available and well used. But how would this work in rural communities, where populations are dispersed and small village schools predominate? Many people are passionate supporters of their local village schools, although the arguments against such institutions are often quite strong in terms of the quality of provision and access to high-quality facilities, and it would be difficult to encourage them to send their children to a large campus which is likely to be miles away from home. A different model is clearly required: groups of schools with central specialist provision. In urban areas, the campus provides the solution; in rural areas, an extended campus or hub could be the answer. Already, of course, we are moving away from the notion of one type of school and, if we were to consider other aspects of educational access and provision, I am sure we would find ourselves looking for additional models to solve the issues which would undoubtedly arise. This does not mean, of course, that we should abandon the notion of a single school type; it merely means that we should stick to it as closely as possible.

We also need to consider the problem of catchment areas. Because of the extreme differences in the social make-up of local communities, schools are bound to attract varied intakes depending upon their location. A comprehensive located in a leafy suburb will obviously attract a very different intake compared to one in a deprived inner-city area. At the moment, these differences are exaggerated by what has been termed 'middle class drift', with well-off parents whose closest school serves a deprived area seeking places at schools in areas they find less intimidating in terms of social composition. The result is a fairly polarised system where social class ends up being reflected in the performance figures of the schools concerned. By insisting that children attend their local school, these differences can be lessened but they will always be there. One solution is perhaps to construct the educational equivalent of electoral districts in order to achieve a balanced social mix; another, and this has already been tried in some schools, is to insist that schools take pupils from all social classes and all attainment bands. Ultimately, however, the solution must lie with the quality of teaching and the degree of support available. Schools in poorer areas need strong support in order to tackle not only the social problems holding children back but their lack of social capital.

Keeping in mind the fundamental principle of a good local school for every child, and assuming that such schools are not only possible but desirable, we now need to consider the age at which children attend the various stages of their education.

Age and stage

When should children start school? As we have seen this is a contentious issue and one that attracts strong arguments on both sides, though these are not always to do with a child's readiness for learning. Many argue that children need to start school as early as possible. This means that they will learn to socialise much more quickly, they will become independent and their learning will be led by experts, rather than in the ad hoc way they might learn at home from their parents. An early start also means that children from poorer families, where social capital may be weak, will have the support they need in order to keep up with their more fortunate peers. Advocates of social equality are generally very supportive of early schooling. On the other hand, there are strong arguments to suggest that children should stay at home with their parents for much longer. This not only strengthens parental bonds but allows children to develop a stronger sense of self, security and belonging. In addition, there is very little evidence to suggest that children in countries where school starts much later, at age 7 for example, underperform in the later stages of their school careers.

There is, of course, an economic argument here. The current structure of the UK economy means that families depend upon two incomes and, for most parents, it is simply unrealistic for one parent to give up work for more than a year or so. The decision to send a child to school, whether it is to a childminder or a nursery, is driven by economics and not necessarily the educational benefits to the child. Unless a much more supportive parental leave system is introduced, this is likely to remain the case for the foreseeable future. An early start is therefore almost inevitable.

Assuming an early start, we now need to consider the various age divisions in schools. Are there any advantages to changing schools at particular ages? Is an infants/juniors/secondary school model any better than a simple primary/secondary approach? Do children benefit more from changing schools at age 11 in the standard model, or is the middle school model where they move on to upper schools at age 13 any better? And how effective are all-through schools? In many ways, these are impossible questions to answer. There is some evidence to suggest that children in middle schools underperform in their key stage 2 tests compared to those in primary schools, but the stakes are much higher in primaries and the tests are accorded much less importance in middles. More to the point, this is a comparison based on accountability structures and not the quality of teaching and learning.

Ultimately, the key point here is that in order to create a more effective, less fragmented system, a standard approach needs to be agreed. This will avoid the confusion outlined in Chapter 6 where we saw that parents potentially have to make decisions about which school to send their children to at the ages of 4, 5, 7, 9, 11, 13 and 16. A local school for every child therefore depends upon more consistent patterns in terms of age and transfer between schools. It could be argued that it doesn't matter whether it's a primary/secondary system or an all-through system, but the confusion needs to be ironed out if the focus is to be on the classroom rather than the institution.

It might, of course, be better to take a more objective view without a preferred structure in mind. This would involve a careful consideration of both what and how children learn at the various stages in their education. We may not be able to determine the best time for children to start school, but it should be possible to use research evidence to consider the most effective ways to structure subsequent learning. A lot of work has been done on the teaching of reading, for example, and, despite the criticisms, there now seems to be a general consensus that carefully designed phonics programmes are effective in this regard. They also prepare children to move on to their first steps in reading with greater fluency. Whether there is enough focus on reading for comprehension is another matter, and this is an area where more work needs to be done. The point is, however, that by focussing on how children learn, we are much more likely to get the age/stage process right.

One of the most contentious areas is the transition between primary and secondary education, and it is here that the system is ripe for overhaul. It has long been known that the transfer between Year 6 and Year 7 often results in a decline in educational attainment and progress. There are lots of reasons for this. Many argue that the long summer holiday creates a gap that is simply too long and that children forget a lot of what they have learned as a result; others point out that the intense focus on the key stage 2 tests means that the gap in reality is much longer, with the tests completed in early May and little serious work undertaken again until September. There is also the problem of the mismatch between primary and secondary curriculums: the focus in primary schools is predominantly on English and mathematics, whereas secondary schools have a much broader approach, with subject specialists teaching a wider range of subjects, of which many primary school children have little experience. Consequently, most secondary schools simply start again so that children go backwards for a while and the momentum of Years 5 and 6 is lost.

In addition, there are other transitional problems caused by the lack of joined-up thinking between primary and secondary teachers. Primary and secondary schools are often seen as two separate worlds, and it is fair to say that, in reality, there is very little contact between the two, even in multi-academy trusts where the links should really be stronger. For example, secondary English teachers often adopt very different approaches to the teaching of reading, writing and grammar. Many, for example, are baffled by the grammatical terminology used at key stage 2, preferring to stick to the more traditional nomenclature they learned at school. Similarly, very few have a good understanding of phonics, and this can be particularly problematic when they are trying to support weaker readers.

We also need to consider readiness to learn. Most parents know that their children are ready to move on to secondary education at some stage in Year 6, and many feel that the move could be made much earlier. Would it be better, therefore, if pupils had access to specialist teachers in, say, Year 5? If so, this would result in a very different system and careful thought would need to be given to the school structures required to make this happen.

The all-through system offers a possible solution, with the curriculum built up in stages: early years where the focus is on reading and basic numeracy (Reception to Year 2); a fluency stage, where children learn to read for understanding and pleasure, and receive a firm foundation in numeracy and arithmetic (Years 3 and 4); a broadening stage taught by specialists (Years 5 to 8); and a specialist stage where pupils really get to grips with a carefully selected range of subjects (Years 9 to 11). This would work in an all-through school, but could it be made to work using the current primary/secondary structure? Theoretically, the answer has to be yes, but it would involve considerable investment to ensure that teachers are available to teach across the traditional primary/secondary divide, not to mention the problems likely to be created by attempting to adapt existing school sites to new modes of working. If a consistent approach is to be adopted across Years 5 to 8, for example, pupils would surely need to be schooled on one site. This would mean the extension of the primary school to accommodate Years 7 and 8, or the extension of secondary schools to accommodate Years 5 and 6. The cost of such a change would undoubtedly be prohibitive. It would also create new transition issues, this time between Years 4 and 5, or 8 and 9.

It could be done, however, with much closer cooperation between primary and secondary schools, and this is where the campus and hub system would come into its own. Schools would be closely linked together; teachers would be able to teach across school sites; and there would be a much more consistent approach to the delivery of the curriculum. This is, of course, one approach; there are bound to be others equally as valid. The most important point is that the system needs to change. It is far too complex and too little attention is paid to the educational needs of the child in the classroom.

In an ideal world, the establishment of a radical new school structure based on the learning needs of all children would be a possibility; in the real world, the best we can hope for is a commitment to simplifying the system in order to put learning centre stage where it belongs. The campus and hub system may be a good idea, but whether it is practicable is another matter; all-through schools could well be part of the answer, but they may not be; and there are bound to be dozens of other ideas which are likely to be equally as compelling.

Avoiding complexity in the system is a complex process. However, there are some basic principles to keep in mind:

1. What and how children learn should be grounded in research and not determined by the way the school system is traditionally structured.

2. Education must be seen as a continuous process of development from the early years to the age of 18 and beyond.

3. The two worlds of primary and secondary education need to be brought together.

4. Teacher training should ensure that teachers understand what and how children learn at all ages, whatever age range they ultimately choose to specialise in.

5. Teachers should be much more involved in decisions regarding the nature and structure of the education system.

6. The end point should be about learning, not examinations.

Above all, the fact that current educational structures are confused and fragmented must be acknowledged. Children are becoming lost in a system which values political experimentation over stability and coherence. A complete overhaul of the system is undoubtedly unlikely, but a switch from a chaotic system characterised by difference and division to one in which every child attends a good local school is perfectly possible. Some call for a revival of local authority control; others insist that an academy structure is the way forward. Ironically, now that the RSCs are creating regional hubs to enable them to control their academies more effectively, we may be seeing the re-emergence of LAs but under another name. Either structure would work, of course, and either could be used to shape and monitor networks of good local schools. Provided independent and grammar schools were removed from the equation, and the various types of schools became one standard type, the result would surely be a highly effective national educational system suitable for children of all classes and abilities.

Governance

Many of the ideas discussed previously depend upon a detailed understanding of education, and yet school structures are determined by politicians who often have little experience of education beyond their own schooling. In addition, local strategies are usually decided by governing bodies with little appreciation of the sophisticated teaching and leadership skills required to make education a success. Teachers and, indeed, school leaders are often marginalised when important decisions are made both nationally and locally. Another vital area of reform, therefore, is governance. Who should be in charge of our schools?

Governors and trustees currently have considerable power and influence. They are responsible for the vision of the school; improvement planning and target setting; analysis of pupil progress; performance management; teachers' pay; property management; setting and overseeing the budget; appointing and disciplining staff; succession planning; adherence to legislation; safeguarding, inclusion, special education needs and disability (SEND); and monitoring the pupil premium. However, governors may have the powers but, in many cases, they simply do not have the expertise to carry out the complex list of duties legally ascribed to them.

If you were to stand back and consider the nature of school leadership from a completely objective standpoint, I think you might begin to wonder how on earth anybody came up with a governance structure like the one currently imposed on schools. Every school in the country has a qualified team of professionals responsible for leading and managing the educational development of large numbers of pupils. These are usually highly qualified individuals who have degrees, postgraduate qualifications, teaching and leadership qualifications, and years of experience. They have been through rigorous assessment procedures, and they are monitored closely by a variety of external agencies, including, for example, Ofsted. So, with a team such as this in place, why would one think it a good idea to impose an additional layer of governance with immense powers, comprising individuals who have very little, if any, understanding of schools and education?

To the casual observer, the idea of assembling a group of between 10 and 20 people who know next to nothing about education or classroom pedagogy and telling them they are in charge must surely seem like lunacy. It is this mismatch between the extent of governors' responsibilities and powers, and their evident lack of expertise which is at the root of so many school improvement issues. If the aim is an educational system fit for the future, then the role of governors and trustees must also be considered.[1]

In reality, headteachers and senior leaders are in control of their schools; nevertheless an additional layer of governance is required for a variety of reasons. The most obvious is that someone needs to appoint and employ the headteacher. There also needs to be some form of monitoring to ensure that the school is being run properly and a level of governance which sits above the day-to-day management structure to ensure that matters such as admissions, complaints and staffing issues are dealt with fairly.

If governance is to be effective, however, governors need to be well trained and knowledgeable. In the current system, parents or members of the local community can join governing boards and quickly take on considerable responsibility without knowing the first thing about education. This cannot be right. Indeed, a great deal of damage is done to schools up and down the country by ill-informed governors asserting their power. So, what might a reformed system of governance look like?

Ultimately, it will be up to the DfE to determine the structure of governance, but whether it is overseen by local authorities, regional school commissioners, charitable trusts or the department itself, there will be a need for local bodies directly connected to individual schools or groups of schools. We should therefore assume some form of representation by the umbrella authority – the equivalent of the local authority governor – but beyond that there should be a degree of flexibility. The fundamental principle, however, must be that governors should have a sufficient level of educational expertise to enable them to engage with schools effectively and skilfully. School governance should not be the pursuit of amateurs.

An expert governing body might look something like this: the headteacher, two members of the leadership team, a teacher and a member of the support staff, a local authority or RSC representative and five or six independent governors. This would achieve a good balance between the school and external governance, but it would also ensure that the leadership team is given appropriate prominence. The independent governors could, of course, be parents, but the aim would be to make sure that several of them had a background in education – recently retired senior leaders, educational consultants and so on. Of course, to attract this level of skill, payment would be required. If governors are to be trained to a high standard, then they must be paid. In effect, good governance depends on the establishment of a new professional class of governors. This is really the only way that governing bodies can be upgraded from groups of well-meaning but often misguided amateurs to professional decision makers.

What can schools do now to put things right?

- **Create stronger links.** The primary/secondary divide is one of the key weaknesses in the education system. Schools need to work together to bridge the gap much more effectively by joint curriculum planning, sharing of staff and agreeing on common learning goals.

- **Read the latest research.** School leaders should keep up to date with the latest educational research and consider the evidence very carefully. They should avoid introducing innovations because they are fashionable, or because all the schools around them seem to be doing so; changes must be carefully thought through, introduced with care and their impact evaluated every step of the way.

- **Take care with governance.** School governors should be selected with care and the constitution of governing bodies carefully thought out. It is up to schools to ensure that governors are adequately trained and recognise that the teachers are the experts. Whenever possible, educational specialists should be appointed to the governing body. Managing the governors is one of the headteacher's key roles.

What should policymakers do to put things right?

- Be brave: abolish faith, grammar and independent schools.

- Base the education system on the fundamental principle of a good local school for every child.

- Take the views of teachers into account when considering any changes to the system.

- Read and commission educational research before suggesting any changes.

- Train more teachers and train them well. Encourage universities to provide specialist provision linked closely to local schools.

- Review the current system of governance to ensure that governors are well trained and adequately remunerated for the work they do. Above all, governors should have the expert knowledge required to participate in the leadership of schools.

Note

1 The role of governance in schools is discussed in more detail in my previous book: R. Steward. 2019. *The Gradual Art of School Improvement*, London, David Fulton.

9 A 21st-century curriculum

The curriculum

Education is in need of reform from top to bottom. So far, we have considered types of schools, school structures, the age at which pupils move on from stage to stage, and governance. Now we need to look more closely at revisions to the school curriculum. As we have seen in Chapters 2, 3 and 4, the school curriculum has always been something of a battleground. The current curriculum is caught between tradition, political ideology, and the educational and social needs of the child. Consequently, it is no longer fit for purpose: it is out of date, it does not meet the needs of all children, and it has not been adapted to take account of the huge changes in society that have taken place in the last 10 or 20 years.

Key issues for young people today include climate change, globalisation, mental and physical health, creativity, new technology, and, of course, social media. The curriculum in schools today may touch on some aspects of these issues, and, as we have seen, the government pays lip service to many of them by constantly expanding the remit of PSHE and citizenship, but they are not given the curriculum time they deserve if pupils are to be appropriately equipped to cope in a rapidly changing world. This does not mean that we need to abandon the current curriculum entirely – there must be a place for traditional subjects – but it does mean a degree of change that cannot be put into effect simply by tinkering with the National Curriculum as it stands. A careful balance needs to be struck between the traditional offer and a more radical plan.

In a way it is a foolish undertaking to suggest a new curriculum plan in a book such as this, but in order to generate debate a starting point is essential. The following is therefore offered as a prompt for discussion; it is certainly not a definitive plan. It is here for readers to argue with, pick holes in and improve. Above all, it is a mere sketch which acknowledges that a much more detailed debate is required.

A 21st-century curriculum – a modest proposal

English

Everything starts with English. Both English language and English literature have to be at the core of any curriculum structure to be followed in England. The study of English is the gateway to all other subjects. As we have seen, however, English in schools has been heavily systematised and heavily politicised. The primary curriculum moves quickly from phonics to a very clinical approach to the study of grammar, with pupils encouraged to spot grammatical features rather than appreciate their effects. Similarly, English at the secondary level currently has a relentless focus on the techniques required to attain a good grade at GCSE, with creativity pushed to the margins, and English literature has been forced down a narrow channel in response to Michael Gove's nostalgic version of Englishness.

A new English curriculum should have both technical proficiency and creativity at its core, and English literature would be considerably enhanced by the adoption of a global perspective. This is not a difficult change to engineer, and it could be put in place in a matter of months. Phonics is undoubtedly a powerful tool for the development of early reading, but it is not the only method, and its importance needs de-emphasising in schools in order to focus on comprehension and enjoyment. Similarly, the focus on grammar currently acts as a barrier to creative writing. Children have become grammar spotters, not writers. A good understanding of grammar of course underpins good writing, but grammatical skills develop as children learn to write. They should not be hammered home before children learn to enjoy writing both to express themselves and to describe the world around them. Writing needs once again to be seen as a creative act, not just a functional one.

The teaching of literature should develop alongside creative writing at all stages of a child's school career. Books need to be carefully chosen to engage and delight; they need to be carefully matched to children's abilities, and they must be updated regularly to ensure that they are in tune with the times. One of the things that has always bothered me is the failure of so many teachers of English to read children's books. Some of the best writing around at the moment, for example, is written for teenagers – Philip Pullman, Philip Reeve, Francis Hardinge, Patrick Ness, Marcus Sedgewick, and so on – and yet so many teachers of English stick to the old favourites they have taught for years. Books need to have the same contemporary currency for children as video games, movies and pop music if their interest is to be engaged fully. It is also important for books to have a global reach. Young people today are global citizens, and they should be aware that books written in English span the globe. Of course, it is important to introduce young people to classic English literature – no child should leave school without having read Dickens, Shakespeare and *Wind in the Willows* – but they should also be aware of novels written in English from America, Africa, India and so on. To focus on 19th-century English literature is to deny the power of English as a global language.

A new English curriculum also needs to take account of how we now read and write. How many of us nowadays still use a pen or pencil to write? How many of us actually write letters? The majority of our writing is done on computers, tablets or mobile phones. It is also done much more quickly than ever before, whether it is via text message, Snapchat, Twitter or email. The teaching of English should teach children both traditional writing skills as well as the techniques needed to cope in the digital world. Similarly, a huge amount of reading is done online, whether it is whole books via apps like Kindle or Apple Books, digital newspapers and magazines, or snippets of information on Twitter. Learning to read social media demands a whole new set of skills. English as a subject still sits at the heart of the curriculum, but it is in urgent need of updating to reflect the digital world.

Mathematics

Mathematics is the other cornerstone of the curriculum, but how relevant to children's lives are some of the maths currently taught in schools, especially at the secondary level? A huge amount of time is now devoted to the teaching of maths in primary schools – in most, every morning is taken up with English and mathematics – and children are now learning to become competent in both numeracy and arithmetic. When they move up to the secondary school, they should be well prepared to tackle the greater demands of the National Curriculum. However, it is at this stage that questions need to be asked. Do children really need this much maths? At the moment there seems to be an implicit assumption in most educational thinking that all children need to be educated in maths to a very high level. This is partly due to pressure from the technology industries but also due to the political obsession with the mathematical prowess of children in Asia, and China in particular.

I suspect few would argue with the relevance and usefulness of the topics set out in the National Curriculum programmes of study for key stage 3 where pupils are expected to extend their understanding of the number system and place value to include decimals, fractions, powers and roots. By the time they get to key stage 4, however, it is surely right to question whether pupils really need the specialist mathematical skills demanded at this level. A glance at some of the subject content in the key stage 4 programmes of study make this clear. For example, pupils should be taught to:

- calculate with roots, and with integer (and fractional) indices

- calculate exactly with fractions (surds) and multiples of π (simplify surd expressions involving squares [for example $\sqrt{12} = \sqrt{(4 \times 3)} = \sqrt{4} \times \sqrt{3} = 2\sqrt{3}$] and rationalise denominators)

- calculate with numbers in standard form $A \times 10^n$, where $1 \leq A < 10$ and n is an integer

- simplify and manipulate algebraic expressions (including those involving surds [and algebraic fractions]) by:

  - factorising quadratic expressions of the form $x^2 + bx + c$, including the difference of 2 squares (factorising quadratic expressions of the form $ax^2 + bx + c$);

  - simplifying expressions involving sums, products and powers, including the laws of indices

- use the form $y = mx + c$ to identify parallel (and perpendicular) lines; find the equation of the line through 2 given points, or through 1 point with a given gradient

- recognise, sketch and interpret graphs of linear functions, quadratic functions, simple cubic functions, the reciprocal function $y =$ with $x \neq 0$ (the exponential function $y = k^x$ for positive values of k, and the trigonometric functions [with arguments in degrees] $y = \sin x$, $y = \cos x$ and $y = \tan x$ for angles of any size)[1]

Is it any wonder that so many 16-year-olds fail their maths GCSEs? The teaching of maths to this level will undoubtedly ensure that a proportion of the population is mathematically highly literate, but how many of us really need this depth of mathematical knowledge? The study of maths undoubtedly develops pupils' reasoning and problem-solving skills, but surely this can be done without so much attention being given to the kind of maths only ever likely to be used in universities and highly technical industries.

The first step towards a new maths curriculum, therefore, should surely involve a closer look at the skills young people really need to engage with the modern world, and there is undoubtedly a case for slimming down the current programmes of study. Pupils need to be mathematically literate, not mathematical experts. There is also a gap to be filled. Survey after survey concludes that what young people really want from their maths lessons is financial and economic literacy. They want to know how to manage their finances, how interest rates work, how to apply for mortgages, what impact taxation will have on their lives, what national insurance contributions are for and how much student loans will really cost them. They need to be educated to understand stocks and shares, the housing market, value added tax and investment accounts. This all requires a good understanding of maths but, at the moment, despite having the ability to solve quadratic equations, most pupils do not have the knowledge they feel they need to navigate the world. A revised mathematics curriculum therefore needs to ensure that children are not only proficient in the use of numbers, good at problem solving and well equipped with reasoning skills, but financially and economically literate.

Science

As we saw in Chapter 3, science in primary schools is marginalised due to the dominance of English and maths, not to mention the fact that it is often poorly taught due to a lack of expertise on the part of the teacher, and in secondary schools the curriculum is overloaded. From learning a few basic, often disconnected skills at key stage 2, children move on to an overloaded key stage 3 curriculum which most teachers find almost impossible to get through in the time available. The first step, as with maths, must therefore be some form of simplification. This will involve careful consideration of what children really need to know, and, of course, what skills they need to progress to further study. Much of the content is lost as children simply cannot remember it all, so a focus on the key elements of scientific knowledge much be considered essential. This will mean a shift to a more skills-based approach where scientific method is privileged over factual recall. A basic foundation of knowledge is of course required, but it is important to ensure that this vital knowledge does not become buried in the content mountain.

The science curriculum must also pay much more attention to the key issue of our age, and one that children care passionately about, namely climate change. Most schools now include consideration of climate change in science lessons, but the National Curriculum programmes of study suggest very limited coverage. At key stage 3, for example, the only reference is to 'the production of carbon dioxide by human activity and the impact on climate'. There is a bit more detail at key stage 4 which covers

- evidence, and uncertainties in evidence, for additional anthropogenic causes of climate change
- potential effects of, and mitigation of, increased levels of carbon dioxide and methane on the Earth's climate
- common atmospheric pollutants: sulphur dioxide, oxides of nitrogen, particulates and their sources
- the Earth's water resources and obtaining potable water

but this is nowhere near enough to reflect young people's concerns.[2] An up-to-date science curriculum must surely have climate change at its heart.

The humanities

As with science, it is hard to see how the geography curriculum can avoid having climate change as a key topic. Once again, the National Curriculum offers limited guidance here, merely stating that pupils should be taught to 'understand how human and physical processes interact to influence and change landscapes, environments and the climate; and how human activity relies on the effective functioning of natural systems'.[3] It is fair to say, of course, that most teachers of geography spend a great deal of time exploring climate change with their classes – how could they not do so? – but it is clear that the current curriculum does not give it sufficient prominence. A reformed curriculum would surely need to have a much greater emphasis on environmental science and close links with the study of ecology in the science curriculum.

Geography is also key to the notion of global education. Pupils need to develop a detailed understanding not only of the geographical features shaping the world but Britain's place in it. They need the knowledge that will allow them to understand the influence of the rise of China on the world economy, for example, as well as a clear understanding of the countries and regions most likely to be affected by climate change. They also need to understand migration patterns and the impact of conflicts. Traditionalists often call for a return to the more basic teaching of geographical facts (e.g. capital cities, mountain ranges and major rivers), but teaching facts in isolation is pointless. Facts are quickly learned and soon forgotten. This kind of information needs to be tied to contemporary issues. Pupils should be taught not simply that the capital city of the USA is Washington, DC, the names of the 50 states, and a few details about the Grand Canyon and the Rockies, but about the complexity of the country, its diversity, its economic policies and its relationship with the rest of the world. They need to recognise key locations where contemporary issues are played out: New York, the states that border Mexico, the states most likely to be affected by hurricanes, the 'fly-over states' and so on. The contemporary study of geography cannot be confined to explanations of geographical features and farming methods; it must provide the vital background information which pupils need to understand global issues.

The same global approach is also essential in history lessons, and the tendency to retreat into the cosy vision of Englishness promoted by Michael Gove needs to be reversed. Of course, children growing up in England need to understand the importance of key events in our history, and they must develop a good understanding of chronology at an early age, but they should also surely be encouraged to appreciate the history of Britain from a global perspective. The ability to list important battles in chronological order, or to recite the kings and queens of Tudor England, may give the impression of historical understanding, but how deep is that understanding? Most children study the Roman empire at some stage in their school careers, but they end up with a fairly shallow grasp of its key features. They may learn about the Coliseum, gladiators and a few mad emperors, and they are very likely to have lessons on Roman Britain, but how often are they taught about the impact of empire, the nature of dictatorship and the influence of Rome on the rest of the world? More to the point, how often do they get to compare the Roman empire with the equally powerful and civilised empires of the east – Persia, Parthia, China and so on – which traditional history teaching tends to ignore?

In light of the Windrush scandal, the study of empire is currently a topic for national debate, but it serves as a useful reminder that history is so much more than a list of English kings and queens. A deeper understanding of key historical events, which does not shy away from awkward questions such as the crimes of empire, or the bombing of Dresden, or Britain's role in the slave trade, will give pupils real insight into why contemporary society is the way it is. Geography and history must be considered key subjects in helping pupils understand the world.

The final strand of the humanities triumvirate, religious education, is equally important if we are to teach our children how to live in a multi-cultural, multi-faith society. A new RE syllabus should be founded, however, on the knowledge that we now live in a secular society. Britain is Christian in name only, and the role of the Church of England in the functioning of the state little more than an historical anachronism. This means that RE should explore the purpose of religion, its effects on society, its potential for both peace and conflict and the issues it poses for contemporary society and governance. The tenets of the major religions will need to be taught, along with key historical, mythological and cultural information, but the emphasis should be on the purpose of religion and its impact on people around the world. Nor should we shy away from discussing atheism, agnosticism and, of course, extremism. To be fair, teachers of RE are often lightyears ahead of the National Curriculum and GCSE specifications, and many of the principles outlined earlier feature regularly in their lessons, but there does need to be formal recognition that RE is no longer about teaching pupils a few facts about world religions in a predominantly Christian country, it is about the importance and impact of religion on British society and global politics.

Together, humanities subjects should also help develop pupils' understanding of politics. This is, of course, a topic as sensitive in many ways as the teaching of religion, but young people do need to be properly equipped to be able to enter into the political life of the country. History teachers are on fairly safe ground when planning lessons exploring the origins of the democratic institutions which shape our constitution, but I think schools need to do more to help pupils understand how democracy works and how it compares with other systems of government around the world. They also need to understand the nature of political parties and the differences between them, and how politics in action relates, for example, to their concerns about the environment and globalisation. Such questions form a key part of Politics A-level, but they should surely be introduced lower down the school if we are to produce well-informed, educated political thinkers capable of taking part confidently in our democratic institutions.

The arts

The arts have seen a dramatic decline in schools in recent years for a variety of reasons which together have created something of a perfect storm. The exclusion from the Ebacc of art, music, drama and dance meant the instant devaluing of these subjects in the eyes of school leaders, parents and, saddest of all, pupils. Russell group universities then added to the problem by omitting the arts from their list of facilitating subjects, and the promotion of STEM added another hammer blow, as more and more pupils were encouraged to abandon the arts in favour of science and maths. As a consequence of all this, schools began to drop arts subjects from the curriculum, first at key stage 3 and then at key stage 4. This led to a dramatic decline in the number of GCSE entries and, unsurprisingly, even greater falls in the number of students taking arts subjects at A-level. Even in schools where commitment to the arts was strong, a lack of funding meant that small examination classes became unsustainable. Most schools manage to offer art at GCSE, but music is disappearing as a GCSE subject in many. Music A-level is now rare indeed. Drama is often offered at GCSE but cut from key stage 3, and dance available only in very large schools where there are more pupils to make up a sustainable set.

I don't think I really need to make a case for the arts in schools – the case has been made over and over again – but one or two key arguments should be emphasised:

- A school that abandons drama at key stage 3 rips one of the most important subjects out of the curriculum. It not only teaches children to be creative but equips them with the vital skills for which businesses and industrialists clamour: oral skills, presentation skills, confidence, empathy and self-possession. Students who study drama or theatre studies at GCSE and A-level are often exactly the composed, intelligent and mature individuals for which they are looking.

- Dance gives pupils an opportunity to do something that is completely unique in the school curriculum. It combines creativity and self-expression with intense physical fitness. It also offers a welcome change to what can seem like a relentless series of desk-bound lessons.

- Art is everywhere and skilled artists are in high demand. Whether it is the high art on display in galleries around the world, the artwork vital to the success of advertising campaigns or the graphic art driving the digital games industry, it is obvious that art helps shape our world.

- Music is perhaps the most worrying loss, and as a school subject it has its own particular difficulties. It is the only subject, for example, which requires extensive knowledge beyond the curriculum if a pupil is to do well. To gain a good grade at GCSE, and especially at A-level, candidates need to be competent musicians; they need to have learned to play an instrument in their own time and, usually, over a number of years. This means that the majority of pupils are effectively excluded from the subject, and this is especially true of poorer pupils who have not had the opportunity to learn an instrument privately. Music is also difficult and demanding, requiring a good musical ear, strong performance and compositional skills, and some understanding of music history. It is not surprising, therefore, that music has fast become the preserve of grammar and independent schools. Finally, it is vital to point out the importance of music in training the brain, and there has been a great deal of research that shows that children who learn music are better able to cope with other subjects, and maths in particular, than those who do not.

A 21st-century curriculum must therefore have a strong arts base. All schools should include art, music, drama and dance as part of the core. Pupils should have opportunities to engage in the arts from an early age and be positively encouraged to take part. There is no reason, for example, why all children should not have the opportunity to learn a musical instrument in primary school, and there is a strong case for arguing that individual instrumental tuition should not only be available but compulsory up to key stage 3. Of course, it would be expensive, but the benefits would be immeasurable.

The other key requirement here is political. The importance of the arts to the intellectual and productive life of the nation must be acknowledged. Politicians currently pay lip service to the arts, but they need to adopt a genuinely supportive stance backed up by revisions to the National Curriculum, DfE performance tables and university entrance requirements. Making an arts subject compulsory at key stage 4 would be a good first step.

Languages

Language learning starts too late in English schools. In most European countries, children begin to learn a second language at an early age and, as a consequence, they become fluent much more quickly. There have been botched attempts by successive governments to introduce languages into primary schools, but these have been thwarted by a chronic lack of funding and a national shortage of language teachers. If the UK is serious about language learning, then major structural change is essential. Young children pick up other languages very quickly. Anyone who has worked in a school where a child with no English at all has been introduced will know how quickly he or she learns to speak fluently and accurately. If children begin learning languages when they are 7 or 8, they will learn much faster than 11-year-olds.

The key here, of course, is high-quality teaching, and this is where structural change is essential. First, we need to train language graduates to become primary teachers, or, more feasibly, train potential primary teachers to become competent language teachers. Given the decline in language learning at both A-level and degree level, this is an ambitious goal to say the least. Employing native speakers may perhaps be the answer, but we need to be aware that native speakers are not always the best teachers. Further training would be essential if this were to be the solution adopted.

To ensure that every primary school has a competent language teacher is clearly a long-term plan and, as we know, politicians rarely plan much further than the next election. It is, however, the only effective way of ensuring that language learning is revived in the UK. At the moment, primary language learning is a mess. It is there because it is part of the National Curriculum, but it is taken seriously in only a few schools with the resources and the commitment to insist upon specialist teaching. Most pupils reach secondary school with a ragbag of French, Spanish or German, and then struggle to engage with language lessons which, by then, seem almost pointless. If they were to join Year 7 with three or four years of real language learning behind them, there would surely be a dramatic difference: pupils would be much more confident about learning a language, already fairly fluent and more likely to continue their language studies to a higher level.

The choice of language is important only in the sense that the language taught in primary schools should match that taught in the local secondaries to ensure continuity. The logical consequence of this is, of course, either a nationally agreed second language or, at the very least, a choice agreed at the county or regional level. There are strong arguments for French, as the language of our nearest neighbour, not to mention the number of French teachers already in our schools; for Spanish, due to its popularity, its global reach and the not-necessarily-accurate view that it is easier to learn than other languages; and German as the language of a key European ally. Many argue that Mandarin is the language of the future, but the complexity of the language and the lack of Mandarin teachers are both significant barriers to learning. Whatever language is chosen equips children with the skills they need to learn other languages, so the initial choice is, in effect, not that important. In fact, the idea of learning one language in order to lay the foundations of future language learning is perhaps the strongest argument for the retention of Latin in the curriculum.

Whatever the choice of language, it is important that languages form a key part of the curriculum. English may well be spoken globally, but if we are serious about understanding other cultures and interacting with other countries, the ability to learn a language is surely a vital skill.

Physical education

As we saw in Chapter 4, physical education as it is currently delivered in schools is hopelessly out of date. The PE curriculum owes more to the games played on a Saturday morning in 19th-century public schools than to genuine concerns about health and fitness. The subject is dominated by team games, and those who teach it are more often than not the ex-stars of their school football, rugby, netball or hockey teams and thus happy to maintain the dominance of what is essentially a wildly outdated ideology. A glance at the physical activities in which adults take part makes this abundantly clear. Certainly, a few participate in team games, but the vast majority concentrate on individual fitness through walking, running, yoga, Pilates and membership of the local gym. Far too many, however, turned off exercise by their memories of team games in school, do no exercise at all. Team games are spectator sports; they are not the route to health and fitness.

A radical approach to PE is therefore required and one focussed on health and fitness rather than games and competition. The starting point is best characterised by Juvenal's famous prescription, *mens sana in corpore sano* (a healthy mind in a healthy body). Pupils need to be taught how to keep healthy both physically and mentally. Exercise is vitally important, but it must be offered in ways that ensure far greater numbers participate willingly rather than reluctantly. This will be expensive and will involve establishing and equipping large gyms in schools along the lines of commercial operations; however, it will have an impact not only on pupils' health but on their ability to perform in academic subjects. Exercise, however, must be put in context. Therefore, it is important to ensure that physical activity is underpinned by an understanding of why exercise is necessary and how the body works. In other words, an academic underpinning. The next step is to establish a link between exercise and food and nutrition so that pupils understand how what they eat determines their physical health. They should also be made aware of the beneficial effects of exercise on their mental health, as well as ways of coping with mental health issues.

This many seem a long way from the traditional PE curriculum and, in many ways, it is a totally new subject. It will require highly skilled teachers and considerable investment, but when the health of the nation is at stake, it is vital that the funds are found to make it happen. Obesity and mental illness epidemics cannot be tackled by dreaming about the playing fields of Eton; a new subject for a new world is needed.

Digital technology

Over the past few years the school curriculum has been trying painfully to adapt to the digital world. Educationalists and politicians all acknowledge that the world has changed, but they are simply not reacting quickly enough to ensure that the curriculum in schools keeps up with the pace of change and is thus able to equip pupils with the skills they need to navigate the modern world. Developing a thorough and up-to-date understanding of digital technology must therefore be a key aim of a more relevant curriculum plan.

As the pace of change quickens, the study of digital and media technology is likely to become as important to young people as English and maths. So, what might such a subject include? The first step must be one of the foundation stones of media studies, namely representation. Pupils need to understand that as soon as something appears in the media – in any form – it has been re-presented. In other words, it has been changed. They need to be alert to the way media imagery is manipulated, whether it is in the careful doctoring of photographs or through complex and lengthy campaigns. They not only need to understand the basic techniques – cropping, framing, juxtaposition, selection, editing, point of view, digital alternations and so on – but the way media manipulation alters our perception of the world. From advertising to fake news, pupils should be taught how to discriminate and how to form their own opinions.

Pupils also need to understand how to use social media. This initially seems like an absurd idea: if anyone knows how to use social media, surely it is young people. However, simply because they use it a lot does not mean that they use it effectively or, indeed, safely. Social media posts need to be analysed and discussed in the classroom in the same way that English teachers analyse literary texts. Pupils need to learn how to identify authorship and to detect bias; they need to learn how to seek alternative, balanced views; they need to be able to identify which sites are credible and which are not; and, above all, they need to be taught how to respond, and whether or not to respond at all.

They need to become skilled at recognising traps and dangers. Media producers are masters of manipulation, whether through advertising, fake news or simple fraud. These dangers should be explored in the classroom. Pupils should understand, for example, the ease with which people can be drawn into losing thousands of pounds on the web, whether through in-game purchases, gambling sites or credit deals charging exorbitant rates of interest. They need to understand the power of advertising, and the techniques advertisers use to hook gullible members of the public, and they need to learn how to protect their identities online. Then there are the less obvious pitfalls of social media use. Young people tend to live in the moment, and, to them, the future seems too far off to worry about. This means that they post all sorts of things online which may come back to haunt them in the future. Obvious examples include naked selfies or sexualised imagery, but how many 16-year-olds think about the negative impact of a timeline which is open to the world and thus accessible to potential employers years in the future?

Some of the most worrying aspects of internet access are often only dealt with in schools when children become victims. Most schools now teach children to be safe online, but how effective is that teaching when so many children still enter into conversations with complete strangers, some of whom may well be adults posing as children? Protecting children is a fundamental duty of schools, and the only sure way of doing this is teaching internet use in depth and detail accorded to academic subjects. Ironically, that most derided of subjects, media studies, may well turn out to be one of the key elements of a 21st-century curriculum.

Vocational studies

With the exception of the arts and PE, the majority of the time pupils spend in school is devoted to academic study. There are few outlets or opportunities for children who are not academic and who prefer practical activities. It is often assumed that these are the weaker pupils, but this is not necessarily the case. Yes, pupils who struggle with academic subjects are better suited to practical alternatives, but that does not mean that practical subjects should be aimed only at weaker pupils. If these subjects are of a sufficiently high quality, if they are taught well and if they are appropriately challenging, they can easily achieve equivalence with their academic counterparts.

As we saw in Chapter 4, the practical offering in most schools is delivered by a suite of design technology subjects, most of which are not fit for purpose. Food technology has little to do either with design or technology and, as suggested previously, would be more appropriate as part of a health and fitness course. Textiles is essentially an arts subject, or at least it should be, leaving us with product design and resistant materials, both of which have had their practical elements neutered by the examination boards' insistence on the inclusion of pointless planning and evaluation exercises.

Some schools attempt to deliver a few vocational courses, but often these are generic BTEC courses, most of which have now been revised to bring them in line with GCSEs and have therefore become much more academic. They are usually very general – business, health and social care, travel and tourism, and so on – and, ultimately, neither practical nor truly vocational. It is not too cynical to say that most schools use these courses to help weaker pupils gain some kind of qualification without really considering their value as preparation for future careers.

The answer is, of course, to enable schools to offer genuinely vocational courses. All pupils should have the opportunity, ideally from Year 9 onwards, to study practical subjects which lead to real careers. Instead of generic, watered-down pseudo subjects, pupils should be offered courses in engineering, mechanics, carpentry, electronics, hair and beauty, cooking and so on. In other words, the sort of courses offered in Further Education colleges. We need to acknowledge the fact that schools are simply not equipped to offer vocational courses and must therefore draw on the expertise of local FE providers. As always, this is easier said than done, but it can be done.

First, schools have to allocate considerable curriculum time to vocational subjects. Pupils need to be off timetable for at least a day a week if real learning is to be accomplished. Second, there is the issue of access, and this is a huge problem in rural areas. A regular bus service has to be provided to ensure that all pupils can access the courses that really interest them. Third, an accommodation has to be reached with both the FE college and other local schools to ensure that timetables are made to match. All this sounds like something of an administrative nightmare, but it can be done, and it has already been done in lots of schools. The reason that such schemes eventually fail, however, is nearly always due to funding issues. The combination of transport costs, timetabling adjustments and course provision is often prohibitive. When such schemes are successful, however, they provide young people with high-quality vocational experiences impossible to obtain in school settings.

Pupils' access to work experience should also be broadened to occupy a key position in the school curriculum. At the moment, most schools offer one or two weeks of work experience in Years 10 or 11, but these are essentially taster opportunities to give pupils an idea of what working life will be like. For pupils aiming for practical careers, a day a week is surely a reasonable proposition. Why shouldn't schools offer a four-day academic curriculum plus a day's work experience? In this way we might see a return to genuine apprenticeships as employers would not have the burden of wages to consider for the first two years at least. The young people involved would also be happier, more engaged with their learning and much more likely to do well in all areas of study.

Vocational study is vital to a 21st-century curriculum, but it must be genuinely vocational; work experience is essential, but it must offer long-term learning opportunities. At the moment, commitment to providing practical opportunities for young people is half-hearted to say the least. If we are serious about vocational alternatives, then we have to pay for them.

A commitment to change

The curriculum outlined in this chapter is merely one possibility. It is not particularly radical, but it does challenge some of the obvious weaknesses in the curriculum currently on offer in most schools. Many of the proposals could be implemented fairly easily, but others require major changes to the provision of education in the UK, not to mention changes to the teaching profession itself. The point, however, is that the curriculum as it stands is out of date, paralysed by custom and practice, and based on an ideological vision of Englishness which is becoming increasingly irrelevant in a global society. Change is long overdue.

Summary: a curriculum model for the future

English
- English for fluency
- Reading
- Writing
- Reading and writing in a digital world
- Oracy

English literature
- Classic literature
- Contemporary literature
- Texts in English from around the world
- Media texts

Mathematics
- Academic maths
- Practical maths

- Maths for personal finance and business

Science
- Key concepts and key knowledge
- Climate change science

The humanities
- Geography with environmental science
- History – local, national and global
- Politics – the institutions underpinning democracy
- RE – the nature of religion and its impact of religion on society

The arts
- Art
- Music
- Drama
- Dance

Languages
- A first language agreed locally or nationally
- Second and third languages dependent on the context of the school or staff expertise

Physical education
- Health and fitness
- Food and fitness
- Individual fitness
- PSHE – taught by specialists

Digital technology
- Media studies
- Social media
- Textual analysis

- Staying safe online
- Digital communication skills

Practical and vocational studies

- Genuine practical courses leading to qualifications recognised by trades and industries
- High-quality work experience

Notes

1 *National Curriculum in England: Mathematics Programmes of Study*, July 2014. www.gov.uk/government/publications/national-curriculum-in-england-mathematics-programmes-of-study/national-curriculum-in-england-mathematics-programmes-of-study
2 *National Curriculum in England: Science Programmes of Study*, May 2015. www.gov.uk/government/publications/national-curriculum-in-england-science-programmes-of-study/national-curriculum-in-england-science-programmes-of-study
3 *National Curriculum in England: Geography Programmes of Study*, September 2013. www.gov.uk/government/publications/national-curriculum-in-england-geography-programmes-of-study/national-curriculum-in-england-geography-programmes-of-study

Conclusion
De-toxifying the classroom

The two great positives of the English education system are undoubtedly teachers and their pupils. Despite the chaos and confusion outlined in the previous chapters, it is impossible not to acknowledge the fact that teachers are better educated, more highly trained and, on the whole, more dedicated than they have ever been before. As a result, children are healthier, brighter and better equipped to enter society than those of any preceding generation. However, the skill and professionalism of teachers is rarely acknowledged nowadays; nor do we celebrate and value the achievements of young people as often as we should. Children seem to thrive in spite of the educational system, not because of it. How much better, therefore, would it be, and how much greater the achievements of the young, if teachers were truly valued, systems were simplified and a love of learning established as the core purpose of education.

Much of this book has explored the damage done to education in recent years due to constant change, underfunding, an outdated curriculum, a lack of parental support, an extreme testing regime, over-regulation, a suffocating accountability culture and political short-termism. The inability of the education system to respond to changes in society, coupled with what has become a national obsession with assessment and testing, has resulted in a generation of children suffering more stress and anxiety than ever before. A toxic environment indeed. And yet, education in England has the potential to be outstanding and a model for the rest of the world. The fundamental ingredients are in place; they just have to be managed more effectively. The changes required to create a world class education system are easily within our grasp, provided the political will is there and the funding made available. First of all, real change requires the decoupling of education and politics. Education is too important to be left to politicians.

The system as it stands is far too complicated and must be simplified. There is also a need for a truly innovative curriculum based on breadth and depth which teaches children really to enjoy learning, thus preparing them for further learning in adult life. The natural corollary of an engaging curriculum is a non-threatening assessment system which checks pupils' learning in order to improve it rather than merely report it. Above all, a change of culture is essential, one that values teachers and sees learning as fundamental to a happy and productive life, rather than simply as preparation for employment.

Why are children learning and what for?

Whenever politicians discuss education on the television or the radio, they tend to start with the assumption that the underlying purpose of education is based on an economic model. Pupils attend school to become good citizens, by which they mean productive economic units. They are there to be taught technical and scientific skills which will enable them to get well-paid jobs and thus contribute to the national economy. This is all very well, but what about the whole child? Yes, we want our children to be well equipped in order to secure employment as adults but, surely, we also want them to be well-rounded individuals, creative thinkers and enthusiastic learners. There is a world beyond work where the real pleasures and challenges of life will be played out. A child who has learned to learn, rather than simply to pass examinations, will be much better equipped to navigate the world than one simply prepared for work.

There is a strong argument to suggest that it doesn't really matter what children learn, as long as they are enjoying it and learning how to learn. As we have seen, when as adults we look back at our own education, we find that we can remember very little of what we learned in lessons. Some of it sticks, of course; usually the things we found most interesting. Most of it is lost and forgotten, however. This doesn't mean that it is inevitable that the things learned in school are bound to be forgotten in later life. Probably the main reason why we have forgotten so much is that most of it was irrelevant to our daily lives. Children must above all learn to learn, but they are likely to learn much more if they follow an up to date curriculum suitably adapted to their needs.

They are also likely to learn more if they are happy in school. As we have seen, the government is desperately concerned with the UK's ranking in the PISA tests, and we are constantly reminded that pupils' performance in reading, maths and science is not good enough. Rarely, however, is much attention paid to the PISA survey comparing what school means for students' lives. In the 2018 survey, published in December 2019, 53% of students in the United Kingdom reported that they are satisfied with their lives, compared to 67% on average across OECD countries.[1] Given the issues outlined earlier, it is hardly surprising that children in this country are not as happy as those in other countries. Whenever parents are asked what they most want from a school, the first thing they say is that they want their children to be happy. In the uniquely pressurised environment of the current system of schooling in the UK, children's happiness appears to come a poor second to examination success.

Putting things right

A love of learning should be the aim of the curriculum and the proper function of the school system. Putting learning at the heart of the education system will almost certainly result in greater engagement, a clear sense of direction and, ultimately, much happier students. But there are changes to be made:

The classroom should be situated at the core of any educational discussion. The question – what will be the impact of this on a child's learning in the classroom? – should always be the first question asked. What is taught, how it is taught and how learning is checked are the fundamentals of any pedagogical discussion. This means that the role of the teacher is of paramount importance. Governors may oversee the strategic vision of the school, leaders may ensure that the school runs smoothly, but it is classroom teachers who teach children to learn.

Teachers therefore need to be valued. Teaching should be regarded as a high-status profession, as it is in other countries, and the voice of the teacher should always be heard when changes to the education system are being discussed. In order to make this happen, there is no escaping the fact that teachers will need to be well paid, highly trained, and, above all, given the time to do the job properly.

Curriculum design should be focussed on learning, not outcomes. It should respond both to the needs of society and the needs of children, planning for the future and not the past. There is obviously a need for a National Curriculum, but it should be flexible enough to allow schools to adapt it to their local context. The pet ideologies of political parties, or individual politicians, should have no place in curriculum design. The current Ofsted model of intent, implementation and impact is perfectly sound, provided the emphasis is on implementation.

Assessment is a necessary evil, but under the current regime children are tested to death and to little purpose. The assessment culture needs to be dismantled and re-thought. Tests today focus on the accountability of schools and not the needs of the child; they test the ability to cram for tests rather than measuring how well children are learning. Assessment as children move up through the system must be formative, only becoming summative in the final years of schooling. There is very little need to test 4-year-olds, and then to test them again when they are 5, 7, 11 and so on. Teachers know how well their pupils are performing, and their judgements should be trusted. A system focussed on learning will keep summative testing to a minimum. Do we really need, therefore, public examinations at any time other than when students leave school at 16 or 18? Common sense tells us that we need a sensible assessment system which measures performance humanely and yet ultimately offers credible qualifications at the end of a pupil's school career.

League tables tell us very little about how well schools are really doing and should undoubtedly be abolished. A glance at *The Sunday Times* list of the top state schools tells us everything we need to know since the vast majority of the schools listed are highly selective grammar schools located in wealthy suburbs. Admittedly, government performance tables focus on progress rather than attainment, but the patterns of success are not wildly different. Selective schools inevitably achieve very positive progress scores, but how can they not do so? League tables do not tell us how good a school really is; that is a much more complicated judgement than examination percentages can ever reveal.

Behaviour in schools is much better than the tabloid press would have us believe, but it could be better. Good behaviour does not depend, however, on the imposition of oppressive regimes and draconian punishments; it depends upon good teaching. If pupils are engaged, if the curriculum is adapted to their needs, and they are happy in school, behaviour improves dramatically.

Social care has been driven down into the education system as a result of chronic underfunding. As social services across the country have been pushed toward collapse, schools have been forced to take up the slack. As we have seen, teachers now spend as much time dealing with social issues than with learning in the classroom. This is a problem that educationalists cannot address in isolation, but it is important to lay down a marker saying clearly that education is the job of schools and it is wrong for politicians to expect schools to solve society's problems. If social services are properly funded, then the pressure on schools will inevitably decrease, and teachers will be released to get on with the day job. Of course, teachers should be well trained in safeguarding, and they will always see pastoral care as a high priority, but something is seriously wrong when schools are seen as responsible for the prevention of knife crime, radicalisation and female genital mutilation.

Extra-curricular provision is vital to the development of the whole child and should be considered to be a fundamental part of the curriculum. Co-curricular provision gives pupils opportunities to explore the world and learn about themselves in ways which complement their classroom learning. And it all begins in play which should have its proper place not only in early years education but at every stage of a pupil's school career.

Innovation should be research based, not dependent on political or educational faddism. Too many school leaders leap on the latest fashionable ideas because of their popularity rather than their effectiveness. In recent years we have seen countless revolutionary pedagogies, some of which have added something to the classroom but many of which have disappeared without trace.[2] In too many schools, too little thought is given to their impact on teaching and learning. They are tried out, then abandoned, leaving staff bewildered and pupils confused. In all walks of life, the best practitioners innovate, and schools should be no different, but innovation must be carefully considered and thoroughly thought through. It then becomes a powerful driver of change and is genuinely able to enrich the learning process. The most effective teachers are those who are always looking at ways to improve their classroom pedagogy but who think deeply about whether new ideas will work; the most effective school leaders are those who look to the future, adapting the curriculum to meet the needs of pupils as society changes around them but who innovate slowly and with great care.

Creativity is one of the most vital aspects of education and one which recent trends have tended to suppress. As we have seen, the arts have been driven out of the curriculum thanks to the Ebacc, Progress 8 performance tables, the Russell Group's facilitating subject list and years of underfunding. It is essential therefore not only that schools are encouraged to reinstate arts subjects, but that creativity is built into all aspects of the curriculum. Creative thinking is surely one of the key drivers of a successful and prosperous society.

Systems and structures are currently far too complicated. Parents and pupils are lost in a maze of academies, free schools, LA schools, studio schools, independents, faith schools, grammar schools and so on. Put simply, the system is in a mess. The aim should surely be a good local school for every child. This will mean serious and far-reaching changes, including the abolition of independent schools and selective education, but the result will be a much fairer and much more effective system of education in this country. Moreover, it will mean high-quality education for all children, not just the privileged few.

The future is the province of the young, and schools should regard this as a fundamental principle. It means that much more attention should be paid not only to the issues which really concern young people but to the issues which are beginning to shape our world. Children should be taught to understand and participate in the digital world from an early age; they should learn to cope with its dangers and exploit its opportunities. They should be taught about climate change and globalisation, and their learning should be shaped to enable them rapidly to navigate changes in society. In other words, it is the job of education to future proof our young people.

Painting in oils

As we saw in the Introduction, the Mock Turtle from *Alice's Adventures in Wonderland* outlined a school curriculum that included 'fainting in coils' and this has indeed proved to be a convincing metaphor to describe the experiences of a child in school today. Surely it is time, therefore, to re-set the system to ensure that children get the chance to do what they should have been doing all along: painting in oils. The English classroom has undoubtedly become a toxic place to learn but, as I hope I have made clear, antidotes are available.

Notes

1 What School Life Means for Student Lives, *Programme for International Student Assessment (PISA), Results from 2018 Country Note*, p. 7. www.oecd.org/pisa/publications/PISA2018_CN_GBR.pdf
2 The educational website @Teacher-Toolkit, for example, list three decades of educational fads. www.teachertoolkit.co.uk/2016/07/10/education-fads/. These include:

- Learning styles
- Lesson objectives
- Assessing Pupil Progress (APP)
- Chinese teaching
- Personal, Learning, Thinking Skills (PLTS)
- Textbooks
- iPads
- Sitting in rows
- Zero tolerance
- Brain gym
- The four-part lesson
- Lollipop stick questioning
- Verbal feedback stamps
- Triple marking
- Starters, middles, plenaries
- The purple pen of progress
- Mindfulness
- Praise
- Classroom displays
- A 'knowledge-rich' curriculum
- Growth mindset
- Knowledge organisers
- One-to-one devices
- Phonics
- Genius hour

Appendix
List of common SEND acronyms

ADD	Attention Defect Disorder
ADHD	Attention Deficit Hyperactivity Disorder
AEN	Additional Educational Needs
AS	Asperger Syndrome
ASD	Autistic Spectrum Disorder
ASN	Additional Support Needs
AUT	Autism
BDD	Body Dysmorphic Disorder
BESD	Behavioural, Emotional and Social Difficulties
CFS	Chronic Fatigue Syndrome
CLD	Complex Learning Needs
DAMP	Deficits in Attention, Motor Control and Perceptual Abilities
DCD	Development Co-ordination Difficulties (Dyspraxia)
DSD	Developmental Co-ordination Disorder
DVD	Developmental Verbal Dyspraxia
DYSC	Dyscalculia
DYSL	Dyslexia
DYSP	Dyspraxia
EAT	Eating Disorders
EBD	Emotional and Behavioural Difficulties
FAS	Foetal Alcohol Syndrome
FASD	Foetal Alcohol Spectrum Disorders
GLD	Generic Learning Difficulties
GLD	Global Learning Delay
HI	Hearing Impairment
LDD	Learning Difficulties and Disabilities
ME	Myalgic Encephalomyelitis
MLD	Moderate Learning Difficulties
MSI	Multi-Sensory Impairment
OCD	Obsessive Compulsive Disorder

ODD	Oppositional Defiance Disorder
PCTs	Primary Care Trusts
PD	Physical Difficulties/Disabilities
PDA	Pathological Demand Avoidance Syndrome
PDD	Pervasive Development Disorder
PMD	Physical and Medical Difficulties
PMLD	Profound and Multiple Learning Difficulties
PNI	Physical and Neurological Impairment
PSI	Physical and Sensory Impairment
RAD	Rapid (or Reactive) Attachment Disorder
S&L	Speech and Language
SCD	Speech and Communication Difficulties
SEAL	Social and Emotional Aspects of Learning
SEBD	Social, Emotional and Behaviour Difficulties
SM	Selective Mutism (formally EM, Elective Mutism)
SPD	Semantic Pragmatic Disorder
SPDs	Sensory Processing Disorders
SpLCN	Specific Language and Communication Difficulties
SpLD	Specific Learning Difficulties
VI	Visual Impairment

Index

academies 85, 110–111
admissions 123–124
Anderton Park Primary School 47
An Inspector Calls (Priestley) 46
arts education 69–72, 89, 157–159
assessment 92–108, 169

Balls, E. 25
Birdsong (Faulks) 46
Black, S.E. 5
Blair, T. 38, 110
Blake, W. 2
Blower, C. 95
Bousted, M. 95
Bradbury, A. 6
business studies 81

Carroll, L. 1
Catcher in the Rye, The (Salinger) 46
Churchill, W. 2
Cider with Rosie (Lee) 6
citizenship 18, 30, 77–80
City Technology Colleges (CTCs) 85
Cognitive Abilities Tests (CATs) 101
computing 56–58
creationism 56
curriculum 24–42, 151–166, 169

Dearing, R. 25, 34, 86
Department for Education (DfE) 46, 49, 63
design technology (DT) 72–74, 89
Devereux, P.J. 5

Dickens, C. 2
digital technology 161–162
Dyson, J. 73

early years education 4, 94–96, 135
Early Years Foundation Stage profile 4, 5, 26–28, 94
educational health care plan (EHC) 120
Education Policy Institute 49
Eisner, E.W. 71
Eley, C. 22
Emmanuel Schools Foundation 56
English 43–48, 152–153
English Baccalaureate (Ebacc) 32, 61, 69, 102, 109
Every Child Matters 77
exclusions 124–125
extra-curricular education 86–88, 170

faith schools 118–119, 142
Famous Five (Blyton) 17
Finland 5, 84, 130
free schools 111–112
fundamental British values (FBV) 79, 136

Gandiban, J.M. 22
Gibb, N. 108
Ginsberg, K.R. 7
global citizenship 136–138
Goodnight Mister Tom (Magorian) 46
Gove, M. 25, 26, 43, 47, 62, 69, 152
governance 147–149

grammar schools 115–116, 141
Great Gatsby, The (Fitzgerald) 46
Guardian, The 11, 19, 62, 72

Harford, S. 26
Hart, B. 9
Hattie, J. 11
Higgins, J. 56
home education 126, 128
humanities 61–65, 155–157
Humphrys, J. 80

Independent, The 62
independent schools 116–117, 140

Juvenal 160

languages 29, 58–61, 67, 159–160
Lichtenstein, P. 22
local authorities (LAs) 109
Long Revolution, The (Williams) 39
Lord of the Flies (Golding) 12

mathematics 48–52, 153–154
McAdams, T. 22
media studies 81–83, 89, 162
mental health 14
mindfulness 17, 21
multi-academy trusts (MATs) 113
Mumsnet 16

Narusyte, J. 22
National Curriculum 24, 43, 54, 61, 62, 77, 88, 97, 126
National Foundation for Educational Research (NFER) 93, 101, 114
Neiderhiser, J.M. 22

Oates, T. 25
Ofqual 44
Ofsted 25, 53, 55, 56, 74–75, 106–107, 120

Palmer, S. 19
parents 7, 20
performance tables 7, 32, 170

phonics 43, 106, 152
physical education (PE) 74–76, 89, 160–161
PISA tests 51, 168
PixL 101
play 7, 20
post-16 education 33, 86, 104
Progress 8 33, 41, 69, 103, 114
Personal, Social and Health Education (PSHE) 77–80, 135
psychology 81
Pupil Premium 8, 20, 89
Pupil Referral Units (PRUs) 122

Rand, A. 134
reading 20, 43, 66, 132–133
reception baseline assessment (RBA) 95
Regional Schools Commissioner (RSA) 111
religious studies 64–65, 67, 157
Resolution Foundation, The 9
Risjsdijk, F.V. 22
Risley, T. 9
Robert-Holmes, G. 6
Rosen, M. 72

safeguarding 19
Salvanes, S.G. 5
Schama, S. 25, 62
Schleicher, A. 57
science 53–56, 154–155
science, technology, engineering and maths (STEM) 51, 66, 69, 73, 99, 133
Secular Society, The 119
Sex and Relationship Education (SRE) 56, 79, 135
sexualisation 14, 21
Sharp, C. 5
Shindler, J. 6
Sidelsky, R. 63
Snowling, M.J. 108
social media 12, 21, 82, 139
sociology 80
special educational needs and disability (SEND) 16, 120–123
special schools 120–122

Spielman, A. 120
Spotts, E.L.
Stripp, C. 48, 52
studio schools 85, 112

Technical and Vocational Education Initiative (TVEI) 84
testing 11, 20, 31, 41, 92–108
Thunberg, G. 55
To Kill a Mockingbird (Lee) 46
Toxic Childhood (Palmer) 19
transition 135

UNICEF 5
university education 37, 51
university technical colleges (UTCs) 112

vocational education 83–86, 162–164

Weale, S. 22, 68
White, J. 39
Williams, R. 39
Wind in the Willows (Grahame) 39, 152

Young, T. 42, 112

Taylor & Francis eBooks

www.taylorfrancis.com

A single destination for eBooks from Taylor & Francis with increased functionality and an improved user experience to meet the needs of our customers.

90,000+ eBooks of award-winning academic content in Humanities, Social Science, Science, Technology, Engineering, and Medical written by a global network of editors and authors.

TAYLOR & FRANCIS EBOOKS OFFERS:

- A streamlined experience for our library customers
- A single point of discovery for all of our eBook content
- Improved search and discovery of content at both book and chapter level

REQUEST A FREE TRIAL
support@taylorfrancis.com

Printed in Great Britain
by Amazon